WILLIAMS-SONOMA

NEW AMERICAN COOKING

THE BEST OF CONTEMPORARY REGIONAL CUISINES

General Editor

Chuck Williams

Recipes

Beth Dooley, Janet Fletcher, Jean Galton,
Kathi Long, Ray Overton, Molly Stevens

Photographs

Leigh Beisch

Oxmoor House®

Contents

New American Cooking

Contemporary American regional fare is constantly evolving. Just as America is often described as a dynamic country, so too does our cooking seem to be always absorbing new influences and techniques. Some of our families' recipes remain unchanged while others change over time as different ingredients and updated methods enter the American repertoire, some of which will become the classics of our day.

The vastly varying geography of the United States greatly affects the character of our cuisines. Recipes that come out of the northern forests are quite unlike those from the southwestern deserts. And these varying climates play out in cooking: sweltering Southern summers and long, cold New England winters yield very different traditions at the table. Local harvests also influence regional culinary trademarks—there's maple syrup from New England, okra from the South, wild rice from the heartland, pinto beans from the Southwest, hazelnuts from the Pacific Northwest, and figs from California.

Many dishes of early immigrants are now firmly part of our heritage, and as new populations arrive, the culinary traditions of their cultures inspire native cooks in novel ways. Each group brings with it ingredients that, like lemongrass or chiles, seem exotic at first but then often become part of our everyday cooking. Meanwhile, more and more farmers are proudly turning to organic and sustainable agriculture, while cooks rededicate themselves to the bounty found at local farmers' markets and from artisanal producers.

New American Cooking embraces tradition and innovation, seasonal foods, and a sharing of cultures to bring you the best of today's American home cooking.

NEW ENGLAND

A vibrant heritage enriches the cuisine of the Northeast region of the United States, one that has significantly influenced American cooking overall, especially our holiday traditions. Early settlers like the Scots and Welsh brought stews and oat breads. Portuguese fishermen adapted their traditional foods to the climate of southern Massachusetts and Rhode Island. Much of Boston cooking reflects the long-standing Irish community, but today the city, and others in the region, has a large Asian population contributing to the rich culinary feast that is New England.

New Englanders have a deep connection to the land and to the sea. Off the craggy coast of this region, the cold waters of the Atlantic provide a great variety of seafood, including lobster, cod, herring, clams, and oysters. Inland, rugged pastures and fertile farmlands sustain the production of the milk, cream, and cheese key to many local recipes such as milk-based soups, scalloped dishes, and custard pies. Cranberries still grow in bogs around Cape Cod and blueberries flourish further north on mountaintops and coastal islands. Hearty recipes like chowders and baked beans were no doubt inspired by the region's bitter winters.

Today the number of small-scale specialty farms in New England that emphasize organic and sustainable practices is growing, and the heirloom produce, artisanal cheeses, and organic meats they produce are being embraced by home cooks and local chefs alike.

New American Cooking is a mix of tradition and innovation. Many dishes are shared among regions, while a good number are still considered local specialties. Lobster Salad with Cucumber & Dill, left, announces the arrival of summer in New England. Old-Fashioned Vanilla Seed Pound Cake, above, is a mark of Southern hospitality.

THE SOUTH

Contemporary Southern cooking is the result of a convergence of multiple factors. Many ingredients now considered Southern, such as black-eyed peas, sweet potatoes, okra, and watermelon, came to the region with slaves from Africa, who as cooks at the great plantation houses used their native ingredients along with local squashes, rice, and wild game. Necessity required cooks to use every part of the domesticated pig, the region's favorite meat: knuckles and feet were pickled, neck bones were stewed with greens, and pig fat was rendered for lard for deep-frying and baking. Lard, together with native soft-wheat flour, creates the region's flaky piecrusts, which marry so well with local peaches and pecans.

In Bayou country, French-influenced recipes that made thrifty use of local game and seafood evolved into the now-familiar traditions of Cajun and Creole cooking. Spain, Great Britain, and the Caribbean have also left marks on American Southern cuisine.

Southerners are proud of their heritage, and Southern hospitality is legendary. Stories about classic dishes such as light-as-air biscuits and fried chicken, or tales of how goat cheese made its way into the grits often lead to an invitation to "come on down and try it."

THE HEARTLAND

What is knowns as the heartland of America defies state boundaries. It includes Minnesota, Iowa, Wisconsin, Michigan, Illinois, Indiana, Ohio, northern Missouri, and the eastern lowlands of Kansas, as well as Nebraska and North and South Dakota. This vast area encompasses the northern forests and the Great Lakes, rolling grasslands and open prairies. It's home to Native American tribes and to newcomers from many nations. Each wave of immigrants—Scandinavians, Eastern Europeans, Welsh, Scots, Germans, Russians, Africans, southeast Asians—has contributed to the local larder, planting seeds from their homelands and sharing their skills as dairy farmers, butchers, bakers, and brewers.

In the heartland, everything from pasties (Cornish meat pies) to *sarma* (Croatian cabbage rolls) to Somalian peanut chicken and towering chiffon cakes

are on the menu. The region's rich offerings for hunting and angling are reflected in the variety of favorite meat and fish dishes. A love of state fairs brings its own customs, notably the quest for blue-ribbon pickles, pies, jams, and jellies. Heartland cooking celebrates both long-established culinary traditions and a rich mix of contemporary flavors.

THE SOUTHWEST

Southwestern food, a colorful cuisine with dishes like tamales, posole, and fry bread, reflects the mix of Native Americans, Spaniards, Mexicans, and Anglo Saxons who inhabit New Mexico, Arizona, Southern Colorado, and West Texas. Sharing a border with Mexico inspired such Tex-Mex dishes as fajitas, *cabrito* (barbecued goat), and tacos; avocados, vanilla, and turkeys also crossed over.

Cattle, sheep, and pigs were introduced to the southwestern United States in the sixteenth century, after Spanish explorers had joined the region's Pueblo, Apache, and Navajo residents. Livestock ranching has been an important part of the area's economy ever since, making the territory famous for barbecue. The traditions of cowboy chuck-wagon fare have also influenced the region's cooking.

Today the Southwest table distills these influences into lively, earthy cooking, with an understanding of the history and rich cultural confluence at its heart.

THE PACIFIC NORTHWEST

With its abundant culinary resources, the Pacific Northwest is a cook's paradise. Its maritime bounty includes salmon and Dungeness crab; its forests harbor prized porcino mushrooms and truffles. The region's rich agriculture yields a wide variety of products, from Washington State's famous apples to Oregon's notable wines and Idaho's signature potatoes.

Many Native Americans still live in the diverse region of the Pacific Northwest, and their traditions, such as smoking salmon over alder wood, are still used today. Immigrants from Vietnam, Korea, Laos, and Thailand brought with them recipes and new herbs and spices. These varied ethnic influences are revealed in the practices of both home cooks and professional chefs. What was dubbed "fusion food" in the 1990s has long been characteristic of Pacific Northwest cooking.

The artisanal food movement is strong in the Northwest, where there is a large concentration of rustic bread bakeries, premium wineries, microbreweries, and coffee roasters. These wonderful handmade foods, together with ethnic ingredients and techniques, result in a cuisine that is fresh, simple, and often innovative.

CALIFORNIA

California cuisine is shaped by its ethnic diversity, from the early Italian and Chinese immigrants to the more recent arrivals from Southeast Asia and Central America. In famously eclectic California, "fast food" is as likely to mean Vietnamese pho or Salvadoran pupusas as it is the usual burger.

California is America's number one agricultural producer—it provides half of the country's fruits, nuts, and vegetables.

Local cooks have a plethora of locally grown, fresh produce with which to work and revel in the principle of seasonality, enjoying in turn the bounty of artichokes, avocados, oranges, and other delights. They also have the benefit of a thousand miles of coastline, with more than 250 varieties of fish and shellfish found in state waters from Crescent City in the north to San Diego in the south.

The artisanal food movement seen throughout the nation today arguably started in California, and Old World traditions of bread, cheese, olive oil, and wine making are most widespread here, alongside dishes inspired by new ingredients and global cuisines.

Old-fashioned or new-fangled—it's all become part of the American culinary repertoire. Photos on page 8: the Heartland's Blue Ribbon Cinnamon Buns, far left, and the Southwest's Salmon Cakes with Jalapeno Remoulade, left. Photos on this page: the Pacific Northwest's Penne with Morels and Spring Vegetables, left, and California's Focaccia-Stuffed Artichokes, above.

Starters, Soups & Salads

Sautéed Pea Shoots with Singing Scallops

3 tablespoons unsalted butter

1½ lb (750 g) pea shoots, rinsed but not dried

½ teaspoon salt

½ teaspoon freshly ground pepper

2 shallots, finely chopped

16 singing scallops in the shell, well rinsed, or 1 lb (500 g) other scallops

¼ cup (2 fl oz/60 ml) dry white wine

3 tablespoons finely diced tomato

2 tablespoons finely chopped mixed fresh herbs such as flat-leaf (Italian) parsley, mint, and thyme

1 teaspoon grated lemon zest

Singing scallops, delicately flavored bivalves, get their whimsical name because their pretty pink shells gape open. They're widely available in the Northwest, retrieved from the ocean floor by divers. If they're not available, you can use bay or sea scallops without the shells. They will take slightly less time to cook; add the remaining ingredients at the same time as you add the scallops.

1. In a large frying pan over medium-high heat, melt 1 tablespoon of the butter. Add the damp pea shoots and ¼ teaspoon each of the salt and pepper. Cover and cook, stirring occasionally, until wilted, 1–2 minutes. Uncover and transfer to individual plates. Keep warm.

2. Return the pan to medium-high heat and add 1 tablespoon of the remaining butter. When it melts, add the shallots and cook, stirring frequently, until soft, 2–3 minutes. Stir in the scallops and cook for 1 minute. Add the wine, tomato, herbs, lemon zest, and the remaining ¼ teaspoon each salt and pepper and 1 tablespoon butter. Simmer until the scallops are opaque throughout, about 1 minute.

3. Spoon the scallop mixture over the pea shoots and serve immediately.

SERVES 4

NUTRITIONAL ANALYSIS PER SERVING
Calories 411 (Kilojoules 1,726); Protein 34 g; Carbohydrates 52 g; Total Fat 11 g; Saturated Fat 6 g; Cholesterol 61 mg; Sodium 510 mg; Dietary Fiber 0 g

Sopa de Lima

1 lb (500 g) skinless, boneless chicken breasts

1 large, ripe Hass avocado

6 cups (48 fl oz/1.5 l) chicken stock

¼ cup (2 fl oz/60 ml) fresh lime juice, plus 6 lime wedges

kosher salt to taste

¾ cup (4½ oz/140 g) diced ripe plum (Roma) tomato

6 tablespoons (2 oz/60 g) finely chopped red onion

3 serrano chiles, minced

3 tablespoons coarsely chopped fresh cilantro (fresh coriander)

You'll find small, spherical, yellow-green limes, the *limas* of southern Mexico, in ethnic markets in the Southwest. The fruit has a flavor reminiscent of bergamot, the citrus fruit whose oil scents Earl Grey tea, and it contributes a light, refreshing quality to this chicken-and-vegetable soup. Similar Key limes make a good substitute, although you can also use common Persian limes.

1. In a saucepan, combine the chicken with water to cover by 3 inches (7.5 cm). Bring to a boil over high heat, reduce the heat to medium-low, and simmer the chicken gently until opaque throughout, about 10 minutes. Remove from the heat and let the chicken cool in the liquid. Lift out the chicken and discard the water. Using your fingers, shred the chicken into strips.

2. Halve and pit the avocado, then peel. Cut each half in half again lengthwise, then cut crosswise into ½-inch (12-mm) cubes.

3. In a saucepan, bring the stock to a boil. Season with the lime juice and salt. Divide the chicken, avocado, tomato, onion, chiles, and cilantro evenly among individual bowls. Ladle the hot stock over the top, again dividing evenly. Serve immediately, accompanying each bowl with a lime wedge for diners to add more juice to taste.

SERVES 6

NUTRITIONAL ANALYSIS PER SERVING
Calories 195 (Kilojoules 819); Protein 21 g; Carbohydrates 8 g; Total Fat 9 g;
Saturated Fat 2 g; Cholesterol 44 mg; Sodium 1,057 mg; Dietary Fiber 1 g

Lobster Salad with Cucumber & Dill

1 lb (500 g) fresh-cooked lobster
    meat (from about 5 lb/2.5 kg
    lobster in the shell), picked over
    for shell fragments and cut into
    bite-sized chunks

1 cucumber, peeled, seeded, and diced

2½ tablespoons fresh lemon juice

1 teaspoon grated lemon zest

1 small shallot, minced

salt and freshly ground pepper
    to taste

⅓ cup (3 fl oz/80 ml) extra-virgin
    olive oil

2 tablespoons minced fresh dill

4 cups (4 oz/125 g) loosely packed
    watercress sprigs, tough stems
    removed

Lobster fishing defines the very soul of Maine, whose rock-bound shoreline is shrouded in dense fog and salty seaside air. Although lobster is available year-round, it's most plentiful in the summer. Serve this elegant seasonal salad with toasted brioche slices and a chilled Chardonnay.

1. In a bowl, combine the lobster and cucumber. Set aside.

2. In a small bowl, whisk together the lemon juice, lemon zest, shallot, salt, and pepper. Whisk in the olive oil. Stir in the dill, then taste and adjust the seasoning. It should be quite zesty.

3. Pour the dressing over the lobster and cucumber and toss to coat evenly. Cover the salad and refrigerate to chill and marinate for at least 30 minutes or as long as several hours.

4. Divide the watercress sprigs among chilled salad plates. Top evenly with the lobster salad and serve at once.

SERVES 4

NUTRITIONAL ANALYSIS PER SERVING
Calories 284 (Kilojoules 1,193); Protein 24 g; Carbohydrates 5 g; Total Fat 19 g;
Saturated Fat 3 g; Cholesterol 82 mg; Sodium 447 mg; Dietary Fiber 1 g

Potato Crisps with Northwest Caviar

¾ lb (375 g) Yukon gold or russet potatoes, peeled and very thinly sliced

2 tablespoons olive oil

½ teaspoon fine salt

¾ cup (6 oz/180 g) crème fraîche or sour cream

3½ oz (105 g) ikura or other salted salmon roe

8 large fresh basil leaves, finely shredded

Chum salmon, the least popular salmon variety, produces the most sought-after ikura, or salted salmon roe. The lovely orange eggs make an affordable caviar. Prepare these crisps ahead of time and top them at the last minute. To slice the potatoes quickly and uniformly, use a mandoline.

1. Preheat the oven to 450°F (230°C).

2. Spread out the potato slices on 2 nonstick baking sheets and brush both sides with the olive oil. Do not overlap the slices. Sprinkle evenly with the salt.

3. Bake the potato slices until crisp, browned, and tender, 15–20 minutes. Remove from the oven and let cool completely.

4. To serve, top each potato slice with a dollop of crème fraîche or sour cream (about 1 teaspoon) and a bit of ikura (about ¼ teaspoon). Sprinkle the basil over the tops and arrange on a platter. Serve immediately.

MAKES ABOUT 40 CRISPS; SERVES 6

NUTRITIONAL ANALYSIS PER SERVING
Calories 197 (Kilojoules 827); Protein 6 g; Carbohydrates 11 g; Total Fat 15 g; Saturated Fat 5 g; Cholesterol 114 mg; Sodium 458 mg; Dietary Fiber 1 g

Warm Baked Olives with Garlic & Fennel

1 cup (5 oz/155 g) Niçoise olives

¼ cup (2 fl oz/60 ml) extra-virgin olive oil

2 large cloves garlic, sliced

½ teaspoon fennel seeds, coarsely crushed in a mortar or spice grinder

1 tablespoon fresh lemon juice

A daylong stay in a garlicky marinade infuses olives with flavor, and warming them intensifies the flavor even more. Serve these olives as a cocktail nibble along with toasted almonds with sea salt. If you can't find Niçoise olives, substitute Kalamata olives or even green Picholines.

1. Rinse the olives well and pat thoroughly dry.

2. In a frying pan over medium heat, warm the olive oil. Add the garlic and heat until fragrant and just starting to color, about 1 minute. Stir in the olives and fennel seeds and cook until the olives are hot throughout, about 2 minutes. Remove from the heat and let cool. Stir the lemon juice into the cooled olives and transfer to a tightly covered container. Let stand for at least 8 hours or as long as 24 hours at room temperature, shaking the container occasionally to redistribute the seasoning.

3. To serve, preheat the oven to 350°F (180°C). Put the olives and their marinade in a baking dish and bake until they are warmed throughout, about 10 minutes.

4. Using a slotted spoon, lift the olives out of the marinade and transfer to a serving dish. Serve warm, not hot.

SERVES 6

NUTRITIONAL ANALYSIS PER SERVING
Calories 122 (Kilojoules 512); Protein 2 g; Carbohydrates 2 g; Total Fat 13 g;
Saturated Fat 1 g; Cholesterol 0 mg; Sodium 284 mg; Dietary Fiber 2 g

Olives &
Olive Oil

When the Spanish missionaries arrived in California over two centuries ago, they brought more than religion. At every mission they founded, they planted olive trees, some of which still stand. What is known today as the Mission olive may or may not be the same variety that the friars planted, but it is the cornerstone of the state's huge canned olive industry.

From thirty-five thousand acres (14,170 hectares) of olive trees in its warm inland valleys, California's canneries produce three-quarters of the ripe olives consumed in the United States. But in truth, the word *ripe* is a misnomer. The olives are picked green, lye-cured to remove their natural bitterness, and then oxygenated to turn them from green to black.

Compared to the canning industry, the olive oil business in California is small but rapidly changing. In recent years, several entrepreneurs have taken steps to make the state as well known for its olive oil as it is for its wine. Importing the best French and Italian trees, they have established plantings—mostly in Northern California—and have sought international advice on how to make top-quality extra-

virgin oil. The California Olive Oil Council, founded in 1992, has established a certification program to ensure that California oils labeled "extra virgin" meet international standards. High land costs mean the state probably will never be a major producer, but some of the high-priced boutique oils are earning acclaim.

From extra-virgin olive oil, extracted without the use of heat or chemicals, to stuffed olives and Mediterranean style tapenades, the olive products from California are rich and varied.

Achiote Shrimp Tostadas

MARINADE

2 tablespoons roasted garlic *(page 36)*

1 package (3½ oz/105 g) *achiote* paste, crumbled

¼ cup (2 fl oz/60 ml) thawed frozen orange juice concentrate

⅓ cup (3 fl oz/80 ml) fresh grapefruit juice

¼ cup (2 fl oz/60 ml) water

2 tablespoons cider vinegar

1 teaspoon cumin seeds, toasted and ground

1 teaspoon freshly ground canela or ½ teaspoon ground cinnamon

pinch of ground allspice or cloves

pinch of kosher salt, or to taste

24 shrimp (prawns), peeled and deveined

MAYONNAISE

1 can (7½ oz/235 g) chipotle chiles in adobo sauce

3 tablespoons roasted garlic *(page 36)*

1 whole egg plus 1 egg yolk

1 tablespoon balsamic vinegar

¾ cup (6 fl oz/180 ml) safflower oil

kosher salt to taste

12 white corn tortillas, each 5 inches (13 cm) in diameter

safflower oil for frying

⅓ cup (½ oz/15 g) snipped fresh chives or coarsely chopped fresh cilantro (fresh coriander)

This appetizer gets its distinctive flavor from two traditional Mexican ingredients, *achiote* paste and chipotle chiles, and a contemporary addition: balsamic vinegar.

1. To make the marinade, in a food processor, combine the garlic, *achiote,* orange juice concentrate, grapefruit juice, water, vinegar, cumin, canela or cinnamon, allspice or cloves, and salt. Purée until smooth.

2. In a bowl, combine the shrimp and ½ cup (4 fl oz/125 ml) of the marinade. Mix well, cover, and set aside at room temperature for 1 hour.

3. To make the mayonnaise, place the chipotle chiles in a blender and purée until smooth. Pass through a fine-mesh sieve. In the food processor, combine ¼ cup (2 fl oz/60 ml) of the purée, the garlic, the whole egg and egg yolk, and the vinegar. Process to blend. Then, with the motor running, slowly add the oil to form a smooth purée. It should be a little thicker than heavy (double) cream. Season with salt. Cover and refrigerate until serving.

4. Using a 2-inch (5-cm) round cookie cutter, cut out 2 rounds from each tortilla. Pour safflower oil to a depth of ¼ inch (6 mm) into a frying pan and heat over medium-high heat. When the oil is hot, add the tortilla rounds, in batches, and fry until crisp, 1–1½ minutes. Using tongs, transfer to paper towels to drain. Pour off all the oil from the pan.

5. Drain the shrimp well. In the frying pan over medium-high heat, warm 2 tablespoons safflower oil. Add half of the shrimp and cook, turning once, until opaque throughout, 4–6 minutes total. Transfer to a plate. Repeat with the remaining shrimp, adding oil as necessary.

6. Place 1 shrimp on each tortilla round and drizzle with ½ teaspoon of the mayonnaise. (Reserve the remaining mayonnaise for another use.) Sprinkle with chives or cilantro and serve immediately.

SERVES 6

NUTRITIONAL ANALYSIS PER SERVING
Calories 680 (Kilojoules 2,856); Protein 14 g; Carbohydrates 53 g; Total Fat 47 g; Saturated Fat 5 g; Cholesterol 132 mg; Sodium 799 mg; Dietary Fiber 4 g

Silken Lima Bean Soup with Ham Croûtes

SOUP

4 lb (2 kg) fresh limas, shelled (about 4 cups), or 2 bags (1 lb/500 g each) frozen lima beans, thawed

8 cups (64 fl oz/2 l) chicken stock

1 russet potato, peeled and cut into ½-inch (12-mm) dice

1 yellow onion, chopped

2 cloves garlic, chopped

1 carrot, peeled and chopped

½ teaspoon salt

½ teaspoon freshly ground pepper

½ cup (4 fl oz/125 ml) heavy (double) cream

1 tablespoon fresh thyme leaves

CROÛTES

6 slices French bread, each 1 inch (2.5 cm) thick

½ cup (3 oz/90 g) chopped country ham

⅓ cup (1½ oz/45 g) shredded cheddar cheese

2 tablespoons cream cheese, at room temperature

1 tablespoon mayonnaise

freshly ground pepper to taste

Lima beans grow in gardens all over the South and are available fresh from June to September. Fordhooks, a favorite variety, are larger and have a fuller flavor than those known as baby limas. If using fresh beans, choose pods that are firm, plump, and dark green, and shell them just before cooking.

1. To make the soup, in a large saucepan over high heat, combine the lima beans, chicken stock, potato, onion, garlic, carrot, salt, and pepper. Bring to a boil, reduce the heat to low, cover partially, and cook, stirring occasionally, until the vegetables are very soft, about 1 hour.

2. Meanwhile, make the croûtes: Preheat the oven to 400°F (200°C). Arrange the bread slices on a baking sheet and toast until golden brown, about 10 minutes. Remove from the oven and turn the oven to broil (grill). Position a rack 6 inches (15 cm) from the heat source.

3. In a small bowl, stir together the ham, cheddar cheese, cream cheese, mayonnaise, and pepper. Divide among the bread slices and spread evenly.

4. When the soup is ready, ladle it into a food processor, in batches if necessary, and purée until smooth. Return the purée to the saucepan and stir in the cream.

5. While the soup is reheating, broil (grill) the croûtes until the topping is bubbly and golden, about 2 minutes.

6. Ladle the soup into warmed bowls, sprinkle with the thyme leaves, and serve the croûtes on the side.

SERVES 6

NUTRITIONAL ANALYSIS PER SERVING
Calories 547 (Kilojoules 2,297); Protein 25 g; Carbohydrates 68 g; Total Fat 20 g; Saturated Fat 9 g; Cholesterol 51 mg; Sodium 2,311 mg; Dietary Fiber 8 g

Spinach, Orange & Beet Salad

4 small (but not baby) beets, about ½ lb (250 g) total weight, trimmed leaving 1 inch (2.5 cm) of stem

2 large navel or blood oranges

¾ lb (375 g) baby spinach, stems removed

DRESSING

3 tablespoons extra-virgin olive oil

1 tablespoon fresh lemon juice, or to taste

1 shallot, minced

salt and freshly ground pepper to taste

California's plump, sweet navel oranges turn up frequently in winter salads—and not just in fruit salads. They add appealing color and tang to this mix of beets and spinach, a good prelude to a main course of pork chops or duck. Red-fleshed blood oranges would also work here.

1. Preheat the oven to 375°F (190°C). Put the beets in a baking dish and add water to a depth of ¼ inch (6 mm). Cover and bake until the beets are tender when pierced, 45–60 minutes.

2. Meanwhile, cut a slice off the top and bottom of 1 orange to expose the fruit. Stand the orange upright on a cutting surface and thickly slice off the peel in strips, cutting around the contour of the orange to expose the flesh. Holding the orange over a bowl, cut along either side of each section to free it from the membrane, letting the section drop into the bowl. Repeat with the remaining orange. Put the spinach in a large bowl.

3. To make the dressing, in a small bowl, whisk together the olive oil, 1 tablespoon lemon juice, shallot, salt, and pepper. Let stand for 30 minutes to allow the shallot flavor to mellow.

4. When the beets are ready, remove from the oven and let cool until they can be handled. Peel and cut into wedges about the size of the orange sections. Put the beet wedges in a bowl and toss with just enough of the dressing to coat them lightly.

5. Using a slotted spoon, transfer the orange sections to the bowl holding the spinach. (Reserve any collected juice for another use.) Add the remaining dressing and toss to coat. Taste and adjust the seasoning, adding more lemon juice if desired.

6. Divide the spinach and oranges among individual plates. Top each serving with an equal amount of the beets. Serve immediately.

SERVES 6

NUTRITIONAL ANALYSIS PER SERVING
Calories 108 (Kilojoules 454); Protein 2 g; Carbohydrates 11 g; Total Fat 7 g;
Saturated Fat 1 g; Cholesterol 0 mg; Sodium 52 mg; Dietary Fiber 3 g

Chorizo Empanadas with Ancho Chile Sauce

DOUGH

2 cups (10 oz/315 g) all-purpose (plain) flour

¾ teaspoon kosher salt

6 tablespoons (3 oz/90 g) chilled unsalted butter, cut into 6 pieces

6 tablespoons (3 oz/90 g) lard, bacon fat, or vegetable shortening

4–5 tablespoons (2–2½ fl oz/ 60–75 ml) ice water

SAUCE

3 ancho chiles

1 tablespoon roasted garlic *(page 36)*

2 tablespoons cider vinegar

1 cup (8 oz/250 g) chilled unsalted butter, cut into 8 pieces

kosher salt to taste

FILLING

2 tablespoons olive oil

½ white onion, finely chopped

2 cloves garlic, minced

1 teaspoon cumin seeds, toasted

½ teaspoon dried Mexican oregano

½ teaspoon freshly ground canela or ¼ teaspoon ground cinnamon

½ lb (250 g) bulk chorizo

1 egg white, lightly beaten with ¼ teaspoon water

1 whole egg, lightly beaten with 1 tablespoon heavy (double) cream

½ cup (2½ oz/75 g) crumbled *queso fresco* or *queso añejo*

1. To make the dough, in a food processor, combine the flour and salt and pulse to mix. Add the butter and the lard or other fat and process until the mixture resembles coarse crumbs. Add the water, 1 tablespoon at a time, until the mixture comes together. Turn out onto plastic wrap, shape into a disk, wrap, and refrigerate for 1 hour.

2. To make the sauce, in a small frying pan over medium-high heat, toast the chiles, turning once, until fragrant, 1–2 minutes. Immerse in hot water for 30 minutes. Drain, reserving the water, and discard the stems. In a blender, combine the chiles and ½ cup (4 fl oz/125 ml) of the soaking water and purée until smooth. If too thick, add a little more water. Pass through a medium-mesh sieve and reserve.

3. To make the filling, in a frying pan over medium-high heat, warm the olive oil. Add the onion and garlic and sauté until softened, 3–4 minutes. Add the cumin, oregano, and canela and cook for 1 minute. Crumble in the chorizo and cook until browned, 4–5 minutes. Drain in a sieve.

4. Preheat the oven to 425°F (220°C). Line a baking sheet with parchment (baking) paper. On a lightly floured work surface, roll out the dough ⅛ inch (3 mm) thick. Using a 4½-inch (11.5-cm) round cookie cutter, cut out as many rounds as possible. Reroll the scraps and cut out additional rounds. You should have 16 rounds. Place 1 tablespoon of the filling in the center of each round. Brush the edges with the egg white and fold in half. With floured fork tines, press the edges together to seal. Place on the prepared baking sheet and brush generously with the egg-cream mixture. Bake until golden brown, about 20 minutes. Let cool for 10 minutes.

5. Finish the sauce: In a saucepan over low heat, warm the ancho purée, roasted garlic, and vinegar. Add the butter, 2 pieces at a time, whisking well after each addition. Season with salt.

6. Top the empanadas with the sauce and cheese, then serve.

MAKES 16 EMPANADAS; SERVES 4

NUTRITIONAL ANALYSIS PER EMPANADA
Calories 368 (Kilojoules 1,546); Protein 7 g; Carbohydrates 17 g; Total Fat 31 g; Saturated Fat 15 g; Cholesterol 77 mg; Sodium 288 mg; Dietary Fiber 1 g

Green Chile Stew

3 tablespoons toasted peanut oil or vegetable oil

2 lb (1 kg) boneless pork shoulder or butt, trimmed of excess fat, cut into ¾-inch (2-cm) cubes

1 white onion, chopped

2 cloves garlic, minced

½ lb (250 g) white or brown fresh mushrooms, brushed clean and quartered through the stem end

¾ lb (375 g) small yellow-fleshed potatoes, quartered lengthwise

1½ teaspoons coriander seeds, toasted and ground

1 teaspoon dried Mexican oregano

2 bay leaves

6 cups (48 fl oz/1.5 l) chicken stock

2 teaspoons kosher salt, or to taste

12–16 New Mexico green chiles (about 2 lb/1 kg total), roasted, peeled, and seeded *(page 311),* then chopped (about 3 cups/18 oz/560 g)

6 tablespoons (3 oz/90 g) crema or crème fraîche

Commonly called simply *chile verde,* or "green chile," this easy-to-make, delicious dish is one of New Mexico's most popular traditional stews. Regional markets sell the state's green chiles both fresh and frozen. If you cannot find them, substitute Anaheim or poblano chiles, both close cousins.

1. In a large saucepan over high heat, warm the oil. In batches, add the pork and brown well on all sides, 6–8 minutes. Using a slotted spoon, transfer to a plate and set aside.

2. Add the onion to the oil remaining in the pan over medium-high heat and sauté until lightly golden, about 4 minutes. Add the garlic and sauté for 1 minute longer. Add the mushrooms and sauté until the edges are browned, 3–4 minutes. Add the potatoes, coriander, oregano, and bay leaves and return the meat to the pan. Stir well, pour in the stock, and add 1 teaspoon of the salt. Bring to a boil, reduce the heat to medium, and simmer, uncovered, until the meat is just tender, about 30 minutes.

3. Add the green chiles and continue to simmer, uncovered, for 20 minutes longer until the chiles are heated through and the meat is very tender. Stir in the remaining 1 teaspoon salt, then taste and adjust with more salt if necessary.

4. Ladle into warmed bowls and garnish with the crema or crème fraîche. Serve at once.

SERVES 6

NUTRITIONAL ANALYSIS PER SERVING
Calories 478 (Kilojoules 2,008); Protein 36 g; Carbohydrates 24 g; Total Fat 27 g; Saturated Fat 9 g; Cholesterol 114 mg; Sodium 1,631 mg; Dietary Fiber 3 g

Southwest Chiles

A bewildering number of distinct chile species and varieties exist, all with different heat levels and flavors and in different shapes, sizes, and shades. A green chile and a red, orange, or yellow chile may simply be different stages of ripeness of the same pepper. Green signals the unripened stage, while the other colors characterize a ripened, or mature, chile. The same chile can also have different names, depending on whether it is fresh or dried and sometimes where it is grown.

Ancho Dried form of poblano, wrinkled and filled with sweet heat. Also ground.

Chile Caribe Finely crushed dried New Mexico red chiles.

Chipotle Dried, smoked version of a jalapeño varietal. Available canned *en adobo,* in a spicy tomato-vinegar sauce.

Jalapeño Popular thick-fleshed fresh green or red chiles that carry high heat. Available pickled, labeled *en escabeche*.

Morita Deep red, wrinkly skinned dried chile with smoky high heat.

New Mexico Green Fresh green chile varying between mild and medium-hot.

New Mexico Red Dark red mature form of the New Mexico green, used fresh and dried. Those grown in the Chimayó region of New Mexico are known for their intense flavor. Available dried whole or ground.

Poblano Medium-sized, cone-shaped fresh chile, available both dark green and dark red-brown, mild to pleasantly hot.

Serrano Small, slim green or red fresh chiles with bright, clean searing heat.

A sampling of fresh and dried chiles of the Southwest (clockwise from left): purple and orange habaneros, chilacas, serranos, güeros, and red jalapeños.

Minted Double Pea Soup

2 tablespoons unsalted butter

2 small inner celery stalks with
leaves, chopped

1 yellow onion, chopped

6 cups (48 fl oz/1.5 l) chicken stock

1 baking potato, peeled and sliced

2 fresh thyme sprigs

⅛ teaspoon freshly grated nutmeg

2 lb (1 kg) sugar snap peas, chopped

2 lb (1 kg) English peas, shelled,
or 2 cups (10 oz/315 g) frozen
shelled English peas, thawed

¼ cup (¼ oz/7 g) fresh flat-leaf
(Italian) parsley leaves

¼ cup (2 fl oz/60 ml) heavy (double)
cream, or to taste

2 tablespoons fresh lemon juice

salt and freshly ground pepper to taste

2 tablespoons chopped fresh mint,
plus 4–6 sprigs

The sugar snap, darling of pea lovers, is a cross of the snow pea (mangetout) and the English pea and is sweeter and more succulent than its forebears. At the farmers' markets in Minneapolis and St. Paul, Hmong farmers (refugees from northern Laos) sell sugar snaps on the vine by the case. If you can find them this way, remove the pea pods and steep the vines for a few moments in the stock before making the soup, to add more luscious, rich, sweet pea flavor.

1. In a heavy soup pot over medium heat, melt the butter. Add the celery and onion and sauté until the onion is translucent and the celery is soft, about 5 minutes. Add the stock, potato, thyme, and nutmeg and bring to a boil. Reduce the heat to medium-low, partially cover the pot, and simmer until the potato slices are very tender, about 10 minutes.

2. Add the sugar snap peas and simmer until tender, 10–15 minutes. Add the English peas and simmer until cooked, 3–5 minutes. Stir in the parsley.

3. In a blender or food processor, purée the soup, in batches, until smooth. Pour through a sieve placed over a bowl resting in a bowl of ice. Stir the soup slowly until it has cooled to room temperature (this sets the green color). Stir in the cream, lemon juice, salt, and pepper, then remove the soup from the ice bath.

4. If serving the soup warm, return to the pot over low heat and heat through; do not allow it to boil. Or, if serving the soup cold, cover the bowl and refrigerate until well chilled.

5. Just before serving, taste and adjust the seasoning, stir in the chopped mint, and ladle into bowls or cups. Garnish with the mint sprigs and serve.

SERVES 4–6

NUTRITIONAL ANALYSIS PER SERVING
Calories 285 (Kilojoules 1,197); Protein 11 g; Carbohydrates 33 g; Total Fat 12 g; Saturated Fat 6 g; Cholesterol 29 mg; Sodium 1,223 mg; Dietary Fiber 8 g

Poached Egg & Chanterelle Salad

6 tablespoons (3 fl oz/90 ml) extra-virgin olive oil

1 tablespoon fresh lemon juice

¾ teaspoon coarse salt

¾ teaspoon freshly ground pepper

2 bunches watercress, tough stems removed

4 large slices artisan bread, each ½ inch (12 mm) thick

¾ lb (375 g) fresh chanterelle or other wild or cultivated mushrooms such as oyster, cremini, or portobello, rinsed quickly or wiped clean, and halved if large

1 tablespoon chopped fresh flat-leaf (Italian) parsley

4 eggs

Chanterelles are beautiful wild or cultivated mushrooms with ruffled tops and a distinctive woodsy flavor. They come in several colors, but the yellow chanterelle is the most common. If they are very dirty, rinse them quickly and pat dry.

1. Preheat the broiler (griller).

2. In a jar, combine 3 tablespoons of the olive oil, the lemon juice, and ¼ teaspoon each of the salt and pepper. Cover and shake well.

3. Place the watercress in a bowl. Drizzle with 2 tablespoons of the dressing and toss well. Divide among individual plates.

4. Brush the bread slices on both sides with 1 tablespoon of the oil and place on a baking sheet. Slip under the broiler and toast, turning once, until golden brown, about 1 minute on each side. Cut in half and set aside.

5. In a large frying pan over medium-high heat, warm the remaining 2 tablespoons oil. Add the mushrooms and sauté until tender, 3–5 minutes. Season with the remaining ½ teaspoon each salt and pepper, and add the parsley. Toss, remove from the heat, and keep warm.

6. Meanwhile, pour water into a shallow saucepan or sauté pan to a depth of 2 inches (5 cm) and bring to just under a boil. One at a time, and working quickly, break the eggs into a saucer and slip into the water. Cook until the whites are firm and the yolks are glazed but still liquid, 3–4 minutes, or until done to your liking.

7. Using a wire skimmer or slotted spoon, carefully remove each egg, and blot the bottom by resting the skimmer or spoon briefly on paper towels. Place 1 egg in the middle of each bed of watercress. Spoon the mushrooms and some of their juices around the eggs and slide 2 bread slice halves under the watercress on opposite sides of each plate. Drizzle the remaining dressing over the eggs and serve.

SERVES 4

NUTRITIONAL ANALYSIS PER SERVING
Calories 440 (Kilojoules 1,848); Protein 15 g; Carbohydrates 35 g; Total Fat 28 g; Saturated Fat 5 g; Cholesterol 213 mg; Sodium 706 mg; Dietary Fiber 5 g

Potato & Roasted Garlic Soup

1 whole head garlic

1 teaspoon olive oil

¼ cup (2 oz/60 g) unsalted butter

1 large yellow onion, minced

2 lb (1 kg) russet potatoes, peeled
and cut into large chunks

2 cups (16 fl oz/500 ml) chicken stock

2 cups (16 fl oz/500 ml) water

1 bay leaf

1¾ cups (14 fl oz/430 ml) milk,
or as needed

salt and freshly ground pepper to taste

3 tablespoons thinly sliced fresh chives

Garlic cloves become soft and mild when roasted whole. Here, the aromatic cloves are added to a creamy potato soup to give it a flavor boost. Look for heavy garlic heads with large, firm cloves and no sooty spots. Serve this soup as a first course, followed by roast pork with steamed chard.

1. Preheat the oven to 400°F (200°C). Put the head of garlic on a sheet of aluminum foil and drizzle with the olive oil. Seal the foil around the garlic to make a package. Bake until the garlic is fragrant and the cloves feel soft, about 40 minutes. You will need to unwrap the package to check for doneness; if the cloves are still firm, reseal and continue baking. When done, set aside to cool. When cool, peel the cloves; they should slip easily from their skins. Set aside.

2. Meanwhile, in a large saucepan over medium heat, melt the butter. Add the onion and sauté, stirring, until soft, about 10 minutes. Add the potatoes, stock, water, and bay leaf and bring to a simmer. Cover, adjust the heat to maintain a gentle simmer, and cook until the potatoes are tender, about 25 minutes. Remove the bay leaf and discard.

3. Working in batches, transfer the potato mixture to a food processor or blender and add the garlic cloves. Secure the lid and cover with a kitchen towel. Process until completely smooth. Return to a clean saucepan and stir in 1¾ cups (14 fl oz/430 ml) milk, or enough to thin the soup to your taste. Season with salt and pepper and reheat gently over medium heat.

4. Divide the soup among warmed bowls. Garnish with the chives, dividing evenly. Serve immediately.

SERVES 6

NUTRITIONAL ANALYSIS PER SERVING
Calories 264 (Kilojoules 1,109); Protein 7 g; Carbohydrates 34 g; Total Fat 12 g;
Saturated Fat 7 g; Cholesterol 31 mg; Sodium 382 mg; Dietary Fiber 3 g

Garlic Galore

Every July, nearly 120,000 people descend on the central California town of Gilroy for a three-day celebration of garlic. During this long weekend, they consume truck-loads of the "stinking rose" in such dishes as stuffed mushrooms and pasta with pesto. Judges select the best garlic recipes in a consumer cooking contest, and hundreds of volunteers work to raise money that they donate to local charities.

Launched in 1979, the Gilroy Garlic Festival has generated so much publicity that Gilroy now proudly proclaims itself the Garlic Capital of the World. Some credit the media coverage with helping to almost triple America's fresh garlic consumption over the last 20 years.

Today, the state of California produces nearly 90 percent of the domestic garlic crop, growing more than 500 million pounds (250 million kg). About three-quarters of the crop is dehydrated for garlic salt, garlic powder, and processed foods. The rest is savored fresh in home kitchens and restaurants.

In California, commercial garlic is planted in the fall from individual cloves. The sprouting cloves produce straplike leaves that resemble leeks, while the bulb

matures underground. When the leaves begin to turn yellow in summer, farmers stop watering the plants. When the tops are dry, the garlic is pulled and dried in the sun for a week or more. Then the tops are trimmed and the bulbs sorted and readied for shipping to garlic lovers throughout the country and around the world.

Garlic lovers enjoy abundant fresh garlic shipped fresh from California growers to markets all over the country.

Fried Scallops & Parsley

1 lb (500 g) sea scallops or large bay scallops

vegetable or peanut oil for deep-frying

1½ cups (6 oz/185 g) fine cracker crumbs or dried bread crumbs

salt and freshly ground pepper to taste

2 eggs

1 cup (1 oz/30 g) loosely packed curly-leaf parsley sprigs

1 lemon, cut into wedges

Cracker crumbs are a popular Yankee coating for fried and broiled seafood. Make your own by putting oyster crackers or unsalted soda crackers in a plastic bag and crushing them with a rolling pin. Traditionalists serve tartar sauce with fried scallops, but a more contemporary approach is lemon wedges.

1. Remove the small, opaque white muscle that wraps partway around the circumference of each scallop. Cut any sea scallops that are more than 1 inch (2.5 cm) thick in half horizontally. Rinse the scallops, pat dry with paper towels, and set aside.

2. Preheat the oven to 200°F (95°C). Pour the vegetable or peanut oil to a depth of 2 inches (5 cm) into a deep-fat fryer or a deep, heavy saucepan and heat to 365°F (185°C) on a deep-frying thermometer.

3. While the oil is heating, spread the cracker crumbs or bread crumbs on a plate and season with salt and pepper. In a shallow bowl, lightly beat the eggs with a few drops of water until blended. Dip the scallops into the eggs, then roll them, a few at a time, in the crumbs to coat. Arrange the breaded scallops on a large plate; do not allow them to touch one another.

4. Carefully add the scallops, a few at a time, to the hot oil. Do not crowd the pan. Deep-fry, turning once, until the scallops are golden brown, 1–1½ minutes total for sea scallops and 30–60 seconds for bay scallops. Using a slotted spoon, transfer the scallops to paper towels to drain. Keep warm in the oven. Repeat until all the scallops are cooked.

5. Carefully toss the parsley sprigs into the hot oil and fry until crisp, 5–10 seconds. Scoop out with a wire skimmer and place on paper towels to drain briefly. Sprinkle with salt.

6. Pile the scallops onto warmed individual plates and top with the fried parsley. Serve immediately with the lemon wedges.

SERVES 4

NUTRITIONAL ANALYSIS PER SERVING
Calories 420 (Kilojoules 1,764); Protein 27 g; Carbohydrates 37 g; Total Fat 19 g; Saturated Fat 11 g; Cholesterol 144 mg; Sodium 771 mg; Dietary Fiber 1 g

Squash Blossom Quesadillas

12 flour tortillas, each 7–8 inches (18–20 cm) in diameter

1½ cups (6 oz/185 g) shredded Monterey jack cheese

¾ cup (4 oz/125 g) crumbled *queso fresco* or mild feta cheese

leaves from 6 fresh epazote sprigs

4 large fresh *hoja santa* leaves, cut lengthwise into strips ½ inch (12 mm) wide

3 or 4 serrano chiles, roasted, peeled, and seeded *(page 311),* then thinly sliced on the extreme diagonal

18 squash blossoms, stems and pistils removed and cut crosswise into strips ½ inch (12 mm) wide

kosher salt to taste

Native Americans of the Southwest—especially the Zunis, who live in western New Mexico—have long eaten the delicate golden blossoms of squashes, the best of which come from zucchini (courgettes). Although they may be stuffed and deep-fried, the flowers are used here to add bright color and subtle flavor to the region's distinctive version of the grilled cheese sandwich.

1. Preheat the oven to 350°F (180°C).

2. Sprinkle 6 of the tortillas evenly with both cheeses, the epazote leaves, the *hoja santa* strips, the chiles, and the squash blossom strips. Sprinkle with salt and place a second tortilla on top of each filled one, pressing down gently. Transfer the quesadillas to 2 ungreased baking sheets.

3. Bake the quesadillas until the cheese starts to melt, 4–5 minutes. Carefully flip the quesadillas over and continue to bake until the cheese is melted, about 4 minutes longer. Remove from the oven and slide the quesadillas onto a cutting board. Cut each round into 6 pieces. Transfer to a serving platter and serve immediately.

SERVES 6–8

NUTRITIONAL ANALYSIS PER SERVING
Calories 339 (Kilojoules 1,424); Protein 14 g; Carbohydrates 34 g; Total Fat 16 g; Saturated Fat 8 g; Cholesterol 37 mg; Sodium 532 mg; Dietary Fiber 2 g

Sweet Corn Chowder

8–10 large ears of corn, husks and silk removed

4 slices thick-cut bacon, cut into ½-inch (12-mm) pieces

1 yellow onion, chopped

½ lb (250 g) red or white boiling potatoes, peeled and chopped

4 cups (32 fl oz/1 l) vegetable or chicken stock

1 bay leaf

2 tablespoons chopped fresh thyme or 2 teaspoons dried thyme

1½–2 cups (12–16 fl oz/375–500 ml) milk, or as needed

1 red bell pepper (capsicum), seeded and diced

1–3 tablespoons Canadian whiskey, to taste (optional)

generous pinch of red pepper flakes, or to taste

salt and freshly ground black pepper to taste

¼ cup (⅓ oz/10 g) chopped fresh flat-leaf (Italian) parsley

In late summer, the corn in Iowa is so sweet that the farmers at markets give out samples cut right off the cob. Less than an hour out of the field, fresh corn hardly needs to be cooked. A splash of Canadian whiskey, made of distilled corn and other grains, gives this sweet, smooth chowder a nice rough edge. Simmer the cobs in the stock for extra flavor.

1. Working with 1 ear of corn at a time, hold it stem end down on a cutting board. Using a sharp knife, and starting from the top, carefully cut off the kernels, rotating the ear after each cut until all the kernels are stripped from the cob. Set the kernels and the cobs aside separately. You should have about 4 cups (1½ lb/750 g) corn kernels.

2. In a heavy soup pot over medium heat, fry the bacon until crisp, about 5 minutes. Using a slotted spoon, transfer the bacon to paper towels to drain. Add the onion to the bacon drippings in the pot and sauté over medium heat until translucent, about 10 minutes.

3. Add the potatoes, stock, bay leaf, thyme, 2 cups (12 oz/375 g) of the corn kernels, and the cobs. Simmer, uncovered, until the potatoes are tender, 12–15 minutes.

4. Remove the bay leaf and the cobs and discard. Working in batches, pour the mixture into a blender or food processor and purée until smooth. Return to the pot.

5. Set the pot over low heat and stir in the remaining corn kernels, enough of the milk to arrive at a nice consistency, the bell pepper, the whiskey (if using), and the red pepper flakes. Season with salt and black pepper. Ladle into warmed bowls and sprinkle with the bacon and the parsley.

SERVES 6 AS A FIRST COURSE, OR 4 AS A MAIN COURSE

NUTRITIONAL ANALYSIS PER FIRST-COURSE SERVING
Calories 324 (Kilojoules 1,436); Protein 9 g; Carbohydrates 34 g; Total Fat 19 g; Saturated Fat 7 g; Cholesterol 27 mg; Sodium 894 mg; Dietary Fiber 5 g

Sweet Corn

Come August in the Heartland, corn hangs on residents' minds like a summer haze. The annual rite of husking ears, loosening silk, and letting the juices run free is at hand, and nearly everyone participates.

Today's sweet corn varieties produce ears so sweet that seed catalogs classify them by sugar percentages: "Sweel" (5 to 10 percent sugar) bred for flavor and crispness, and "Sugar Enhanced" (15 to 18 percent sugar) and "Supersweet" (25 to 30 percent sugar), which balance sweetness with juiciness. Popular varieties include Kandy Korn (sweet yellow), Bodacious (supersweet yellow), and Butter and Sugar (sweet bicolor), all types that are particularly good for canning.

Organic corn varieties include red, purple, and bicolored yellow and white and have more complex flavors than their commercial counterparts. Most farmers hand-pick organic corn to ensure that the ears are fully mature and to prevent them from getting bruised or damaged in the process, which often happens during machine-harvesting.

The best way to cook corn? Get the ears from the corn patch into a pot of boiling water as quickly as possible, watch for the color to darken (about a minute or so), and then take the corn out of the water right away. Never salt the water, as it toughens the corn kernels; and although cooks once added milk or sugar to the water to revive overly mature ears, the excellent corn available today makes such additions unnecessary.

Corn on the cob, with plenty of butter, is a uniquely American tradition, especially in the Heartland states.

Mussels in Thai Coconut Broth

2 lb (1 kg) mussels, well scrubbed and debearded

½ cup (4 fl oz/125 ml) dry white wine

1 tablespoon canola oil

2 heads baby bok choy, trimmed and cut into 1-inch (2.5-cm) pieces

1 red bell pepper (capsicum), seeded and finely julienned

2 shallots, thinly sliced

2 teaspoons light brown sugar

1 teaspoon curry powder

large pinch of cayenne pepper

1 can (13 fl oz/430 ml) unsweetened coconut milk, well shaken

¼ cup (¼ oz/7 g) fresh cilantro (fresh coriander) leaves

4 lime wedges

The Northwest is famous for its farmed mussels, most of which come from areas in Puget Sound. Two types are grown: the Mediterranean mussel and the more dominant Penn Cove mussel. Since the two varieties have alternate spawning seasons, mussels are now available year-round. Store mussels for no more than a day after purchase, covered with a damp kitchen towel in your refrigerator, then scrub and debeard them just before cooking.

1. Place the mussels in a large saucepan, discarding any that fail to close to the touch. Add the wine and bring to a boil over high heat. Cover and cook, shaking the pan occasionally, until the mussels open, about 5 minutes. Using a slotted spoon, transfer the mussels to a bowl, discarding any that failed to open; cover and keep warm. Pour the liquid in the pan through a fine-mesh sieve lined with cheesecloth (muslin) and set aside.

2. Wipe out the pan, add the canola oil to it, and place over medium-high heat. When the oil is hot, add the bok choy, bell pepper, and shallots and cook, stirring, until the vegetables are soft, about 5 minutes. Stir in the brown sugar, curry powder, and cayenne. Pour in the coconut milk and the reserved mussel cooking liquid and bring to a boil over high heat.

3. Divide the mussels among warmed bowls and ladle the broth over the top, dividing evenly. Sprinkle with the cilantro and serve immediately with the lime wedges on the side.

SERVES 4

NUTRITIONAL ANALYSIS PER SERVING
Calories 313 (Kilojoules 1,315); Protein 11 g; Carbohydrates 11 g; Total Fat 25 g; Saturated Fat 18 g; Cholesterol 18 mg; Sodium 223 mg; Dietary Fiber 1 g

Garden Gazpacho

1¼ lb (625 g) ripe tomatoes

½ English (hothouse) cucumber, peeled, cut into large chunks

4 large red bell peppers (capsicums) about 1½ lb (750 g) total weight, roasted, peeled, and seeded *(page 311)*

½ yellow bell pepper (capsicum), seeded and cut into ¼-inch (6-mm) dice

2 serrano chiles, minced

1 small red onion, finely chopped

1 clove garlic, minced

2 tablespoons extra-virgin olive oil, plus extra for drizzling

1 tablespoon sherry vinegar

1 teaspoon kosher salt

1 ripe Hass avocado, pitted, peeled, and cut into ¼-inch (6-mm) cubes

1 tablespoon snipped fresh chives

½ teaspoon dried Mexican oregano

Some of the earliest versions of gazpacho, dating back to medieval Spain, were nothing more than cold soups of bread, olive oil, vinegar, garlic, and water. Vegetables, most notably sun-ripened tomatoes, gradually entered the mixture. In this version, garden produce has completely elbowed out the bread, and minced serrano chiles brand the gazpacho with a hint of Southwestern fire.

1. Cut the tomatoes in half crosswise. Using the largest holes on a box grater placed over a bowl, grate the tomato halves. Discard the skins.

2. In a food processor, pulse the cucumber chunks until coarsely puréed. Add to the bowl of tomatoes. Place the red bell peppers in the processor and process until the peppers are coarsely puréed. Add to the tomatoes and cucumber.

3. Stir in the yellow bell pepper, chiles, onion, garlic, 2 tablespoons olive oil, vinegar, and salt. Taste and adjust the seasoning. Cover and refrigerate until slightly chilled.

4. Ladle into bowls and garnish with the avocado. Sprinkle with the chives and oregano, then drizzle with a little olive oil. Serve immediately.

SERVES 4

NUTRITIONAL ANALYSIS PER SERVING
Calories 230 (Kilojoules 966); Protein 5 g; Carbohydrates 24 g; Total Fat 15 g;
Saturated Fat 2 g; Cholesterol 0 mg; Sodium 392 mg; Dietary Fiber 6 g

Focaccia-Stuffed Artichokes

4 large artichokes

1 lemon, halved

about 10 oz (315 g) herbed focaccia, processed into fine crumbs (about 4 cups)

½ cup (2 oz/60 g) freshly grated Parmesan cheese

¼ cup (⅓ oz/10 g) minced fresh flat-leaf (Italian) parsley

2 cloves garlic, minced

¼ cup (2 fl oz/60 ml) olive oil

salt and freshly ground pepper to taste

boiling water, as needed

In spring, when jumbo artichokes flood California's markets, many people make a meal of them. Tuck a stuffing of seasoned focaccia crumbs between their leaves, and you have a substantial lunch or the centerpiece of a meatless dinner.

1. Preheat the oven to 375°F (190°C).

2. To trim each artichoke, cut off the stem flush with the bottom and rub the cut surface with a lemon half. With a serrated knife, cut about 1 inch (2.5 cm) off the top of each artichoke and rub the cut surfaces with lemon. Using scissors, cut off the pointed tips of the leaves. Gently pry open the artichoke leaves without breaking them, loosening the artichoke enough for you to reach the center choke easily. With a spoon or melon baller, scoop out the prickly inner leaves and hairy choke and discard. Squeeze the lemon halves into a large bowl of cold water and submerge the trimmed artichokes in the water as each one is done to prevent the cut surfaces from browning.

3. In a large bowl, combine the focaccia crumbs, Parmesan cheese, parsley, garlic, and olive oil. Stir well. Season with salt and pepper.

4. Drain the artichokes and pat dry. Fill the center cavities with stuffing, then use your fingers to tuck the remaining stuffing between the leaves. The innermost leaves will be too tightly joined, but the outer leaves can be gently separated and the stuffing tucked between them.

5. Stand the artichokes upright in a baking dish just large enough to hold them. Add boiling water to the dish to a depth of ½ inch (12 mm). Cover with parchment (baking) paper, then with aluminum foil. Bake until tender when pierced, 50–60 minutes. Uncover, raise the heat to 400°F (200°C), and bake for about 15 minutes longer to crisp the top crumbs.

6. Transfer to a platter or individual plates and serve warm, not hot.

SERVES 4

NUTRITIONAL ANALYSIS PER SERVING
Calories 441 (Kilojoules 1,852); Protein 19 g; Carbohydrates 49 g; Total Fat 21 g; Saturated Fat 5 g; Cholesterol 13 mg; Sodium 742 mg; Dietary Fiber 10 g

Rhode Island Johnnycakes with Country Ham

1½ cups (7½ oz/235 g) white or yellow cornmeal, preferably stone-ground

1 teaspoon salt

1 teaspoon sugar

1½ cups (12 fl oz/375 ml) boiling water

1 small yellow onion, grated (about ⅓ cup/2 oz/60 g)

¼–½ cup (2–4 fl oz/60–125 ml) milk

½ cup (3 oz/90 g) finely chopped country ham

freshly ground pepper to taste

2–3 tablespoons unsalted butter

Cornmeal pancakes are popular throughout New England, but nowhere are they taken as seriously as they are in Rhode Island. This savory adaptation makes a wonderful hors d'oeuvre or starter served plain or topped with a dollop of crème fraîche flavored with red onions, roasted garlic, or chives.

1. Preheat the oven to 200°F (95°C).

2. In a bowl, using a wooden spoon, stir together the cornmeal, salt, and sugar. Slowly stir in the boiling water, mixing until smooth and quite stiff. Let the batter stand for 5 minutes.

3. Stir in the grated onion. Add enough of the milk to make a batter the consistency of porridge. Stir in the ham and season with pepper.

4. Preheat a griddle or frying pan, preferably nonstick, over medium heat. Add about ½ tablespoon butter. When the butter melts, spoon the batter onto the griddle or pan, using a tablespoon to make bite-sized cocktail cakes or a scant ¼ cup (2 fl oz/60 ml) to make larger cakes for a first course. Flatten the cakes with the back of a spoon so they will cook evenly. Cook, flipping once, until nicely browned and very crisp on both sides, 3–4 minutes on each side for little cakes, and 5–7 minutes on each side for larger ones. Do not let the pan get too hot, or the cakes will cook too quickly. The inside should remain a bit moist, like polenta. Transfer to a platter and place in the oven to keep warm. Repeat with the remaining batter, adding more butter as needed to prevent sticking.

5. Johnnycakes are wonderful served plain, but you may dress them up as described in the note. If serving the cakes with cocktails, arrange them on a large platter for passing. If serving as a first course, divide among individual plates. Serve immediately.

SERVES 8–10 AS AN HORS D'OEUVRE, OR 6 AS A FIRST COURSE

NUTRITIONAL ANALYSIS PER SERVING
Calories 144 (Kilojoules 605); Protein 5 g; Carbohydrates 20 g; Total Fat 5 g; Saturated Fat 3 g; Cholesterol 17 mg; Sodium 520 mg; Dietary Fiber 1 g

Vermont Cheddar & Walnut Crisps

1½ cups (7½ oz/235 g) all-purpose (plain) flour

½ cup (2 oz/60 g) finely chopped walnuts

½ teaspoon salt

½ teaspoon freshly ground pepper

½ cup (4 oz/125 g) chilled unsalted butter, cut into ¼-inch (6-mm) pieces

1¼ cups (5 oz/155 g) shredded sharp cheddar cheese

1 egg yolk

2 tablespoons heavy (double) cream or milk

A perfect snack to serve with cocktails, these savory wafers highlight the much-acclaimed aged cheddar cheeses made in Vermont. A mix of cheddar and Parmesan will work, too.

1. In a food processor, combine the flour, nuts, salt, and pepper. Process briefly to mix. Drop in the butter and pulse until the butter forms pea-sized pieces. Add the cheddar cheese and process until well mixed. Finally, drop in the egg yolk, add the cream or milk, and pulse only until the dough comes together. Alternatively, in a large bowl, stir together the flour, nuts, salt, and pepper. Add the butter and, using a pastry blender or 2 table knives, cut in the butter until it forms pea-sized pieces. Using a rubber spatula, quickly stir in the cheese. Finally, add the egg yolk and cream or milk and work these quickly into the dough using the rubber spatula. Turn the dough out onto a floured work surface and shape it into a thick, flat disk. Wrap in plastic wrap and refrigerate for at least 1 hour.

2. Preheat the oven to 400°F (200°C).

3. Sprinkle the work surface lightly with flour, then roll out the dough about ¼ inch (6 mm) thick. If it begins to crumble, press any fissures together with your fingers. Using a cookie cutter or a knife, cut out shapes of any sort about 1½ inches (4 cm) across. Arrange them on 2 ungreased baking sheets, spacing them about ½ inch (12 mm) apart. Gather up the scraps, reroll, cut out more shapes, and add to the baking sheets.

4. Bake until lightly browned, about 14 minutes, switching the baking sheets halfway through so the crisps cook evenly. To test, break a crisp in half to see if the inside is cooked. If not, bake for a few minutes longer. Transfer to a wire rack to cool.

5. Serve the crisps within a few hours or store in an airtight container at room temperature for up to a few days.

MAKES ABOUT 6 DOZEN CRISPS

NUTRITIONAL ANALYSIS PER CRISP
Calories 38 (Kilojoules 160); Protein 1 g; Carbohydrates 3 g; Total Fat 3 g; Saturated Fat 1 g; Cholesterol 9 mg; Sodium 29 mg; Dietary Fiber 0 g

Farmstead Cheeses

The cheese most closely associated with New England is cheddar. Early settlers brought cheddaring techniques from England and began making the familiar sharp, firm cheese as a way to preserve milk. American-made cheddar was referred to as Yankee cheese, rat cheese, or store cheese and was sold from large blocks in every general store, a practice that continues in many New England towns today.

By the mid-nineteenth century, cheese makers in the United States developed the means to manufacture their products on a large scale. Fortunately, factory cheese making never completely took over, and a few original producers of distinctive hand-made cheddar cheese are still in business today, such as Crowley Cheese Company and Grafton Village Cheese, both of which are in Vermont.

In recent years, these traditional companies have been joined by leagues of cheese artisans, and the range of quality cheese made in the region has increased tremendously. For example, at the 2004 annual conference of the American Cheese Society, an organization that is dedicated to perpetuating superior farmstead cheese nationally, New England took 15 percent of the first-, second-, and third-place ribbons for such products as a peppercorn flavored cheese from Silvery Moon Creamery in Maine; Smoked Capri from Westfield Farm in Massachusetts; and the aged cheddar of Shelburne Farms in Vermont.

The number and variety of New England farmstead cheeses has exploded in recent years and includes artisanal cheeses made from the milk of cows, sheep, and goats.

Grilled Teleme in Chard Leaves

4 large, unblemished Swiss chard
    leaves with no holes

boiling water, as needed

6 oz (185 g) California teleme
    cheese, chilled and evenly divided
    into 4 slices

pinch of red pepper flakes

½ teaspoon chopped fresh oregano

4 slices coarse country bread, about
    ½ inch (12 mm) thick and 4 inches
    (10 cm) long

1 clove garlic, halved

2 tablespoons olive oil

salt to taste

Soft, creamy teleme cheese, especially when it is ripe and runny, takes well to the grill. As it is made in California, this cow's milk cheese has an edible, rice flour–dusted rind and an unctuous texture after a few weeks' aging. This is a knife-and-fork dish. Pair it with a glass of Sauvignon Blanc.

1. Prepare a medium-hot fire in a charcoal grill, or preheat a gas or electric grill.

2. Carefully cut away the white rib from each chard leaf, but leave each leaf in one piece. Put the leaves in a large bowl. Pour in boiling water to cover and let stand for 2 minutes. Transfer to a sieve to drain and place under cold running water until cold. Gently squeeze dry. Lay the chard leaves flat in a single layer on a kitchen towel and pat dry.

3. Put one slice of cheese in the center of each leaf. Sprinkle each piece with a few red pepper flakes and then top evenly with the oregano. Fold the bottom end of each chard leaf over the cheese, fold in the sides, and roll up to form a neat package.

4. Place the bread slices on the grill rack and grill, turning once, until toasted on both sides. Rub one side of each slice with a cut side of garlic. Drizzle the garlic-rubbed side of each slice with 1 teaspoon of the olive oil. Set aside on individual plates.

5. Brush the cheese packages with the remaining 2 teaspoons olive oil and season with salt. Place on the grill rack directly over the coals and heat for 1 minute. Turn and grill on the second side until the cheese feels very soft to the touch, about 1 minute longer.

6. Place a cheese package on each slice of bread and serve immediately.

SERVES 4

NUTRITIONAL ANALYSIS PER SERVING
Calories 269 (Kilojoules 1,130); Protein 11 g; Carbohydrates 17 g; Total Fat 18 g;
Saturated Fat 6 g; Cholesterol 15 mg; Sodium 496 mg; Dietary Fiber 2 g

Roasted Oysters with Leeks & Sorrel

24 small or medium oysters in the shell

1 bunch sorrel, about 2 oz (60 g), stems removed

2 tablespoons unsalted butter

1 large leek, including about 2 inches (5 cm) of pale green parts, finely shredded

1½ teaspoons grated lemon zest

1½ teaspoons grated orange zest

½ teaspoon coarse salt

½ teaspoon freshly ground pepper

⅓ cup (3 fl oz/80 ml) heavy (double) cream

1 tablespoon chopped fresh flat-leaf (Italian) parsley

Oyster fans fall into two camps: those who eat them raw and those who prefer them lightly cooked. For the latter group, these roasted oysters make an elegant first course.

1. Working with 1 oyster at a time, and holding it over a bowl to capture the liquor (liquid), grip each shell, flat side up, with a folded kitchen towel. Push the tip of an oyster knife to one side of the hinge and pry upward to open the shell. Keeping the blade edge against the inside of the top shell, run the knife all around the oyster to sever the muscle that holds the shell halves together. Lift off and discard the top shell. Run the knife underneath the oyster to cut its flesh free from the bottom shell and set the oyster aside. Pour off the liquor from the shell into the bowl. Scrub the bottom shell with a stiff-bristled brush and place on a baking sheet lined with rumpled aluminum foil. When all the bottom shells are on the baking sheet, set an oyster in each shell. Cover and refrigerate until needed. Pour the oyster liquor through a fine-mesh sieve lined with cheesecloth (muslin) set over a small bowl and set aside.

2. Cut the sorrel leaves into a chiffonade: Working in batches, stack the leaves, tightly roll up the stack lengthwise and thinly slice the cylinder crosswise. Set aside. Preheat the oven to 450°F (230°C).

3. In a frying pan over medium heat, melt the butter. Add the leek and cook, stirring occasionally, until very soft, about 5 minutes. Add the sorrel and cook, stirring frequently, until soft, about 5 minutes. Stir in the lemon and orange zests, salt, pepper, cream, and strained liquor. Raise the heat to high and simmer until the liquid is reduced slightly, about 2 minutes. Remove from the heat and top each oyster with a tablespoon of the mixture. Spoon any remaining liquid over the oysters.

4. Bake the oysters until they are bubbling, 9–10 minutes. Divide among individual plates, sprinkle with the parsley, and serve.

SERVES 4

NUTRITIONAL ANALYSIS PER SERVING
Calories 190 (Kilojoules 798); Protein 6 g; Carbohydrates 10 g; Total Fat 15 g;
Saturated Fat 8 g; Cholesterol 75 mg; Sodium 268 mg; Dietary Fiber 1 g

Northwest Oysters

Most folks driving through Willapa Bay, Washington, would see it as a typical coastal town. But oyster lovers will spot the local processors, nondescript warehouses flanked by enormous piles of spent oyster shells. The plump meats taken from those sun-bleached casings probably ended up in a bisque or stew, in a mixed-seafood fry, or in a three-egg omelet.

In 1850, at the height of the California gold rush, oysters fresh from Willapa Bay were crated and placed aboard schooners bound for San Francisco. The bivalves were an immediate hit, and, before long, as many as two hundred thousand bushels were being shipped each year. As a result, by 1895, the native oyster beds were almost completely wiped out.

The first efforts to restore the depleted beds failed miserably. But in 1920, plantings of Japanese seed oysters took, and Willapa Bay was back in business.

These days, several varieties of both cupped and flat oysters are farmed. The most plentiful are the Pacific oysters, cupped specimens with a slightly fruity taste that bear the names of their farm locations, such as Yaquina, Wescott,

Quilcene, and Shoalwater Bays. A second cupped oyster, the Kumamoto, is a tiny Japanese transplant treasured for its remarkably sweet taste. Farmed flat oysters include the native Olympia and the European flat, incredibly slow growers that are perfectly delicious raw with only a spritz of lemon juice.

Succulent oysters from the Pacific Northwest are delicious eaten straight from their shells with a squeeze of lemon juice and some freshly ground black pepper.

New England Clam Chowder

4 lb (2 kg) clams, preferably littlenecks or Maine mahogany, well
  scrubbed

½ cup (4 fl oz/125 ml) water

3 slices thick-cut bacon, cut into
  ½-inch (12-mm) pieces

1 tablespoon unsalted butter

1 large yellow onion, chopped

2 small inner celery stalks with
  leaves, chopped

½ teaspoon fresh thyme, or pinch
  of dried

¾ lb (375 g) red or white boiling
  potatoes, peeled and cut into
  ½-inch (12-mm) dice

2 cups (16 fl oz/500 ml) half-and-
  half (half cream)

1½–2 cups (12–16 fl oz/375–500 ml)
  milk, or as needed

freshly ground pepper to taste

From Massachusetts north, clam chowder is always creamy and white. It is only from Rhode Island south that cooks dare to introduce tomatoes to the pot. Serve the chowder with soda crackers, common crackers, or crusty bread.

1. Discard any clams that are gaping and do not close when tapped. Put the clams and water in a large pot, cover with a tight-fitting lid, and place over high heat. Cook, shaking the pot once or twice to distribute the heat evenly, until the clams have opened, about 4 minutes.

2. Using a slotted spoon, scoop the clams into a bowl to cool, leaving the broth behind. Discard any clams that failed to open. Strain the broth through a double layer of cheesecloth (muslin) to eliminate any sand. Measure and add enough water to make 2 cups (16 fl oz/500 ml). Set aside.

3. In a heavy soup pot over medium heat, fry the bacon until crisp, about 5 minutes. Using a slotted spoon, transfer the bacon to paper towels to drain. Add the butter to the bacon drippings remaining in the pot over medium heat. Stir in the onion, celery, and thyme and cook until the onion is translucent, about 10 minutes. Do not allow to brown. Add the potatoes and the reserved broth and simmer, uncovered, until the potatoes are almost tender, 10–12 minutes.

4. While the potatoes are cooking, remove the clams from their shells, discarding the shells and being careful to capture their juices in the bowl. Add the clams and juices to the soup. Stir in the half-and-half and enough milk to arrive at a nice consistency that appeals to you. Bring to just below a simmer and heat to serving temperature. Do not allow to boil.

5. Add the bacon and season with pepper (it should be plenty salty from the clams). Ladle into warmed bowls and serve at once.

SERVES 8 AS A FIRST COURSE, OR 5 AS A MAIN COURSE

NUTRITIONAL ANALYSIS PER SERVING
Calories 271 (Kilojoules 1,138); Protein 10 g; Carbohydrates 16 g; Total Fat 19 g;
Saturated Fat 9 g; Cholesterol 55 mg; Sodium 178 mg; Dietary Fiber 1 g

Jicama, Carrot & Red Cabbage Salad

DRESSING

1 tablespoon finely chopped shallot

1 teaspoon minced serrano chile

1½ tablespoons white wine vinegar

1 tablespoon fresh lime juice

1 tablespoon sugar

kosher salt to taste

⅓ cup (3 fl oz/80 ml) safflower oil

1 small jicama, about ¼ lb (125 g),
    peeled and julienned

1 carrot, peeled and julienned

¼ small head red cabbage, finely
    shredded

handful of sunflower or radish
    sprouts, root ends trimmed

On hot summer days, Southwest cooks, following the lead of their Mexican counterparts, sprinkle crisp sticks of chilled, raw tropical jicama with coarse salt, ground New Mexico chile, and fresh lime juice. Here, jicama joins carrots, red cabbage, and bright green sprouts in a colorful salad that makes a refreshing side dish for outdoor meals.

1. To make the dressing, in a small bowl, whisk together the shallot, chile, vinegar, lime juice, sugar, and salt. Whisk in the oil. Set the mixture aside for about 10 minutes to allow the flavors to blend. Taste and adjust the seasoning.

2. In a bowl, combine the jicama, carrot, cabbage, and sprouts. Toss thoroughly to distribute the ingredients evenly. Add the dressing, toss, and serve immediately.

SERVES 4

NUTRITIONAL ANALYSIS PER SERVING
Calories 210 (Kilojoules 882); Protein 1 g; Carbohydrates 12 g; Total Fat 18 g;
Saturated Fat 2 g; Cholesterol 0 mg; Sodium 14 mg; Dietary Fiber 3 g

Shellfish & Avocado Cocktail

¾ lb (375 g) large shrimp (prawns), peeled, deveined, and cut into ½-inch (12-mm) pieces

½ lb (250 g) sea scallops, quartered

about 1½ cups (12 fl oz/375 ml) fresh lime juice

1 tomato, halved, seeded, and diced

1 small avocado, pitted, peeled, and diced

½ white onion, minced

¼ cup (⅓ oz/10 g) chopped fresh cilantro (fresh coriander)

1 large clove garlic, minced

2 tablespoons extra-virgin olive oil

1½ teaspoons dried oregano

1 jalapeño or 2 serrano chiles, minced, including seeds

1½ cups (12 fl oz/375 ml) tomato juice, chilled

salt to taste

This refreshing seafood cocktail—a variation of ceviche—is popular in California's Mexican restaurants. It is often served in a large parfait glass, but a martini glass makes a more contemporary presentation. Note that the shellfish needs to marinate for at least twelve hours.

1. In a glass or stainless-steel bowl, combine the shrimp, scallops, and enough lime juice just to cover them. Cover and refrigerate, stirring occasionally, until the shellfish has turned opaque all the way through, indicating that the lime juice has "cooked" it, 12–24 hours.

2. Just before serving, drain the shellfish, reserving the lime juice. Return the shellfish to the bowl and add the tomato, avocado, onion, cilantro, garlic, and olive oil. Add the oregano, crumbling it between your fingers to release its fragrance. Add the minced chile to taste, then add the tomato juice. Toss to mix. Season with salt. Taste and add as much of the reserved lime juice as needed to give the mixture a refreshing tang.

3. Divide among stemmed glasses and serve.

SERVES 6

NUTRITIONAL ANALYSIS PER SERVING
Calories 189 (Kilojoules 794); Protein 17 g; Carbohydrates 10 g; Total Fat 10 g; Saturated Fat 1 g; Cholesterol 83 mg; Sodium 356 mg; Dietary Fiber 1 g

California Avocados

On the short list of foods to consider for your last meal, avocado should be near the top. With a piece of rustic bread, coarse salt, and a lemon, a ripe Hass avocado would satisfy completely. Eat the whole thing with no thought of calories, smearing the smooth, buttery flesh on bread and savoring every bite.

You're not alone if you think of the avocado as a forbidden fruit, an item too rich, too calorie-laden to eat with abandon. A recent industry ad campaign battled that very attitude with a humorous spin on the tag line: "It's Not Wrong to Be in Love with the Avocado."

The avocado has little saturated fat and plenty of nutrients. A New World native, avocados thrive in California between San Luis Obispo and the border of Mexico, yielding 95 percent of the nation's crop. Most growers cultivate the pebbly-skinned Hass.

About six thousand California growers harvest avocados, so you can see that most orchards aren't very large. A single tree can produce as much as 60 pounds (30 kg)—about 120 avocados—a year. Luckily for the growers, avocados store well on the tree, so there's no mad rush at harvest time. In fact, the longer an avocado hangs, the more oil content— and therefore, more flavor—it will develop. And those little fruits that some markets label "cocktail avocados"? They are the miniature pit-free fruits that inexplicably develop on the trees.

Rich in nutrients and prized for its creamy texture, the avocado is a delicious fruit sliced into a salad or spooned straight from its shell.

Wild Fennel Gravlax

1 teaspoon fennel seeds

¼ cup (2 oz/60 g) sugar

¼ cup (2 oz/60 g) coarse salt

1 teaspoon coarsely ground pepper

2 pieces salmon fillet, each about
½ lb (250 g)

1 cup (1½ oz/45 g) coarsely chopped
fronds and stems from common or
Florence (bulb) fennel

1 tablespoon vodka or aquavit

½ cup (4 oz/125 g) unsalted butter,
at room temperature

24 thin slices brown bread

6 lemon slices

In Seattle, wild fennel usually occupies any space forfeited by blackberry bushes. This fennel is known as common fennel (a different variety than Florence, or bulb, fennel), and its fronds are bushy and flavorful. It makes a nice change from the ubiquitous dill that usually flavors this dish. To ensure that the salmon is safe to eat raw, freeze it for twenty-four hours, then thaw in the refrigerator before using.

1. In a spice grinder or a mortar, coarsely grind the fennel seeds. Pour into a small bowl and add the sugar, salt, and pepper. Stir well.

2. Rub the salmon pieces on both sides with the fennel-seed mixture. Place 1 piece of salmon, flesh side up, on a plate and top with the fennel fronds. Sprinkle with the vodka or aquavit. Top with the second salmon fillet, flesh side down. Wrap the sandwiched fillets in plastic wrap. Place on a clean plate and top with a second plate. Place a 2–3-lb (1–1.5-kg) weight on top (several large cans work well). Refrigerate until the fish is somewhat opaque, about 24 hours.

3. To serve, scrape off the fennel fronds and other seasonings and pat the fish dry. Butter the bread slices. Slice the salmon against the grain about ⅛ inch (3 mm) thick and place on a platter with the lemon slices and buttered bread. Serve immediately.

SERVES 6

NUTRITIONAL ANALYSIS PER SERVING
Calories 432 (Kilojoules 1,814); Protein 20 g; Carbohydrates 31 g; Total Fat 25 g;
Saturated Fat 11 g; Cholesterol 86 mg; Sodium 1,655 mg; Dietary Fiber 3 g

Fish & Shellfish

Broiled Bluefish with Tomato-Basil Relish

RELISH

2 cups (8 oz/250 g) currant or other
small cherry tomatoes, a mixture
of red and yellow if possible,
stems removed

2 or 3 green (spring) onions, white
and pale green parts only, finely
chopped (¼ cup/¾ oz/20 g)

⅓–½ cup (⅓–½ oz/10–15 g) loosely
packed fresh basil leaves, cut into
narrow strips

2 tablespoons extra-virgin olive oil

1 tablespoon capers, roughly chopped

1 small clove garlic, crushed and
minced

1 teaspoon sherry vinegar or red
wine vinegar

salt and freshly ground pepper
to taste

olive oil for brushing

2 small or 1 large bluefish fillet,
preferably with skin on, 1½–2 lb
(750 g–1 kg) total weight

1 teaspoon chopped fresh thyme, or
½ teaspoon dried thyme

salt and freshly ground pepper
to taste

Large schools of beautiful, spirited bluefish migrate to New England's shallow coastal waters every summer. The zesty tomato-basil relish that accompanies the bluefish here is also good with tuna, salmon, or swordfish steaks. Serve the fish with boiled new potatoes, a rice pilaf, or bread.

1. To make the relish, halve the tomatoes, or quarter them if larger than a gumball. Put them in a bowl with the green onions, basil, olive oil, capers, garlic, and vinegar. Toss lightly to combine, then season with salt and pepper. (The relish may be made several hours in advance, but do not refrigerate.)

2. Preheat the broiler (grill). Cover the broiler pan with aluminum foil and brush the foil with olive oil.

3. Arrange the fish, skin side down, on the foil and brush the top with more olive oil. Sprinkle the fish with the thyme, salt, and pepper.

4. Position the broiler pan so that the top of the fish is about 4 inches (10 cm) below the heat source and broil (grill) the fillet(s) for 3–4 minutes if they are less than 1 inch (2.5 cm) thick, or 5–7 minutes for thicker fillet(s). Flip carefully and broil for another 4 minutes for thinner fillet(s), or 6 minutes for thicker fillet(s).

5. Transfer the fish to a warmed platter and divide into 4 serving pieces. Spoon the tomato relish over the top and serve at once.

SERVES 4

NUTRITIONAL ANALYSIS PER SERVING
Calories 311 (Kilojoules 1,306); Protein 38 g; Carbohydrates 4 g; Total Fat 15 g;
Saturated Fat 3 g; Cholesterol 110 mg; Sodium 214 mg; Dietary Fiber 1 g

Grilled Coho Salmon with Cucumber Relish

CUCUMBER RELISH

CUCUMBER RELISH

3 small English (hothouse) cucumbers, peeled and diced

1 jalapeño chile, seeded and finely chopped

3 tablespoons finely chopped fresh flat-leaf (Italian) parsley leaves

3 tablespoons finely chopped fresh mint leaves

3 tablespoons extra-virgin olive oil

3 tablespoons fresh lemon juice, or to taste

pinch of sugar

salt and freshly ground pepper to taste

4 coho salmon, about ¾ lb (375 g) each, cleaned

12 fresh flat-leaf (Italian) parsley sprigs

olive oil for coating

4 fresh mint sprigs

Midwest coho salmon is farm-raised in cold, clear stream-fed ponds. Its flesh is firm and sweet like that of trout but with the light pink color of salmon. Serve the cohos with this refreshing, spicy cucumber-mint relish.

1. To make the relish, in a bowl, stir together the cucumbers, chile, parsley, mint, olive oil, lemon juice, and sugar. Season with salt and pepper. Set aside while you cook the salmon.

2. Prepare a fire in a charcoal grill, or preheat a gas or electric grill.

3. Rinse the salmon inside and out under cold running water and pat them dry with paper towels. Place 3 parsley sprigs in the cavity of each salmon. Place the fish in a shallow nonaluminum pan and coat them all over with olive oil.

4. Place the salmon on the grill rack and cook until the skin begins to tighten over the flesh, about 4 minutes. Flip and cook until the flesh is opaque throughout, 3–4 minutes longer.

5. Transfer the salmon to warmed individual plates. Garnish each fish with a mint sprig and 1 or 2 spoonfuls of relish. Pass the remaining relish at the table.

SERVES 4

NUTRITIONAL ANALYSIS PER SERVING
Calories 471 (Kilojoules 1,978); Protein 50 g; Carbohydrates 6 g; Total Fat 27 g; Saturated Fat 5 g; Cholesterol 100 mg; Sodium 106 mg; Dietary Fiber 3 g

Grilled Spot Prawns

1½ lb (750 g) fresh or frozen spot prawns in the shell

3 tablespoons extra-virgin olive oil

2 tablespoons chopped fresh flat-leaf (Italian) parsley

1 teaspoon coarse salt

1 teaspoon coarsely ground pepper

grated zest of 2 lemons

Spot prawns are sweet shrimp that live in the waters off the coasts of Alaska, Washington, and Oregon. The females often come with the orange roe attached, an added treat. Here, the prawns are grilled with their shells on. Make sure the grill is very hot, so the fire can burnish the shells and give them a nice smoky flavor.

1. Prepare a hot fire in a charcoal grill, or preheat a gas or electric grill.

2. In a large bowl, combine the prawns, olive oil, parsley, salt, pepper, and lemon zest. Mix well to coat the prawns evenly.

3. When the grill is very hot, place the prawns on the grill rack and grill, turning once, until they turn opaque and are just cooked through, 1–2 minutes on each side. Transfer to a platter and serve immediately.

SERVES 4

NUTRITIONAL ANALYSIS PER SERVING
Calories 96 (Kilojoules 403); Protein 10 g; Carbohydrates 1 g; Total Fat 6 g;
Saturated Fat 1 g; Cholesterol 70 mg; Sodium 253 mg; Dietary Fiber 0 g

Crisp Salmon with Warm Potato Salad

POTATO SALAD

1 tablespoon white wine vinegar

1½ teaspoons Dijon mustard

3 tablespoons olive oil

⅓ cup (1 oz/30 g) minced green (spring) onion, white and pale green parts only

1 tablespoon chopped capers

2 teaspoons chopped fresh tarragon

salt and freshly ground pepper to taste

1 lb (500 g) small boiling potatoes, unpeeled, quartered

3 teaspoons olive oil

6 skinless salmon fillets, ½ lb (250 g) each

salt and freshly ground pepper to taste

½ lb (250 g) watercress, thick stems removed

6 lemon wedges

Searing fish in a hot frying pan to produce a crisp, browned surface is a popular technique among California chefs. To prevent the fillets from overbrowning before they are done, chefs finish the cooking in a moderate oven. The method works best with a fatty fish such as Pacific king salmon.

1. To make the potato salad, in a small bowl, whisk together the vinegar and mustard. Gradually whisk in the olive oil to make an emulsion. Whisk in the green onion, capers, and tarragon. Season generously with salt and pepper.

2. In a saucepan over high heat, combine the potatoes with salted water to cover. Bring to a boil, adjust the heat to maintain a gentle simmer, and cook, checking often, until just tender when pierced, about 10 minutes. Drain thoroughly, then transfer to a large bowl and add the dressing. Toss to coat evenly. Let stand until warm, tossing occasionally so the dressing penetrates the potatoes evenly.

3. Meanwhile, preheat the oven to 375°F (190°C). Heat 2 large ovenproof frying pans over medium-high heat until hot. Add 1½ teaspoons of the oil to each pan, swirl to coat, and heat until the oil is almost smoking.

4. Season the salmon fillets on both sides with salt and pepper, then immediately put them in the pans, flat side (skin side) up. Cook until golden brown and crusty without moving the salmon, 1–2 minutes; lift a fillet slightly to check the progress. When browned, turn the fillets carefully and transfer the pans to the oven. Bake uncovered until the fillets are just opaque throughout, about 8 minutes. Transfer the fillets to paper towels briefly to drain any fat, then to individual plates.

5. Add the watercress to the potatoes and toss to coat with the dressing. Taste and adjust the seasoning. Divide the salad evenly among the plates. Garnish each portion with a lemon wedge and serve immediately.

SERVES 6

NUTRITIONAL ANALYSIS PER SERVING
Calories 567 (Kilojoules 2,381); Protein 48 g; Carbohydrates 16 g; Total Fat 34 g; Saturated Fat 6 g; Cholesterol 134 mg; Sodium 249 mg; Dietary Fiber 2 g

Steamer Clams with Broth & Drawn Butter

4 lb (2 kg) steamer clams, well scrubbed

1 cup (8 oz/250 g) butter, melted and kept warm

This recipe comes from one of the best steamer cooks of coastal Massachusetts, who scorns the addition of any ingredient that would adulterate the natural, sweet flavor of the clams. Melted butter, of course, is acceptable. You can use salted or unsalted, whichever you prefer.

1. Before steaming the clams, ready the table: Have enough warm soup mugs and small ramekins to serve a mug of clam broth and a ramekin of melted butter per person. Also, set out a large bowl to collect the empty shells.

2. Pour water to a depth of ½ inch (12 mm) into a pot large enough to accommodate the clams and not be more than two-thirds full. (If you have a large pot outfitted with a steamer basket, use it.) Discard any clams that are gaping and do not close when tapped. Put the clams in the pot, cover with a tight-fitting lid, and place over high heat. Cook, shaking the pot once or twice to distribute the heat evenly, until all the clams have opened, 8–10 minutes from the time steam appears.

3. Using a large spoon, scoop the clams into large soup bowls, dividing them evenly and discarding any that failed to open. Pour the broth through a fine-mesh sieve into the mugs, trying to leave any grit behind in the bottom of the pot. Distribute the melted butter evenly among the ramekins at each place setting. Serve the clams immediately while they are piping hot. The best way to eat them is to pry open each shell with your fingers and pull the clam from it. Remove the membrane from the dark-colored "neck," or "foot." Dip the clam first in broth to rinse off any remaining sand, then in butter, and then pop it into your mouth. Some people like to sip the clam broth. Be careful, as there is always some sand at the bottom of the mug.

SERVES 4–6

NUTRITIONAL ANALYSIS PER SERVING
Calories 366 (Kilojoules 1,537); Protein 7 g; Carbohydrates 1 g; Total Fat 37 g; Saturated Fat 23 g; Cholesterol 118 mg; Sodium 406 mg; Dietary Fiber 0 g

Clams

The bounty of clams found in shallow tidal waters of the North Atlantic is one of New England's greatest natural resources. Two main types of clams exist here: hard-shell clams, also known as quahogs, and soft-shell clams, referred to as pisser, steamer, or long-neck clams.

Quahogs (pronounced "coe-hogs"), which are round and have tightly closed shells, are categorized by size. The smaller and younger the clam, the more tender the meat. The largest quahogs (chowder clams) are most often used in chowders, pies, and stuffings. Smaller hard-shell clams, called littlenecks and cherrystones, are eaten raw or steamed or used in pasta sauces and soups.

Steamer clams, with thin oval shells about 3 to 4 inches (9 to 12 cm) long, have a brittle, elongated shell with a protruding black "neck," or "foot." Although steamers, as their name suggests, are typically steamed and served with clam broth and butter, they can also be breaded and deep-fried. Connoisseurs of fried clams will tell you that only clam bellies, or whole clams, are worth eating. Clam strips, from which the bellies have been removed, are considered a distant second.

While many locals still dig for clams at low tide, more folks choose to wait in line at the casual eateries, affectionately referred to as clamshacks, that operate up and down the coast. Two classic spots— the Clam Box, in Ipswich, Massachusetts, and Woodman's, in nearby Essex—promise generous plates of fried fresh clams.

Larger quahogs, and smaller littlenecks and cherrystones are also referred to as "hard-shell" clams, to distinguish them from the thinner-shelled steamers.

Baked Snapper with Melon-Mango Salsa

SALSA

¼ honeydew melon, about 1 lb (500 g), seeded, peeled, and cut into ½-inch (12-mm) dice

2 mangoes, about ¾ lb (375 g) each, pitted, peeled, and cut into ½-inch (12-mm) dice

3 kiwifruits, about ¼ lb (125 g) each, peeled and cut into ½-inch (12-mm) dice

1 red onion, finely chopped

2 green (spring) onions, white and tender green parts only, chopped

3 cloves garlic, finely chopped

2 jalapeño chiles, seeded and finely chopped

½ cup (¾ oz/20 g) chopped fresh cilantro (fresh coriander)

¼ cup (2 fl oz/60 ml) fresh lime juice

salt and freshly ground pepper to taste

1 red snapper, 3–3½ lb (1.5–1.75 kg), cleaned, with head and tail intact

4 carrots, peeled and quartered lengthwise

1 Vidalia or other sweet onion, sliced

3 tablespoons olive oil

salt and freshly ground pepper to taste

1 lemon, sliced

1 lime, sliced

a few sprigs fresh dill

1½ cups (12 fl oz/375 ml) dry white wine

The sweet and spicy salsa, inspired by the kitchens of both south Florida and Cuba, pairs beautifully with the delicate flavor of a roasted whole red snapper. Do not be intimidated by the thought of roasting a whole fish. It is much simpler than you might imagine and makes a stunning presentation.

1. To make the salsa, in a large bowl, toss together the honeydew, mangoes, kiwifruits, red onion, green onions, garlic, chiles, cilantro, lime juice, salt, and pepper. Cover and let stand at room temperature for at least 4 hours to blend the flavors, or refrigerate for up to 1 day.

2. Preheat the oven to 400°F (200°C). Select a baking dish large enough to accommodate the fish. Lightly coat the dish with vegetable oil.

3. To prepare the fish, rinse and pat dry. Using kitchen shears, snip away the fins. Layer the carrots in the prepared baking dish and top them with the onion slices. Lay the fish on top and brush the cavity and the surface with the olive oil. Season generously inside and out with salt and pepper. Cut 1 lemon slice into quarters and set aside. Arrange the remaining lemon slices and all the lime slices inside the cavity of the fish, overlapping them. Place the dill on top of the citrus slices and sew the cavity closed with a trussing kneedle and kitchen string. Pour the wine around the fish.

4. Measure the thickest part of the stuffed fish; plan on 8 minutes roasting for each 1 inch (2.5 cm) of thickness. Roast until the flesh is opaque at the bone when tested with a knife or fork, about 20 minutes. Remove from the oven and let stand for 10 minutes. With kitchen shears, carefully snip and remove the kitchen string.

5. Transfer the fish to a large platter. Surround with the salsa and garnish with the reserved lemon slice. To serve, cut along the gill line and down the backbone, carefully lifting the flesh from the bone, then turn and repeat on the other side.

SERVES 4

NUTRITIONAL ANALYSIS PER SERVING
Calories 533 (Kilojoules 2,239); Protein 45 g; Carbohydrates 64 g; Total Fat 14 g; Saturated Fat 2 g; Cholesterol 71 mg; Sodium 182 mg; Dietary Fiber 9 g

Louisiana Crawfish Boil

4–6 oz (125–185 g) packaged crab and crawfish boil or Creole seasoning

1–2 tablespoons cayenne pepper (optional)

3 bay leaves

1 lemon, sliced

1 cup (8 fl oz/250 ml) cider vinegar

18 lb (9 kg) crawfish in the shell

18 small new potatoes

6 ears of yellow corn, husks and silk removed and ears halved

A crawfish boil is to the South what a clambake is to the Northeast. This feast is ideal for a casual gathering of friends who know one another well enough to dive into a heaping mound of steaming crawfish, corn, and potatoes with bare fingers and good appetites. Serve with lots of napkins, cocktail sauce and clarified butter for dipping, and ice-cold beer.

1. Fill a very large stockpot about two-thirds full with water. Add the seasoning, cayenne pepper to taste (if using), bay leaves, lemon slices, and vinegar and bring to a boil over high heat. Add about one-third of the crawfish. Bring back to a boil and cook until the crawfish are firm and bright, about 3 minutes. Using a slotted spoon, transfer to a large, clean bowl and cover. Repeat with the remaining crawfish in two more batches, adding them to the bowl as they are done.

2. Add the potatoes to the boiling water and cook for 15 minutes. Add the corn and continue cooking until the corn is just tender, about 4 minutes longer. Using the slotted spoon, transfer the potatoes and corn to another bowl.

3. Heap the cooked crawfish onto several large serving platters (or cover a picnic table with newspapers for dining al fresco). Serve with the potatoes and corn.

SERVES 6

NUTRITIONAL ANALYSIS PER SERVING
Calories 575 (Kilojoules 2,415); Protein 63 g; Carbohydrates 70 g; Total Fat 5 g; Saturated Fat 1 g; Cholesterol 404 mg; Sodium 1,034 mg; Dietary Fiber 8 g

Rice & Crawfish

According to legend, rice cultivation in South Carolina began in 1620, when the captain of a British merchant ship that sailed into Charleston from Madagascar gave his plantation-owner host a handful of so-called Golde Seede Rice. The plantation fields were flat, fertile, and well irrigated—ideal conditions for rice production. By the early 1700s, rice was a major crop in South Carolina, and the port of Charleston was exporting annually huge shiploads of Carolina Golde to England. By the mid-1800s, rice production began to move west to Mississippi, Louisiana, Arkansas, and Texas. Today, these states produce almost 80 percent of the rice eaten in the United States.

A second legend—an old wives' tale, actually—accounts for another famous Southern food. When the Acadians, later known as Cajuns, left Nova Scotia for Louisiana, a school of lobsters followed. The lobsters molted repeatedly during the long journey, so that by the time they reached Louisiana, they had become the tiny morsels known affectionately as crawfish, crayfish, crawdads, or mudbugs.

Although crawfish look like miniature lobsters, these tasty freshwater denizens are only distant cousins. Today most crawfish are farm raised, with the harvest beginning in December and lasting until May or June. After the rice harvest, some ambitious farmers seed their fields with crawfish eggs, knowing they will hatch and feed on the rice stubble that is left behind, producing a second cash crop for the season.

Unlike the lobster, which it resembles in appearance, the crawfish grows in freshwater.

Fish Tacos with Pickled Onions & Chiles

PICKLED ONIONS

1 cup (8 fl oz/250 ml) red wine vinegar

6 tablespoons (3 fl oz/90 ml) frozen orange juice concentrate, thawed

⅓ cup (3 oz/90 g) sugar

1½ teaspoons dried Mexican oregano

2 bay leaves (optional)

kosher salt to taste

2 large red onions, thinly sliced

MARINADE

1 large white onion, cut up

2 cloves garlic

3 serrano chiles, stems removed

1 bunch fresh cilantro (fresh coriander), cut into large pieces

1 cup (8 fl oz/250 ml) fresh lime juice

2–3 tablespoons honey

kosher salt to taste

1½ lb (750 g) Chilean sea bass fillet, cut into large cubes

kosher salt and freshly ground pepper to taste

3–4 tablespoons (1½–2 fl oz/ 45–60 ml) olive oil

1½ cups (3 oz/90 g) romaine (cos) lettuce, finely shredded

12 corn tortillas, heated

½ cup (3 oz/90 g) canned pickled jalapeño strips

¾ cup (6 fl oz/180 ml) crema

6 lime wedges

Fish tacos have swept the Southwest in reaction to the growing popularity of fresh seafood. Red snapper or another sea bass can be used in place of the Chilean sea bass, and any leftover pickled onions are good on grilled fish. Serve with fresh salsa.

1. To make the pickled onions, in a bowl, combine the vinegar, orange juice concentrate, sugar, oregano, bay leaves (if using), and salt. Stir until the sugar is dissolved. Add the onions and stir to coat evenly. Cover and let stand at room temperature, stirring occasionally, for 6–8 hours. Refrigerate, covered, until ready to use. The pickled onions will keep for up to 1 month.

2. To make the marinade, in a food processor, combine the onion, garlic, chiles, cilantro, and lime juice. Process until a coarse purée forms. Season to taste with honey and salt. The flavor should be a balance of tart, sweet, salty, and spicy. Pour into a bowl, add the fish, and turn to coat. Cover and marinate at room temperature for 2 hours or refrigerate for up to 4 hours.

3. Remove the fish from the marinade, scraping off the excess marinade, and set aside on paper towels. Sprinkle the fish with salt and pepper.

4. In a large frying pan over medium-high heat, warm the olive oil. Add half of the fish and brown, turning as necessary, until well seared, 1–2 minutes on each side. Transfer the fish to a plate. Repeat with the remaining fish. Break the cubes of cooked fish into smaller pieces and keep warm.

5. To assemble each taco, place 2 tablespoons of the lettuce in the center of a warm corn tortilla and top with about one-twelfth of the fish. Add 2 or 3 strips pickled jalapeño and 1 tablespoon pickled onions. Drizzle with 1 tablespoon of the crema. Serve with the lime wedges.

MAKES 12 TACOS; SERVES 6

NUTRITIONAL ANALYSIS PER TACO
Calories 277 (Kilojoules 1,163); Protein 14 g; Carbohydrates 31 g; Total Fat 11 g; Saturated Fat 4 g; Cholesterol 36 mg; Sodium 200 mg; Dietary Fiber 2 g

Cornmeal-Crusted Trout with Corn Relish

4 ears of corn, husks and silk removed

1 small white onion, sliced ½ inch (12 mm) thick

1 small red bell pepper (capsicum), roasted, peeled, and seeded *(page 311)*, then diced

1 large poblano chile, roasted, peeled, and seeded *(page 311)*, then diced

¼ cup (⅓ oz/10 g) coarsely chopped fresh cilantro (fresh coriander)

1–2 tablespoons white wine vinegar

2–3 tablespoons toasted peanut oil

kosher salt to taste

CORNMEAL COATING

1½ cups (7½ oz/235 g) stone-ground yellow cornmeal

¼ cup (1½ oz/45 g) *masa harina*

6 tablespoons (1 oz/30 g) ground Chimayó chile

1½ teaspoons freshly ground coriander

1 teaspoon freshly ground cumin

1 tablespoon kosher salt

1 teaspoon freshly ground pepper

1 cup (5 oz/155 g) unbleached all-purpose (plain) flour

3 eggs

6 boneless whole trout

kosher salt and freshly ground pepper to taste

3 tablespoons olive oil

Mountain trout is one of the few fish varieties that exist in New Mexico's high desert. A town in the northeastern part of the state has even honored the prized fish by taking its Spanish name, *Truchas*.

1. To make the relish, working with 1 ear of corn at a time and holding it with tongs, toast over a gas flame or under a broiler (grill) until evenly charred in spots. Let cool, then, steadying the stalk end on a cutting board, strip off the kernels with a sharp knife. There should be about 2 cups (12 oz/375 g). Char the onion slices in the same way, let cool, and chop finely. In a bowl, combine the corn, onion, bell pepper, chile, cilantro, and the vinegar, peanut oil, and salt to taste. Set aside.

2. Preheat the oven to 475°F (245°C). Line a baking sheet with aluminum foil.

3. To make the coating, in a bowl, combine the cornmeal, *masa harina*, ground chile, coriander, cumin, salt, and pepper. Whisk to combine. Transfer to a shallow dish large enough to accommodate 1 trout.

4. Spread the flour on a flat plate. Beat the eggs in a shallow dish large enough to accommodate 1 trout. Season each trout cavity with salt and pepper and dust the outside with the flour, shaking off the excess. Dip the trout into the beaten eggs, then coat it with the cornmeal, pressing lightly to adhere. Transfer to a rack and repeat with the remaining trout.

5. In a nonstick frying pan over medium-high heat, warm the oil. Add 2 trout and brown, turning once, for 1–2 minutes on each side. Transfer to the prepared baking sheet and repeat with the remaining trout.

6. Bake the trout until opaque throughout when pierced with a knife, about 5 minutes. Transfer to warmed individual plates, spoon some corn relish over each fish, and serve.

SERVES 6

NUTRITIONAL ANALYSIS PER SERVING
Calories 810 (Kilojoules 3,402); Protein 60 g; Carbohydrates 70 g; Total Fat 33 g; Saturated Fat 6 g; Cholesterol 238 mg; Sodium 902 mg; Dietary Fiber 7 g

Seafood Grill with Nasturtium Butter

BUTTER

6 tablespoons (3 oz/90 g) unsalted
butter, at room temperature

2½ tablespoons chopped organic
nasturtium blossoms
(6–8 blossoms)

2 teaspoons finely grated and
drained radish (1 small radish)

salt and freshly ground pepper
to taste

1 lb (500 g) sea scallops

3 salmon steaks, each about ½ lb
(250 g) and 1–1½ inches (2.5–4 cm)
thick

1½ lb (750 g) swordfish steaks, each
about 1–1½ inches (2.5–4 cm)
thick

¼ cup (2 fl oz/60 ml) olive oil

salt and freshly ground pepper
to taste

organic nasturtium blossoms

Brightly colored nasturtiums trail from window boxes and garden plots all summer long. The blossoms contribute a peppery bite to this compound butter for grilled seafood.

1. First, make the butter: Several hours before serving, combine the butter, chopped nasturtiums, and radish in a small bowl. Work together with a wooden spoon to mix evenly. Season lightly with salt and pepper. Scoop the butter onto a sheet of waxed paper and shape it into a log about 1½ inches (4 cm) in diameter. Wrap securely in waxed paper and refrigerate or freeze until firm. Just before putting the fish on the grill, slice the butter into disks about ⅛ inch (3 mm) thick and return the disks to the refrigerator.

2. Prepare a medium-hot fire in a charcoal grill, or preheat a gas or electric grill. Soak 8 bamboo skewers in water for 30 minutes.

3. Drain the skewers. Remove the small white muscle that wraps partway around the circumference of each scallop. Holding 2 skewers parallel, thread one-fourth of the scallops onto them. Repeat with the remaining scallops and skewers. Brush the scallops, salmon, and swordfish on both sides with the olive oil and season with salt and pepper.

4. Arrange the salmon and swordfish on the grill rack and grill, turning once, until just opaque throughout, 5–6 minutes on each side. After turning the fish, put the scallops on the grill and cook, turning once, until opaque throughout, 2–3 minutes on each side.

5. Transfer the seafood to a warmed platter. Slide the scallops from the skewers. Peel the skin from each salmon steak and remove the center bone. This will separate each steak into halves. Cut the swordfish into 6 equal pieces. Top each steak and every other scallop with a disk of butter. Garnish with nasturtiums and serve immediately.

SERVES 6

NUTRITIONAL ANALYSIS PER SERVING
Calories 514 (Kilojoules 2,159); Protein 53 g; Carbohydrates 2 g; Total Fat 31 g;
Saturated Fat 11 g; Cholesterol 154 mg; Sodium 274 mg; Dietary Fiber 0 g

Grilled Black Cod with Cucumbers & Ginger

2 English (hothouse) cucumbers, very
thinly sliced

1 cup (3½ oz/105 g) very thinly
sliced red onion

2 teaspoons coarse salt

3 tablespoons chopped pickled ginger

1 tablespoon unseasoned rice vinegar

3 tablespoons canola oil

4 black cod fillets, about 1½ lb
(750 g) total weight

½ teaspoon freshly ground pepper

Black cod, or sablefish, is a mild, buttery fish with a firm texture. It is fished from Southern California to the Bering Sea, from January through September. If unavailable, Chilean sea bass or halibut would make a fine substitute.

1. Prepare a hot fire in a charcoal grill, or preheat a gas or electric grill. Oil the grill rack.

2. In a bowl, combine the cucumbers and onion and sprinkle with 1½ teaspoons of the salt. Let stand for 15 minutes. Stir in the ginger, vinegar, and 2 tablespoons of the canola oil. Set aside.

3. Brush the fish fillets on both sides with the remaining 1 tablespoon oil. Sprinkle with the remaining ½ teaspoon salt and the pepper.

4. Place the fish, skin side down, over the fire and grill, turning once, until just opaque throughout, about 8 minutes total.

5. Transfer the cod fillets to warmed individual plates. Serve immediately with the cucumber salad.

SERVES 4

NUTRITIONAL ANALYSIS PER SERVING
Calories 290 (Kilojoules 1,218); Protein 33 g; Carbohydrates 13 g; Total Fat 11 g;
Saturated Fat 1 g; Cholesterol 73 mg; Sodium 881 mg; Dietary Fiber 3 g

Seafood Stew in Smoky Tomato Broth

TOMATO BROTH

3 tablespoons extra-virgin olive oil

1 small white onion, slivered

2 cloves garlic, minced

1 teaspoon dried Mexican oregano

1 bay leaf

1 can (15 oz/470 g) whole tomatoes
with juice, puréed

1 can (15 oz/470 g) diced tomatoes
with juice

3 chipotle chiles in adobo sauce,
finely chopped

pinch of sugar

kosher salt and freshly ground pepper

STEW

3 tablespoons olive oil

2 cloves garlic, minced

18 extra-large shrimp (prawns),
peeled and deveined

18 small mussels, well scrubbed and
debearded

18 small hard-shell clams, well
scrubbed

3 cups (24 fl oz/750 ml) bottled
clam juice

1½ cups (12 fl oz/375 ml) water

kosher salt to taste

2 cups (10 oz/315 g) Seasoned White
Rice (page 315)

2 tablespoons coarsely chopped fresh
cilantro (fresh coriander), plus
sprigs for garnish

1 lime, cut into 6 wedges

This recipe owes its existence to Above Sea Level, a fish purveyor in Santa Fe, who consistently provides good fresh seafood. It resembles a traditional Mexican *sopa de mariscos* (shellfish stew), with the flourish of a smoky tomato broth that adds a north-of-the-border influence.

1. To make the tomato broth, in a large saucepan over medium-high heat, warm the olive oil. Add the onion and sauté until translucent, about 3 minutes. Add the garlic, oregano, and bay leaf and sauté for 1 minute. Add the puréed and diced tomatoes and juice and the chipotles and season to taste with sugar, salt, and pepper. Simmer, uncovered, until slightly thickened, about 20 minutes. Set aside.

2. To make the stew, in a large, deep frying pan over medium-high heat, warm the olive oil. Add the garlic and sauté for 1 minute. Add the shrimp and sauté until they just turn pink and are opaque throughout, 2–3 minutes. Remove the shrimp from the pan and keep warm. Add the mussels and clams, discarding any that fail to close to the touch. Pour in the tomato broth, bottled clam juice, and water and season with salt. Cover and simmer until the mussels and clams open, 3–4 minutes. Uncover and discard any shellfish that failed to open.

3. Place a scoop of rice in the center of each of 6 large, wide-rimmed soup plates. Arrange 3 shrimp, 3 mussels, and 3 clams around the rice. Stir the chopped cilantro into the remaining broth. Taste and adjust the seasoning. Ladle enough of the broth into each of the soup plates to fill just below the rim. Garnish each serving with a cilantro sprig along with a wedge of lime, to be squeezed onto the stew before eating. Serve at once.

SERVES 6

NUTRITIONAL ANALYSIS PER SERVING
Calories 373 (Kilojoules 1,567); Protein 30 g; Carbohydrates 26 g; Total Fat 17 g;
Saturated Fat 2 g; Cholesterol 161 mg; Sodium 641 mg; Dietary Fiber 2 g

Walleye in Parchment with Lemon & Dill

6 tablespoons (3 oz/90 g) unsalted butter, at room temperature

4 walleye fillets, 4–6 oz (125–185 g) each

1 lemon, thinly sliced

4–8 fresh dill sprigs

4–8 fresh flat-leaf (Italian) parsley sprigs

8 dashes of Tabasco or other hot-pepper sauce

salt and freshly ground pepper to taste

Walleye, often called the sole of freshwater fish, is snowy white, fine flaked, sweet, and tender. Although sometimes called walleye pike, the fish is not a pike at all, but instead a member of the perch family and closely related to the sweet yellow perch. On the Wolf River in Wisconsin, walleyes migrate a hundred miles upstream from Lake Winnebago, to the delight of northern Heartland sport fishers. If walleye is not available, substitute sole, snapper, or flounder in this recipe.

1. Preheat the oven to 350°F (180°C). Cut four 24-by-12-inch (60-by-30-cm) pieces of parchment (baking) paper. Using 2 tablespoons of the butter, liberally butter each sheet.

2. Rinse the fillets and pat dry with paper towels. Place 1 walleye fillet at one wide end of the parchment, leaving about 2 inches (5 cm) of paper uncovered at the bottom. Put 2 or 3 slices of lemon, 1 or 2 dill sprigs, and 1 or 2 parsley sprigs on top of each fillet. Shake 2 dashes of hot-pepper sauce over each fillet. Season the fish with salt and pepper. Dot each fillet with equal amounts of the remaining 4 tablespoons (2 oz/60 g) butter.

3. To close the parchment paper, moisten the edges of the paper with water. Fold the free half of the paper over the fish, closing it like a book. Fold the edges of the paper over, crimping as you go, to enclose the fish. Assemble the remaining 3 packets, and place all the packets on a baking sheet.

4. Bake until the parchment paper is puffed and brown, 10–12 minutes.

5. Place the packets on individual plates. Slit open carefully, avoiding the steam, and fold back the parchment. Serve at once.

SERVES 4

NUTRITIONAL ANALYSIS PER SERVING
Calories 215 (Kilojoules 903); Protein 28 g; Carbohydrates 3 g; Total Fat 10 g; Saturated Fat 6 g; Cholesterol 145 mg; Sodium 80 mg; Dietary Fiber 1 g

Salt & Pepper Squid

2 lb (1 kg) squid

1 cup (5 oz/155 g) all-purpose (plain) flour

1 tablespoon coarse salt

1 teaspoon coarsely ground pepper

canola oil for deep-frying

lemon wedges

Squid is wonderfully light and crisp when treated to a dusting of flour and a brief dunking in very hot oil. Coarse salt and pepper and a crowning spritz of fresh lemon juice complete the dish.

1. To clean each squid, grip the head and pull it and the attached innards from the body. Squeeze out the small, hard beak at the base of the tentacles. Using a small, sharp knife, cut away the eyes; set the tentacles aside. Pull out the transparent quill-like cartilage from the body and discard, then, using a finger, clean out the body pouch, holding it under cold running water as you work. Rub off the mottled skin on the outside of the pouch. Rinse the pouch and tentacles well. Cut the bodies into rings ½ inch (12 mm) wide; leave the tentacles whole. If you are using already cleaned squid, simply cut the bodies into rings.

2. In a shallow bowl, stir together the flour, salt, and pepper.

3. Pour canola oil into a deep, heavy saucepan to a depth of 3 inches (7.5 cm) and heat to 375°F (190°C) on a deep-frying thermometer. When the oil is ready, add about one-third of the squid to the flour mixture, turn to coat evenly, and then shake off the excess. Add the squid to the oil, stir briefly, and cook for 1 minute. The squid should be opaque and perfectly tender. Using a wire skimmer, lift out the squid and place on paper towels to drain briefly. Repeat with the remaining squid in two batches.

4. Transfer the squid to a warmed platter and serve immediately with lemon wedges.

SERVES 4

NUTRITIONAL ANALYSIS PER SERVING
Calories 271 (Kilojoules 1,138); Protein 25 g; Carbohydrates 13 g; Total Fat 12 g; Saturated Fat 1 g; Cholesterol 362 mg; Sodium 437 mg; Dietary Fiber 0 g

Sand Dabs with Meyer Lemon & Capers

2 Meyer lemons

2 sand dabs, about ½ lb (250 g) each

salt and freshly ground pepper to taste

about ½ cup (2½ oz/75 g) all-purpose (plain) flour

2 teaspoons olive oil

2 teaspoons plus 3 tablespoons unsalted butter

2 tablespoons chopped capers

1 tablespoon minced fresh flat-leaf (Italian) parsley

Sand dabs are typically cooked on the bone, which keeps them intact and contributes to their excellent flavor. If you prefer, you can substitute petrale sole fillets, but they will cook faster.

1. Cut a slice off the top and bottom of 1 lemon to expose the flesh. Stand the lemon upright on a cutting board and, using a sharp knife, thickly slice off the peel in strips, cutting around the contour of the fruit to expose the flesh. With the knife, cut along both sides of each lemon section to free it. Cut the sections into small, neat dice. Using the second lemon, squeeze enough juice to measure 1 tablespoon.

2. Season the sand dabs generously with salt and pepper. Spread the flour on a plate, then dip each fish in the flour, coating both sides. Shake off the excess flour and put the fish on a rack.

3. Heat a large nonstick frying pan over medium-high heat. Add the olive oil to the hot pan. When the oil is hot, add the 2 teaspoons butter. When the butter melts, foams, and just begins to color, add the fish. Reduce the heat to medium. Cook on the first side until it is well browned and the fish are cooked halfway through, 3–4 minutes, depending on their size. Turn the fish gently with a spatula. Cook on the second side until the fish are no longer pink at the bone, 3–4 minutes longer. Remove the fish to a warmed platter.

4. Pour off any fat in the pan and return to low heat. Add the remaining 3 tablespoons butter to the pan along with the diced lemon, lemon juice, capers, and parsley. Swirl the pan until the butter melts. Pour over the fish and serve at once.

SERVES 2

NUTRITIONAL ANALYSIS PER SERVING
Calories 528 (Kilojoules 2,218); Protein 46 g; Carbohydrates 24 g; Total Fat 29 g; Saturated Fat 14 g; Cholesterol 166 mg; Sodium 570 mg; Dietary Fiber 1 g

Meyer Lemons

Although it has been cultivated in California since the early 1900s, the delicate, sweet-scented Meyer lemon has only recently come into its own. For years it was mainly a backyard fruit with little commercial presence. But when contemporary California chefs began to celebrate the locally grown, they rediscovered the Meyer lemon and sparked demand for this unusual citrus.

Discovered in China by an American agricultural explorer in 1908, the Meyer lemon has a mysterious family tree. Some say it may be a cross between a lemon and a mandarin orange. Whatever its parentage, its lemon-orange flavor enhances seafood, asparagus, ice cream, and cake.

Compared to the two most common lemons in California, the Eureka and the Lisbon, the Meyer has a thinner skin with a richer yellow-orange color. Scratch that skin and you release a powerful floral fragrance. Inside, it has tender walls and a goodly amount of low-acid juice.

In fact, if chefs have one complaint about the Meyer, it's that it is not tart enough for some preparations. Where more tartness is desirable—say, in vinaigrettes—they may choose to supplement the Meyer lemon juice with some conventional lemon juice or vinegar.

Thanks to the renewed interest in Meyer lemons, a few commercial growers have planted them. But Meyers are still rare enough in the marketplace that the Californians who love them often plant their own.

Chefs prize the Meyer lemon for its vibrant color and mild citrus flavor, which makes it a particularly good ingredient in desserts.

Lobster Rolls

1 lb (500 g) fresh-cooked lobster meat (from about 5 lb/2.5 kg lobster in the shell), picked over for shell fragments and cut into bite-sized chunks

1 celery stalk with leaves, finely minced (⅓ cup/2 oz/60 g)

⅓ cup (3 fl oz/80 ml) mayonnaise

1 tablespoon capers, chopped (optional)

salt and freshly ground pepper to taste

4–6 hot-dog rolls, preferably split-top, or sandwich rolls

1½ tablespoons unsalted butter, at room temperature

Every summer, when Maine's Route 1 is jammed with north-bound vacationers, there is always a waiting line at Maine Diner in Wells. A favorite menu item is the famous lobster roll—a buttered and grilled hot dog–style roll stuffed with chunks of lobster meat. Coleslaw is the likely side.

1. In a bowl, combine the lobster meat, celery, mayonnaise, and the capers, if using. Fold together gently so as not to break up the meat. Season with salt and pepper. (The mixture may be made ahead, covered, and refrigerated overnight.)

2. Split the rolls, if necessary, and butter the outsides. Preheat a griddle or large frying pan over medium heat. When the pan is hot, place the rolls, buttered sides down, on the hot surface and toast until lightly browned, about 3 minutes.

3. Transfer the rolls to individual plates and divide the lobster mixture evenly among the rolls. Serve immediately.

SERVES 4–6

NUTRITIONAL ANALYSIS PER SERVING
Calories 324 (Kilojoules 1,361); Protein 22 g; Carbohydrates 19 g; Total Fat 17 g;
Saturated Fat 4 g; Cholesterol 83 mg; Sodium 631 mg; Dietary Fiber 1 g

Pickled Pepper Shrimp with Okra

3 cups (24 fl oz/750 ml) cider vinegar

1 cup (8 fl oz/250 ml) fresh orange juice

1 cup (7 oz/220 g) firmly packed light brown sugar

2 Scotch bonnet chiles, seeded and thinly sliced

2 tablespoons coriander seeds, crushed

2 tablespoons mustard seeds

2 tablespoons dill seeds

1 tablespoon celery seeds

3 bay leaves, crumbled

12 peppercorns

6 allspice berries

2 teaspoons ground turmeric

2 teaspoons salt

3 lb (1.5 kg) large shrimp (prawns), peeled and deveined

1 lb (500 g) baby okra, no more than 2 inches (5 cm) long, stems trimmed without cutting into pod

1 Vidalia or other sweet onion, thinly sliced

1 red bell pepper and 1 green bell pepper (capsicum), seeded and thinly sliced lengthwise

1 lemon, thinly sliced

3 cloves garlic, chopped

½ cup (4 fl oz/125 ml) extra-virgin olive oil

24 baguette slices, toasted

A classic pickling, or preserving, method of the Deep South joins with the flavors of tropical Florida in this refreshing dish. Be sure to choose small, plump okra pods, or they will be tough and stringy when pickled.

1. In a large nonaluminum saucepan, stir together the vinegar, orange juice, brown sugar, chiles, coriander seeds, mustard seeds, dill seeds, celery seeds, bay leaves, peppercorns, allspice berries, turmeric, and salt. Bring to a boil over high heat, stirring to dissolve the sugar. Reduce the heat to low and simmer, uncovered, until the mixture is slightly reduced and very aromatic, about 10 minutes.

2. Add the shrimp, okra, onion, red and green bell peppers, lemon, and garlic. Return to a boil over high heat, remove from the heat, cover, and let cool to room temperature.

3. Stir the olive oil into the cooled mixture, transfer to a nonaluminum bowl, cover, and refrigerate for at least 8 hours or as long as 2 days, stirring occasionally.

4. Using a slotted spoon, transfer the shrimp and vegetables to small plates. Serve chilled or at room temperature with the baguette slices.

MAKES 3 QT (3 L); SERVES 12

NUTRITIONAL ANALYSIS PER SERVING
Calories 446 (Kilojoules 1,873); Protein 26 g; Carbohydrates 59 g; Total Fat 14 g; Saturated Fat 2 g; Cholesterol 140 mg; Sodium 845 mg; Dietary Fiber 4 g

Creole Vegetables with Crawfish Tails

2 ears of yellow or white corn, husks and silk removed

⅓ cup (3 fl oz/80 ml) bacon drippings or peanut oil

⅓ cup (2 oz/60 g) all-purpose (plain) flour

2 yellow onions, chopped

2 celery stalks, chopped

2 green bell peppers (capsicums), seeded and chopped

4 cloves garlic, chopped

1 or 2 finger hot, bird's eye, or jalapeño chiles, seeded and finely chopped

2 cups (16 fl oz/500 ml) chicken stock

1 can (28 oz/875 g) crushed tomatoes with added purée

1 lb (500 g) baby lima beans, shelled

1 lb (500 g) small okra, sliced

1 lb (500 g) fresh or thawed frozen crawfish tails or small shrimp (prawns), peeled and deveined

3 green (spring) onions, chopped

salt and freshly ground pepper to taste

filé powder for dusting

RICE

2 cups (14 oz/440 g) long-grain white rice

4½ cups (36 fl oz/1.1 l) chicken stock or water

2 tablespoons unsalted butter

salt and freshly ground pepper to taste

The Creoles were the original French and Spanish colonists of New Orleans. The Cajuns were French immigrants from Acadia (now known as Nova Scotia) who subsequently settled on the bayous of the Louisiana swamp country. This basic gumbo combines the cooking styles and ingredients of both heritages.

1. Resting an ear of corn on its stalk end in a shallow bowl, cut down along the ear with a sharp knife, stripping off the kernels and rotating the ear with each cut. Then run the flat side of the blade along the ear to remove any "milk." Repeat with the remaining ear. Set aside.

2. In a large, heavy saucepan over medium heat, warm the bacon drippings or peanut oil. Stir in the flour and cook, stirring constantly, until the mixture (called a roux) is a dark caramel color, about 20 minutes. Do not allow it to burn, or the dish will have a scorched taste.

3. Stir in the onions, celery, bell peppers, garlic, and chiles and cook, stirring occasionally, until the vegetables are soft, about 10 minutes. Add the stock, tomatoes, corn, lima beans, and okra and cook uncovered, stirring often, until slightly thickened, about 40 minutes.

4. Meanwhile, cook the rice: In a large saucepan over medium-high heat, combine the rice, chicken stock or water, butter, salt, and pepper. Bring to a boil, reduce the heat to low, cover, and simmer until the rice is tender, about 20 minutes. Remove from the heat and let stand, covered, for about 10 minutes. Fluff with a fork. Taste and adjust the seasoning.

5. Add the crawfish tails or shrimp and the green onions to the vegetable mixture and cook over medium heat until the shellfish is cooked through and turns coral pink, about 5 minutes. Season with salt and pepper.

6. Spoon the rice onto individual plates. Ladle the vegetables and seafood over the rice. Dust each serving with filé powder and serve at once.

SERVES 6

NUTRITIONAL ANALYSIS PER SERVING
Calories 706 (Kilojoules 2,965); Protein 29 g; Carbohydrates 110 g; Total Fat 17 g; Saturated Fat 6 g; Cholesterol 95 mg; Sodium 1,450 mg; Dietary Fiber 12 g

Roux, Gravy & Sauce

A roux is a flavorful mixture of a flour and a fat, which is sometimes oil, sometimes butter, sometimes lard. It is the base of a gravy or sauce and is also used to thicken such Louisiana dishes as gumbo *(see* Creole Vegetables with Crawfish Tails, *opposite)* and étouffée.

The best vessel to use for making a roux is a heavy pot or cast-iron frying pan. The usual ratio of flour to fat is one to one (by volume). Depending on the desired color, a roux can take anywhere from two minutes (a blond roux) up to an hour (a black roux, most often used in gumbos). Generally, blond and medium roux are used in gravies and sauces.

Although all gravies are sauces, not all sauces are gravies. A gravy is a sauce made from meat juices, usually combined with stock, milk, or cream, and then thickened with a roux or other thickener. Most Southerners love a good gravy. Indeed, most consider it a beverage. Anyone who is unfamiliar with the milk or cream gravy served throughout the region may question the passion for this concoction, but it plays a very important role in Southern cuisine, marrying fried chicken with rice, sausage

with biscuits, and, of course, roast beef and mashed potatoes.

Like a gravy, a sauce is a thickened liquid used to accompany and highlight the flavor of foods. But the similarity stops there. Sauces can be made not only from meat juices, but also from simmered vegetables, puréed fruits, chocolate, or caramel.

The browner the roux, the nuttier its flavor. A medium roux like the one above plays a versatile role in Southern cooking.

Salmon Cakes with Jalapeño Rémoulade

JALAPEÑO RÉMOULADE

1 whole egg plus 1 egg yolk

2 teaspoons Dijon mustard

¾ cup (6 fl oz/180 ml) safflower oil

2 cloves garlic, minced

1 tablespoon capers, rinsed

¼ cup (2 oz/60 g) cornichons, rinsed

6 canned pickled jalapeño strips, plus 1 tablespoon juice from can

¼ cup (¾ oz/20 g) thinly sliced green (spring) onion

¼ cup (⅓ oz/10 g) chopped fresh flat-leaf (Italian) parsley

pinch of kosher salt

SALMON CAKES

2 lb (1 kg) salmon fillets, skinned and cut into chunks

1 large red onion, cut into ¼-inch (6-mm) dice

3 tablespoons chopped fresh tarragon

⅓ cup (2 oz/60 g) diced roasted red bell pepper (capsicum) *(page 311)*

1 cup (2 oz/60 g) fresh bread crumbs

½ teaspoon kosher salt

1 teaspoon white pepper

1 cup (5 oz/155 g) unbleached all-purpose (plain) flour

2 eggs

1 tablespoon water

2 cups (4 oz/125 g) *panko*

½ cup (4 fl oz/125 ml) vegetable oil

Strips of pickled jalapeño chile spike a traditional French-style tartar sauce to give this dish a Southwestern accent.

1. To make the rémoulade, in a food processor, combine the whole egg, egg yolk, and mustard. Pulse to mix. With the motor running, slowly pour in the oil and process until the mixture forms a thick mayonnaise. Add the garlic, capers, cornichons, and jalapeño strips and juice. Pulse until finely chopped. Add the green onion and parsley and pulse to mix. Season with salt, transfer to a bowl, cover, and refrigerate.

2. Rinse the processor bowl. To make the salmon cakes, in 2 batches, place the salmon chunks in the processor and pulse until coarsely chopped. Transfer to a bowl. Add the onion, tarragon, bell pepper, and bread crumbs and mix gently. Season with the salt and white pepper.

3. Line a baking sheet with aluminum foil. With a ¼-cup (2-oz/60-g) measure, scoop out the salmon mixture and shape into flat patties about ¾ inch (2 cm) thick. Arrange on the prepared baking sheet and freeze for 20–30 minutes.

4. Line a baking sheet with paper towels. Spread the flour on a flat plate. In a shallow bowl, lightly beat the eggs with the water. Spread the *panko* on a flat plate. In a frying pan over medium-high heat, warm ¼ cup (2 fl oz/60 ml) of the oil. Coat 3 or 4 of the salmon cakes with flour, shaking off any excess. Dip them into the egg, rubbing it into the flour. Dip the cakes into the *panko,* pressing to adhere. Add the cakes to the hot oil and fry, turning once, until golden and cooked through, 2–3 minutes on each side. Transfer to the prepared baking sheet and keep warm in a low oven. Repeat with the remaining cakes, adding the remaining ¼ cup (2 fl oz/ 60 ml) oil as necessary to prevent sticking.

5. Place 2 salmon cakes on each plate, top with a spoonful or two of rémoulade, and serve.

MAKES 12 CAKES; SERVES 6

NUTRITIONAL ANALYSIS PER CAKE
Calories 475 (Kilojoules 1,993); Protein 20 g; Carbohydrates 22 g; Total Fat 33 g;
Saturated Fat 5 g; Cholesterol 116 mg; Sodium 330 mg; Dietary Fiber 1 g

Panfried Salmon with Pinot Noir & Thyme

4 salmon fillets with skin intact, each 4–5 oz (125–155 g) and ¾ inch (2 cm) thick

¾ teaspoon coarse salt

¾ teaspoon freshly ground pepper

1 tablespoon olive oil

1 cup (8 fl oz/250 ml) Pinot Noir

4 fresh thyme sprigs, plus more for garnish (optional)

1 tablespoon unsalted butter

A bright purple wine sauce looks beautiful drizzled over lustrous pink salmon. For this simple reduction sauce, you need to buy a good-quality Oregon Pinot Noir, some of the best of which come from the Willamette Valley. Remember, the better the wine, the better the sauce. Pour the rest of the bottle to accompany your dinner.

1. Sprinkle the salmon fillets with ½ teaspoon each of the salt and pepper.

2. In a large frying pan over high heat, warm the olive oil. Add the salmon, skin side down, and cook until browned and crisp, 3–4 minutes. Turn the fish and cook for 2–3 minutes longer. The salmon will be slightly rare at the center. If you prefer it fully cooked, continue cooking for another minute or so. Transfer the fish to a warmed platter and cover to keep warm.

3. Add the wine and the thyme sprigs to the pan and bring to a boil over high heat. Cook until reduced by half, about 5 minutes. Remove the thyme sprigs and stir in the remaining ¼ teaspoon each salt and pepper and the butter.

4. Pour the sauce over the salmon. Garnish with additional thyme sprigs, if you like, and serve immediately.

SERVES 4

NUTRITIONAL ANALYSIS PER SERVING
Calories 269 (Kilojoules 1,130); Protein 23 g; Carbohydrates 1 g; Total Fat 19 g; Saturated Fat 5 g; Cholesterol 75 mg; Sodium 346 mg; Dietary Fiber 0 g

Holiday Oyster Stew

6 tablespoons (3 oz/90 g) unsalted
    butter

1 shallot, grated

2 pt (1 l) freshly shucked oysters
    with their liquid

2 cups (16 fl oz/500 ml) heavy
    (double) cream

1 cup (8 fl oz/250 ml) milk

few drops of Tabasco or other
    hot-pepper sauce

salt to taste

2 tablespoons finely chopped fresh
    chervil or chives (optional)

If you're up to the task of shucking the oysters yourself, figure four to five dozen medium-sized oysters for this recipe. Look for the briny-flavored Atlantic oysters such as Wellfleets or Belons, which are harvested in the cold coastal waters of Maine.

1. Preheat the oven to 200°F (95°C). Place individual soup bowls on a baking sheet. Using about 1 tablespoon total of the butter, place a sliver of butter in each bowl and slip the baking sheet into the oven.

2. Select a wide saucepan or deep sauté pan that will accommodate the oysters snugly in a single layer. Add the remaining 5 tablespoons (2½ oz/75 g) butter to the pan and place it over medium heat. When the butter melts, stir in the shallot and cook for a minute or two without browning. Add the oysters and their liquid, and heat until the liquid just starts to simmer and the edges of the oysters begin to curl, 2–5 minutes. Using a slotted spoon, transfer the oysters to a shallow bowl and set aside.

3. Raise the heat to high and cook the liquid until it is reduced by about half, 5–7 minutes. Add the cream and milk and bring to just below a boil. Taste and season discreetly with the Tabasco and salt. (The stew may be plenty salty from the oysters.) Reduce the heat to medium-low and return the oysters to the pan to heat through. Do not allow the stew to boil or stay too long on the heat, or the oysters will toughen.

4. Ladle into the warmed bowls and garnish each serving with a bit of chervil or chives, if desired. Serve piping hot.

SERVES 6–8

NUTRITIONAL ANALYSIS PER SERVING
Calories 443 (Kilojoules 1,861); Protein 13 g; Carbohydrates 9 g; Total Fat 40 g;
Saturated Fat 23 g; Cholesterol 204 mg; Sodium 207 mg; Dietary Fiber 0 g

Oregon Peppered Bacon & Crab BLT

1 red bell pepper (capsicum)

½ cup (4 fl oz/125 ml) mayonnaise

1 tablespoon chopped fresh tarragon

4 thick slices peppered bacon, about
6 oz (185 g) total weight

4 crusty artisan bread rolls, split and
lightly toasted

1½ cups (8 oz/250 g) fresh-cooked
Dungeness crabmeat, picked over
for shell fragments

2 ripe tomatoes, sliced ¼ inch (6 mm)
thick

1 small head butter (Boston) or Bibb
lettuce, leaves separated

This is not your average BLT. The Northwest's popular peppered bacon joins Dungeness crab and tarragon to deliver delightful—and unexpected—flavors to this classic sandwich. For a special-occasion lunch, prepare all the elements ahead of time, then assemble the sandwiches just before serving.

1. Preheat the broiler (griller). Cut the bell pepper in half lengthwise and remove the stem, seeds, and ribs. Place, cut sides down, on a baking sheet. Broil (grill) until the skin blackens and blisters. Remove from the broiler, drape loosely with aluminum foil, and let cool for 10 minutes, then peel away the skin. Chop finely and place in a small bowl. Add the mayonnaise and tarragon and mix well.

2. Meanwhile, in a large frying pan over medium-high heat, fry the bacon until crisp, about 10 minutes. Using tongs, transfer to paper towels to drain.

3. Spread the cut surfaces of the rolls with the mayonnaise mixture, dividing it evenly between the tops and bottoms.

4. Place the bottoms of the rolls on individual plates and top with the crabmeat, tomatoes, bacon, and lettuce. Cover with the roll tops and secure each sandwich with 2 toothpicks. Cut each sandwich in half between the toothpicks and serve.

SERVES 4

NUTRITIONAL ANALYSIS PER SERVING
Calories 500 (Kilojoules 2,100); Protein 21 g; Carbohydrates 34 g; Total Fat 31 g;
Saturated Fat 6 g; Cholesterol 83 mg; Sodium 843 mg; Dietary Fiber 3 g

Dungeness Crab Cakes with Cabbage Slaw

CRAB CAKES

¼ cup (2 fl oz/60 ml) mayonnaise

2 teaspoons dry mustard

salt and cayenne pepper to taste

¼ cup (1½ oz/45 g) finely minced celery

¼ cup (¾ oz/20 g) finely minced green (spring) onion, white and pale green parts only

1 lb (500 g) fresh-cooked Dungeness crabmeat, picked over for shell fragments

2 cups (4 oz/120 g) soft fresh bread crumbs

4 teaspoons olive oil

4 teaspoons unsalted butter

4 lemon wedges

CABBAGE SLAW

¼ cup (2 fl oz/60 ml) buttermilk

¼ cup (2 fl oz/60 ml) mayonnaise

2 tablespoons minced fresh dill

1 clove garlic, minced

4 cups (12 oz/375 g) thinly sliced Napa cabbage

1 cup (4 oz/125 g) grated carrot

¼ cup (¾ oz/20 g) minced green (spring) onion

salt and freshly ground black pepper to taste

fresh lemon juice to taste

Many East Coast cooks add a liberal dash of Old Bay seasoning to their blue-crab cakes, but California cooks using the local Dungeness take a lighter approach. These crab cakes have just enough mayonnaise to hold them together and just enough seasoning to heighten, not hide, the crab flavor.

1. To make the crab cakes, in a bowl, stir together the mayonnaise and mustard. Add a pinch each of salt and cayenne pepper. Stir in the celery and green onion, then gently fold in the crabmeat and 1 cup (2 oz/60 g) of the bread crumbs. Spread the remaining 1 cup (2 oz/60 g) bread crumbs on a sheet of waxed paper.

2. Shape the crab mixture into 8 patties, each 1 inch (2.5 cm) thick. They will only reluctantly hold together, but try not to overwork them. Coat them on both sides with the bread crumbs, then arrange on a baking sheet. Cover and refrigerate for 1 hour.

3. While the crab cakes are chilling, make the slaw: In a small bowl, whisk together the buttermilk, mayonnaise, dill, and garlic. In a large bowl, toss together the cabbage, carrot, and green onion. Add the dressing and salt and black pepper to taste and toss well. Taste and add as much lemon juice as desired.

4. Heat 2 large nonstick frying pans over medium heat. Put 2 teaspoons oil and 2 teaspoons butter in each pan. When the fat is hot, put 4 crab cakes in each pan. Cook until golden brown on the bottom, about 3 minutes. Turn and cook until the second side is well browned and the cakes are hot throughout, 3–4 minutes longer.

5. Transfer to individual plates and serve immediately with the lemon wedges and the slaw.

SERVES 4

NUTRITIONAL ANALYSIS PER SERVING
Calories 510 (Kilojoules 2,142); Protein 28 g; Carbohydrates 24 g; Total Fat 34 g; Saturated Fat 7 g; Cholesterol 142 mg; Sodium 659 mg; Dietary Fiber 3 g

Dungeness Crab

It's a perfect winter lunch: a chunk of sourdough bread with butter, a glass of crisp California Chardonnay, and a heaping platter of cold cracked Dungeness crab. At seafood bars such as the venerable Swan Oyster Depot in San Francisco, crab enthusiasts enjoy the sweet, firm meat of *Cancer magister* with Louis dressing or with extra-virgin olive oil and a spritz of lemon. In California's Chinatowns, chefs pull the crabs live from tanks and stir-fry them with salted black beans or with ginger and green (spring) onions.

The Dungeness crab has been fished commercially—and enthusiastically—in California since the gold rush days. Among the most beloved of California's seafood species, the red-shelled crabs seduce diners with generous portions of snowy white meat found in their claws and body. The whole crabs typically weigh 1½ to 3 pounds (750 g to 1.5 kg) and yield about a quarter of their weight in meat.

From central California north to the Oregon border, fishermen harvest the crab in traps. To ensure future stocks, they keep only male crabs that are over 6¼ inches (15.5 cm) wide. In Northern California, where these shellfish are at their most abundant, the commercial season runs from December 1 to July 15.

Some shoppers buy crab already cooked. Others buy them live and boil them in water, white wine, aromatic vegetables, and herbs. Then they set out crab crackers, whip up a dipping sauce, and sit down to a feast.

The sweet, firm meat of the Dungeness crab is considered as great a treat on the West Coast as lobster is on the East Coast.

Swordfish Paillards with Green Olive Relish

RELISH

½ cup (2 oz/60 g) walnuts

1 large red bell pepper (capsicum)

½ cup (2½ oz/75 g) rinsed, pitted, and finely chopped green olives such as French Picholine

¼ cup (⅓ oz/10 g) finely chopped fresh mint

6 tablespoons (3 fl oz/90 ml) extra-virgin olive oil

2 tablespoons fresh lemon juice

2 cloves garlic, minced

salt and freshly ground pepper to taste

6 swordfish steaks, each about 6 oz (185 g) and a scant ½ inch (12 mm) thick

2 tablespoons extra-virgin olive oil

salt and freshly ground pepper to taste

Paillard is the French term for a thin slice of boneless meat, but some chefs, with poetic license, use the same word for thinly sliced fish. For the relish, choose lightly brined, unseasoned green olives that don't taste too sharp or salty; avoid those packed in vinegar.

1. To make the relish, preheat the oven to 350°F (180°C). Spread the walnuts on a baking sheet and toast in the oven until lightly colored and fragrant, about 15 minutes. Transfer to a cutting board, let cool, and then chop finely.

2. Turn the oven to broil (grill). Cut the bell pepper in half lengthwise and remove the stem, seeds, and ribs. Place, cut sides down, on a baking sheet. Broil (grill) until the skin blackens and blisters. Remove from the broiler (grill), leaving the broiler on. Drape the pepper loosely with aluminum foil and let cool for 10 minutes, then peel away the skin. Finely chop half of the pepper. Reserve the other half for another use.

3. In a bowl, combine the walnuts, chopped bell pepper, olives, mint, olive oil, lemon juice, and garlic. Season with salt and pepper. Set aside until serving.

4. Position the broiler rack about 8 inches (20 cm) from the heat source. Oil the swordfish on both sides with the olive oil. Arrange the fish on a heavy baking sheet. Season with salt and pepper.

5. Broil (grill) the fish until it is opaque throughout and just flakes, about 5 minutes. Transfer to individual plates and top with the olive relish, dividing it evenly. Serve immediately.

SERVES 6

NUTRITIONAL ANALYSIS PER SERVING
Calories 425 (Kilojoules 1,785); Protein 32 g; Carbohydrates 4 g; Total Fat 32 g; Saturated Fat 5 g; Cholesterol 59 mg; Sodium 422 mg; Dietary Fiber 1 g

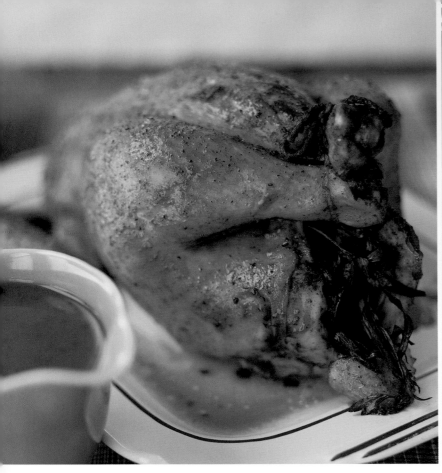

Poultry & Meats

Game Hens with Turnip Green Stuffing

2 tablespoons unsalted butter, at room temperature

4 Cornish hens, 1¼ lb (625 g) each

salt and freshly ground pepper to taste

1 cup (8 fl oz/250 ml) apple cider

STUFFING

6 slices bacon, coarsely chopped

2 leeks, white and light green parts only, chopped (about 1 cup/3 oz/ 90 g)

2 cloves garlic, chopped

1 celery stalk, chopped

1 Granny Smith apple, cored and grated

½ cup (2 oz/60 g) chopped pecans

1 package (10 oz/315 g) frozen chopped turnip greens, thawed and squeezed dry

2 cups (8 oz/250 g) crumbled day-old corn bread

¼ cup (⅓ oz/10 g) chopped fresh parsley

1 tablespoon chopped fresh sage

pinch of freshly grated nutmeg

salt and freshly ground pepper to taste

1 egg, lightly beaten

1½ cups (12 fl oz/375 ml) chicken stock

These stuffed hens are equally suitable for a celebratory dinner or a casual gathering.

1. Preheat the oven to 400°F (200°C). Lightly coat a roasting pan with vegetable oil. Rub the butter over the hens and season with salt and pepper. Place, breast side up, in the pan.

2. To make the stuffing, in a large frying pan over medium-high heat, cook the bacon until it begins to render some fat, about 2 minutes. Reduce the heat to medium and add the leeks, garlic, celery, apple, and pecans. Cook, stirring often, until the vegetables are soft and the nuts are aromatic, about 10 minutes. Remove from the heat and stir in the turnip greens, corn bread, parsley, sage, nutmeg, salt, pepper, egg, and chicken stock. Toss to mix well. Let stand for 10 minutes.

3. Loosely fill the cavities of each hen, including the flap of skin at the neck, with the stuffing. Truss the legs with kitchen string and tuck the wing tips beneath the breasts. Pour the apple cider around the hens. Spoon any remaining stuffing into a small buttered baking dish. Cover the roasting pan and baking dish with aluminum foil.

4. Roast the hens for 45 minutes. Uncover and continue to roast until the skin is crisped and golden brown and the juices run clear when a thigh joint is pierced, or an instant-read thermometer inserted into a breast registers 170°F (77°C), about 30 minutes longer. Slip the small baking dish in the oven for the last 30 minutes. Bake, covered, for 20 minutes, then remove the foil and bake for 10 minutes longer. Remove the hens from the oven and let rest for 15 minutes before serving.

5. Snip the strings and transfer the Cornish hens to a warmed serving platter. Serve immediately with the additional dish of stuffing.

SERVES 4

NUTRITIONAL ANALYSIS PER SERVING
Calories 1,271 (Kilojoules 5,084); Protein 67 g; Carbohydrates 55 g; Total Fat 87 g; Saturated Fat 26 g; Cholesterol 438 mg; Sodium 1,250 mg; Dietary Fiber 7 g

Skirt Steak Fajitas with Avocado Salsa

The orange flavor and smoky heat of the marinade give this skirt steak unforgettable character. Carved into strips after grilling, the meat is served with salsa atop warm flour tortillas for wrapping up, burrito style.

MARINADE

4 small navel or other seedless oranges, peeled, halved, and each half quartered

½ can (7 oz/220 g can) chipotle chiles in adobo sauce

1 white onion, halved and each half quartered

3 large cloves garlic

leaves from 4 fresh rosemary springs

leaves from 3 fresh marjoram sprigs

1 bunch fresh cilantro (fresh coriander), cut crosswise into thirds

1 teaspoon kosher salt

freshly ground pepper to taste

2 lb (1 kg) skirt steak, trimmed of surface fat and silver skin and cut in half horizontally

SALSA

3 ripe Hass avocados, halved and pitted

1 red onion, diced

2 cloves garlic, minced

¼ cup (⅓ oz/10 g) coarsely chopped fresh cilantro (fresh coriander)

2–3 tablespoons fresh lime juice, or to taste

kosher salt to taste

2 limes, quartered

kosher salt and freshly ground pepper to taste

12 flour tortillas, heated

1. To make the marinade, in a food processor, combine the oranges, chipotle chiles, onion, garlic, rosemary, marjoram, and cilantro. Process until the ingredients are thoroughly combined, resulting in a coarse purée. Season with salt and pepper.

2. Pour a thin layer of the marinade into a baking dish, add the steak, and top evenly with the remaining marinade. Cover and refrigerate for at least 6 hours or up to overnight.

3. To make the salsa, cut the avocado halves in half again lengthwise, and then make short horizontal cuts through the flesh of each quarter to create large chunks. Using a spoon, scoop the chunks from the skin into a bowl. Add the onion, garlic, cilantro, lime juice, and salt and stir to combine. Taste and adjust the seasoning. Cover with plastic wrap, pressing it directly onto the surface of the salsa, and set aside.

4. Prepare a fire in a charcoal grill.

5. Remove the meat from the refrigerator 30 minutes before grilling and scrape off the marinade. Squeeze the juice from the limes over the meat and sprinkle with salt and pepper.

6. Place the meat on the grill rack about 4 inches (10 cm) from the coals and grill, turning once, for about 3 minutes on each side. Transfer to a cutting board, let rest for 5 minutes, and then slice into thin strips.

7. Top each warmed tortilla with some of the sliced steak and divide among warmed individual plates. Serve with the salsa.

SERVES 6

NUTRITIONAL ANALYSIS PER SERVING
Calories 682 (Kilojoules 2,864); Protein 38 g; Carbohydrates 57 g; Total Fat 35 g; Saturated Fat 9 g; Cholesterol 75 mg; Sodium 570 mg; Dietary Fiber 6 g

Hunter's Cassoulet

2¼ cups (1 lb/500 g) dried navy beans

1 yellow onion, chopped

2 carrots, peeled and chopped

2 celery stalks with leaves, chopped

4 cloves garlic, crushed

4 fresh thyme sprigs or 1 teaspoon dried thyme

1 bay leaf

¼ lb (125 g) slab bacon or salt pork, in one piece

1 lb (500 g) sweet Italian sausage, cut into 2-inch (5-cm) chunks

1 lb (500 g) boneless pork shoulder or butt, trimmed of excess fat, cut into 2-inch (5-cm) chunks

1 lb (500 g) boneless shoulder or leg of lamb, trimmed of excess fat, cut into 2-inch (5-cm) chunks

1 cup (8 fl oz/250 ml) dry red wine

2 cups (12 oz/375 g) canned plum (Roma) tomatoes, chopped

2 tablespoons tomato paste

3 tablespoons chopped fresh flat-leaf (Italian) parsley

1 tablespoon chopped fresh thyme

2 cloves garlic, chopped

salt and freshly ground pepper to taste

TOPPING

1 cup (4 oz/125 g) toasted bread crumbs

1 cup (1½ oz/45 g) finely minced fresh parsley

This recipe is a shortcut version of the classic French meat-and-bean dish, as warming today as it was for the early French trappers and voyageurs who made new lives in the Heartland.

1. Pick over the beans and discard any stones or misshapen beans. Rinse well, place in a large bowl, and add water to cover. Let soak overnight.

2. Drain the beans and place in a Dutch oven or other large, heavy pot. Add the onion, carrots, celery, garlic, thyme sprigs or dried thyme, bay leaf, and water to cover by about ½ inch (12 mm). Bring to a boil over high heat, skimming off any foam on the surface. Reduce the heat to low, cover partially, and simmer, stirring occasionally, until the beans are tender but still hold their shape, 20–25 minutes. Drain, then return the beans to the Dutch oven or pot, reserving half of the cooking liquid.

3. Meanwhile, in a small saucepan, combine the bacon or salt pork with water to cover. Bring to a boil and cook for about 2 minutes. Drain, dice the meat, and add to the beans. Preheat the oven to 375°F (190°C).

4. In a large frying pan over medium-high heat, cook first the sausage, then the pork and the lamb, in batches, until browned on all sides, about 15 minutes for each batch. Drain off and discard the fat after browning each batch and add each batch of browned meat to the beans as it is finished.

5. Pour the wine into the frying pan and deglaze the pan, scraping up all the browned bits on the bottom. Stir in the tomatoes and tomato paste and simmer until reduced slightly, about 3 minutes. Add to the beans. Stir in the parsley, chopped thyme, garlic, salt, and pepper. Pour in enough of the reserved bean liquid just to cover the beans and stir well.

6. To make the topping, combine the bread crumbs with ¾ cup (1 oz/30 g) of the parsley. Spread it over the beans and place in the oven. Bake until the beans are very tender and the topping is browned, about 45 minutes. Garnish with the remaining ¼ cup (½ oz/15 g) parsley and serve.

SERVES 8–10

NUTRITIONAL ANALYSIS PER SERVING
Calories 592 (Kilojoules 2,486); Protein 42 g; Carbohydrates 48 g; Total Fat 26 g; Saturated Fat 9 g; Cholesterol 104 mg; Sodium 724 mg; Dietary Fiber 7 g

Rubbed Steak with Asparagus

3 tablespoons sesame seeds, lightly
 toasted

3 tablespoons Asian sesame oil

2 tablespoons coriander seeds

2 teaspoons red pepper flakes

2 teaspoons brown sugar

1½ teaspoons coarse salt

3 tablespoons peeled and grated
 fresh ginger

2 cloves garlic, smashed and minced

1 tablespoon minced lemongrass

1 teaspoon soy sauce

4 rib-eye or strip steaks, each
 8–10 oz (250–315 g) and 1 inch
 (2.5 cm) thick

1–1½ lb (500–750 g) asparagus,
 tough ends removed

1½ tablespoons olive oil or
 vegetable oil

New England hasn't been exempt from the wave of fusion cooking that has swept the country, and now many local dishes have an exotic accent. Prepare this recipe in late spring when the days are long and the asparagus is fat and tender.

1. Set aside 1 teaspoon each of the sesame seeds and sesame oil. In a mortar or spice grinder, grind together the remaining sesame seeds, the coriander seeds, red pepper flakes, brown sugar, and coarse salt. In a small bowl, mix the sesame seed mixture with the ginger, garlic, lemongrass, the remaining sesame oil, and ½ teaspoon of the soy sauce. Pat the steaks dry with paper towels and rub this mixture over the entire surface. Cover and refrigerate for at least 30 minutes or as long as 4 hours.

2. Prepare a medium-hot fire in a charcoal grill.

3. Brush the asparagus with a light coating of oil. Place the steaks on the grill rack and grill, turning once, for 5–8 minutes on each side for medium-rare or a minute or so longer for medium. Arrange the asparagus spears on the perimeter of the grill while the steaks cook and turn them often to brown them evenly. To check the steaks for doneness, make a small cut into the center of a steak with a paring knife. The steaks should be slightly less cooked than desired, as they will continue to cook a little more off the fire. When the steaks are done, transfer them to a platter and tent with aluminum foil.

4. Once the steaks are off the grill, shift the asparagus to the center of the grill rack where the fire is hottest and grill, turning as necessary, until tender and browned in spots, 4–5 minutes longer. Transfer the asparagus to a separate platter and season with the reserved 1 teaspoon each sesame seeds and sesame oil and the remaining ½ teaspoon soy sauce.

5. Uncover the steaks and serve immediately with the asparagus.

SERVES 4

NUTRITIONAL ANALYSIS PER SERVING
Calories 806 (Kilojoules 3,385); Protein 52 g; Carbohydrates 11 g; Total Fat 62 g;
Saturated Fat 20 g; Cholesterol 157 mg; Sodium 765 mg; Dietary Fiber 3 g

Herb-Studded Pork Roast

1 tablespoon chopped fresh sage

1 tablespoon chopped fresh marjoram
or oregano

1 clove garlic, minced

½ teaspoon dry mustard

½ teaspoon coarse salt

½ teaspoon freshly ground black
pepper

⅛ teaspoon cayenne pepper

⅛ teaspoon ground nutmeg

1 bone-in pork loin roast, 3–4 lb
(1.5–2 kg), backbone cracked

2 teaspoons olive oil

about 2 cups (16 fl oz/500 ml) dry
white wine, chicken stock, or water

2 tablespoons unsalted butter
(optional)

Gone are the days when every New England homestead raised a few fat pigs to provide meat for the family, but pork remains popular across the region. Ask your butcher to crack the backbone to make carving easy.

1. In a small bowl, stir together the sage, the marjoram or oregano, garlic, mustard, coarse salt, black pepper, cayenne, and nutmeg. With the tip of a sharp paring knife, make 15–20 small slits all over the pork roast. Stuff small pinches of some of the herb mixture into the slits. Rub the roast with the olive oil and spread the remaining herb mixture over the surface of the meat. Cover with plastic wrap and refrigerate for 2–6 hours.

2. Preheat the oven to 450°F (230°C).

3. Set the roast in a roasting pan. Roast for 10 minutes, then reduce the oven temperature to 275°F (135°C) and pour 1 cup (8 fl oz/250 ml) of the wine, stock, or water over the roast. Continue to roast, checking from time to time and adding more liquid if the pan is completely dry, until an instant-read thermometer inserted into the thickest part away from the bone registers 155°F (68°C), about 2 hours. Transfer to a carving board, tent with aluminum foil, and let rest for 10–15 minutes.

4. If you would like to make a simple pan sauce, skim off any fat from the pan juices in the roasting pan and set it on the stove top over medium-high heat. If there is less than ½ cup (4 fl oz/125 ml) pan drippings remaining, add ½ cup (4 fl oz/125 ml) more of the wine, stock, or water. Bring to a boil and deglaze the pan, stirring to scrape up any browned bits stuck to the pan bottom. Whisk in the butter, if using. Season to taste with salt and pepper. Pour into a warmed bowl or gravy boat.

5. Carve the roast into ¼–½-inch (6–12-mm) slices and arrange on a warmed platter. Pass the pan sauce at the table.

SERVES 6

NUTRITIONAL ANALYSIS PER SERVING
Calories 426 (Kilojoules 1,789); Protein 43 g; Carbohydrates 1 g; Total Fat 25 g;
Saturated Fat 9 g; Cholesterol 130 mg; Sodium 210 mg; Dietary Fiber 0 g

Lamb Steaks with Heirloom Beans

1 cup (7 oz/220 g) dried heirloom white beans, preferably Jacob's Cattle beans

½ cup (4 fl oz/125 ml) extra-virgin olive oil, plus 2½ tablespoons, and more for drizzling

¼ cup (2 fl oz/60 ml) fresh lemon juice, plus a few drops for seasoning

1 tablespoon chopped fresh rosemary, plus 2 sprigs

4 cloves garlic, 2 minced and 2 sliced

1 teaspoon dry mustard

2 teaspoons salt, plus salt to taste

½ teaspoon freshly ground pepper

4 lamb steaks cut from the leg, each about ½ lb (250 g) and ¾ inch (2 cm) thick

1 bay leaf

4–5 cups (32–40 fl oz/1–1.25 l) water

1 shallot, minced

2 tablespoons chopped fresh flat-leaf (Italian) parsley

Heirloom beans are available in many varieties. Jacob's Cattle beans, lovely white beans from the Kennebec Bean Company of Maine, have a moist, creamy texture and tender skin.

1. Pick over the beans and discard any stones or misshapen beans. Rinse well, place in a bowl, and add water to cover; let soak overnight.

2. In a shallow nonaluminum dish, stir together the ½ cup (4 fl oz/125 ml) olive oil, the ¼ cup (2 fl oz/60 ml) lemon juice, the chopped rosemary, the minced garlic, the mustard, 1 teaspoon of the salt, and the pepper. Place the lamb steaks in the marinade, turn to coat, cover, and refrigerate, turning two or three times, for 3–4 hours.

3. Drain the beans and put them in a saucepan with the sliced garlic, ½ tablespoon of the remaining oil, the rosemary sprigs, bay leaf, and water to cover by 1 inch (2.5 cm). Place over medium heat, bring to a simmer, cover partially, and simmer very gently until tender, 1–2 hours, adding the remaining 1 teaspoon salt and more water, if needed, after 45 minutes. Remove from the heat and set aside while you cook the steaks.

4. Preheat the broiler (grill) or a stove-top grill pan over high heat.

5. Wipe the excess marinade from the steaks. Position the broiler pan 3–4 inches (7.5–10 cm) below the heat source. Broil (grill) the steaks for 4–5 minutes. Flip them and cook for 4 minutes longer for medium-rare. They are best served still pink in the center.

6. Just before the lamb steaks are done, drain the beans and toss with the shallot, the remaining 2 tablespoons olive oil, and the chopped parsley. Season with a few drops of lemon juice and salt and pepper.

7. Transfer the steaks to warmed individual plates and place a spoonful of beans alongside. Drizzle olive oil over the beans, and serve.

SERVES 4

NUTRITIONAL ANALYSIS PER SERVING
Calories 618 (Kilojoules 2,596); Protein 45 g; Carbohydrates 32 g; Total Fat 35 g; Saturated Fat 11 g; Cholesterol 122 mg; Sodium 751 mg; Dietary Fiber 20 g

Buttermilk-Cornmeal Fried Chicken

2 cups (16 fl oz/500 ml) buttermilk

1 teaspoon Tabasco or other hot-pepper sauce

1 frying chicken, about 4 lb (2 kg), cut into 8 serving pieces

1 cup (5 oz/155 g) yellow cornmeal

1 cup (5 oz/155 g) all-purpose (plain) flour

1 teaspoon salt

1 teaspoon freshly ground pepper

1 teaspoon chopped fresh sage

½ teaspoon paprika

½ teaspoon garlic powder

½ teaspoon onion powder

2 cups (1 lb/500 g) solid vegetable shortening

Ask Southerners to name their favorite dish and the answer is inevitably fried chicken. There are probably as many recipes for this Southern specialty as there are folks who enjoy it. This version uses buttermilk and Tabasco to tenderize and flavor the chicken, and cornmeal for a crisp crust.

1. In a large bowl, stir together the buttermilk and Tabasco. Slip the chicken pieces into the mixture. Cover and refrigerate for at least 4 hours or as long as overnight.

2. In a shallow baking dish, stir together the cornmeal, flour, salt, pepper, sage, paprika, garlic powder, and onion powder. Remove each piece of chicken from the buttermilk, allowing the excess to drip away. Coat the chicken pieces evenly with the seasoned flour and place on a large baking sheet.

3. In a large, deep frying pan over medium-high heat, melt the shortening and heat to 360°F (180°C) on a deep-frying thermometer. Arrange the chicken, skin side down, in the pan, placing the pieces of dark meat in the center and the pieces of white meat around the sides. Allow the pieces to touch slightly, but do not overcrowd the pan. Reduce the heat to medium and cook until the chicken is golden brown, about 12 minutes. Using tongs, turn the chicken, cover, and continue to cook for another 10 minutes. Uncover, turn the chicken once more, and cook until crisp and cooked through, about 10 minutes longer.

4. Using tongs, transfer to paper towels to drain. Serve piping hot, at room temperature, or even chilled, straight from the refrigerator.

SERVES 4

NUTRITIONAL ANALYSIS PER SERVING
Calories 884 (Kilojoules 3,713); Protein 60 g; Carbohydrates 37 g; Total Fat 54 g; Saturated Fat 14 g; Cholesterol 178 mg; Sodium 595 mg; Dietary Fiber 2 g

Linguiça Sausage with Littleneck Clams

3 tablespoons olive oil

1 yellow onion, finely chopped

1 red or green bell pepper (capsicum), seeded and diced

¼ teaspoon coarse salt

pinch of red pepper flakes (optional)

2 or 3 cloves garlic, minced

1 teaspoon sweet paprika

1 lb (500 g) linguiça or other smoked pork sausage such as kielbasa, sliced ¼ inch (6 mm) thick

½ cup (4 fl oz/125 ml) dry white wine

1 can (28 oz/875 g) plum (Roma) tomatoes, drained and chopped

24 littleneck clams, about 2 lb (1 kg) total weight, well scrubbed

2 tablespoons chopped fresh flat-leaf (Italian) parsley

The industrious port city of New Bedford, Massachusetts, has been home to many Portuguese immigrants since the early nineteenth century, a fact reflected in the prevalence of gutsy recipes like this one. Serve the clams and sausage with crusty bread or over rice.

1. In a wide saucepan or large, deep frying pan over medium-low heat, warm the olive oil. Add the onion, bell pepper, coarse salt, and red pepper flakes (if using) and cook, stirring often, until soft, about 15 minutes. Add the garlic and paprika and cook, stirring, for about 1 minute longer. Stir in the sausage and cook, stirring occasionally, until heated through, 2–3 minutes.

2. Raise the heat to high and add the wine and tomatoes. Bring to a simmer and cook for 5 minutes to blend the flavors. Discard any clams that are gaping and do not close when tapped. Add the clams, cover, and cook until the clams open, which will take 6–10 minutes. The clams may not all open at the same time. As they do open, scoop them out with a slotted spoon and set them aside in a large bowl. After 10 minutes, scoop out and discard any clams that failed to open.

3. Return the cooked clams, still in their shells, to the pan. Spoon into warmed pasta bowls and sprinkle with the chopped parsley. Serve immediately with forks and spoons.

SERVES 4

NUTRITIONAL ANALYSIS PER SERVING
Calories 552 (Kilojoules 2,318); Protein 22 g; Carbohydrates 18 g; Total Fat 42 g; Saturated Fat 13 g; Cholesterol 88 mg; Sodium 1,659 mg; Dietary Fiber 3 g

Country-Fried Steak with Vidalia Onion Gravy

4 pieces round steak, ½ lb (250 g) each, trimmed of visible fat

1 cup (5 oz/155 g) all-purpose (plain) flour

2 tablespoons cornstarch (cornflour)

1 teaspoon onion powder

1 teaspoon garlic powder

½ teaspoon salt

½ teaspoon freshly ground black pepper

¼ teaspoon cayenne pepper

2 tablespoons unsalted butter

2 tablespoons olive oil

3 Vidalia or other sweet onions, thinly sliced

2 cups (16 fl oz/500 ml) beef stock

1 cup (8 fl oz/250 ml) milk

Here is a simple recipe that shows off the Southerner's love for gravy—on everything.

1. Using a meat pounder, pound the steaks until slightly flattened and uniform in thickness.

2. In a large lock-top plastic bag, combine the flour, cornstarch, onion powder, garlic powder, salt, black pepper, and cayenne. Seal closed and shake the bag to mix. Remove ⅓ cup (2 oz/60 g) of the seasoned flour mixture and set aside. Add the pounded steaks, one at a time, to the bag. Seal and shake the bag to coat the steaks evenly.

3. In a large frying pan over medium-high heat, melt the butter with the olive oil. Reduce the heat to medium, add the steaks, and cook, turning once, until well browned, about 4 minutes on each side. Transfer to a plate and tent with aluminum foil to keep warm.

4. Add the onions to the pan over medium heat and cook, stirring often, until they begin to soften, 5–7 minutes. Stir in the reserved ⅓ cup (2 oz/60 g) seasoned flour and cook, stirring often, for 1 minute. Add the beef stock and milk, bring quickly to a boil, stirring constantly, and deglaze the pan, stirring to remove any browned bits from the pan bottom. Reduce the heat to low, stir in any accumulated juices from the browned steaks, and then nestle the meat into the simmering gravy.

5. Cover and simmer over very low heat, stirring occasionally, until the gravy is very thick and the meat is fork tender, about 45 minutes. Taste and adjust the seasoning.

6. Transfer to warmed individual plates and serve at once.

SERVES 4

NUTRITIONAL ANALYSIS PER SERVING
Calories 835 (Kilojoules 3,507); Protein 61 g; Carbohydrates 59 g; Total Fat 39 g; Saturated Fat 14 g; Cholesterol 173 mg; Sodium 889 mg; Dietary Fiber 5 g

Beer Brats with Sauerkraut

6 bratwursts

1 red onion, cut into rings 1 inch (2.5 cm) thick

2–2½ cups (16–20 fl oz/500–625 ml) German-style beer

2 cups (1 lb/500 g) sauerkraut

1 tablespoon caraway seeds

1 tart apple, unpeeled, halved, cored, and cut into 2-inch (5-cm) chunks

6 crusty long rolls, split horizontally

Sauerkraut, German for "sour cabbage," is the perfect foil for peppery bratwurst braised in beer. Fresh sauerkraut, sold in delicatessens and the refrigerated section of supermarkets, comes closest to the tangy flavor of homemade "kraut" cured in big wooden barrels. German communities throughout the Midwest hold Oktoberfest celebrations with street fairs where vendors sell grilled bratwurst and sauerkraut on crusty buns.

1. Prepare a fire in a grill, or preheat the broiler (grill).

2. Put the sausages and onion into a wide, deep pan and add beer as needed to cover them halfway. Bring the beer to a gentle boil and cook the sausages for about 10 minutes. Prick the sausages all over with a fork.

3. Place the sausages on the grill rack or on a broiler pan. Grill or broil, turning as needed, until nicely browned on all sides, 3–5 minutes.

4. Meanwhile, in a small saucepan over medium heat, combine the sauerkraut, caraway seeds, and apple. Bring to a gentle boil and cook until the apple is soft, about 5 minutes.

5. Place a sausage on each roll bottom, top with a spoonful of the sauerkraut, and close the rolls. Pass the remaining sauerkraut at the table.

SERVES 4–6

NUTRITIONAL ANALYSIS PER SERVING
Calories 703 (Kilojoules 2,953); Protein 29 g; Carbohydrates 58 g; Total Fat 39 g; Saturated Fat 13 g; Cholesterol 82 mg; Sodium 1,823 mg; Dietary Fiber 5 g

Midwest Microbrews

August Schell Brewery, founded in New Ulm, Minnesota, in 1860, is the grand-daddy of the Midwest microbrewery movement. Best known for Schell Bock and Oktoberfest, rich malty-sweet brews for harvest celebrations, Schell seeded a crop of independent breweries that continue to make beer the old-fashioned way.

Introduced by German immigrants, beer drinking was once a daily ritual in much of the Midwestern region, and the *biergarten* was a place to relax, sing, and play musical instruments. Milwaukee's Pabst, Miller, Schlitz, and Blatz; St. Paul's Hamms; St. Louis's Anheuser-Busch; and LaCrosse's Heilman all got their start by supplying draft kegs to these gathering places. Joseph Schlitz Brewing Company produced the first bottled beer, which quickly "Made Milwaukee Famous."

In the early 1900s, Anheuser-Busch owned and operated its own railroad to export its beer. In 1920, Prohibition put the brakes on industry expansion, and most breweries barely survived until 1933, when the law was repealed.

Since then, mass-produced American beer has become blander, lighter, and more uniform, as the number of breweries in the country has dropped from some two thousand to fewer than fifty. Microbrews, in contrast, are deep in color and have robust flavors. Among them are St. Paul's Summit; Rapid City, South Dakota's Firehouse; Chippewa Falls, Wisconsin's Leinenkugel's; and Lawrence, Kansas's Free State.

The hearty, individual flavors of Midwestern microbrews uphold a rich tradition.

Texas Baby Back Ribs

SAUCE

¾ cup (6 fl oz/180 ml) white wine vinegar

¾ cup (6 fl oz/180 ml) cider vinegar

⅓ cup (3 fl oz/80 ml) Worcestershire sauce

1 tablespoon dried Mexican oregano

2 teaspoons paprika

1 teaspoon *each* garlic salt, garlic powder, onion salt, and onion powder

1 teaspoon *each* coriander and cumin seeds, toasted and ground *(page 314)*

1 teaspoon freshly ground canela or ½ teaspoon ground cinnamon

1 teaspoon dry mustard

½ teaspoon ground allspice

10 shakes of liquid smoke

2 tablespoons chipotle seasoning or 1 tablespoon puréed chipotle chiles in adobo sauce

2 tablespoons ground Chimayó chile

½ cup (4 fl oz/125 ml) chile sauce

½ cup (3½ oz/105 g) firmly packed dark brown sugar

¼ cup (2 fl oz/60 ml) tamarind concentrate

¼ cup (3 oz/90 g) honey

3 sides baby back ribs, 4½–5½ lb (2.25–2.75 kg) total weight

3 tablespoons rendered bacon fat

Even though Texas is beef country, the state's favored spicy, vinegary, not-too-sweet barbecue sauce also goes with the rich, sweet flavor of pork. If you like, though, try this sauce with meaty beef ribs or steaks.

1. To make the sauce, in a bowl, combine the wine vinegar, cider vinegar, Worcestershire sauce, oregano, paprika, garlic salt and powder, onion salt and powder, coriander, cumin, canela or cinnamon, mustard, allspice, liquid smoke, chipotle seasoning or chipotle purée, ground chile, chile sauce, brown sugar, tamarind concentrate, and honey. Mix well. Pour half of the mixture into the bottom of a large baking dish. Trim the membrane from the nonmeaty side of the rib slabs and place the ribs on top of the sauce. Turn them to coat on both sides. Pour the remaining sauce over the ribs, cover, and refrigerate overnight.

2. Preheat the oven to 350°F (180°C). Line a 14-by-18-inch (35-by-45-cm) rimmed baking sheet with 1-inch (2.5-cm) sides with aluminum foil. Place a large wire rack on the baking sheet.

3. Remove the ribs from the sauce, reserving the sauce. Place the ribs, meaty side up, on the rack. Bake, basting with ¼ cup (2 fl oz/60 ml) of the sauce, until the ribs are tender, about 1¼ hours.

4. While the ribs are baking, pour the remaining sauce into a saucepan with the bacon fat. Bring to a boil, reduce the heat to medium, and simmer, uncovered, until thickened, 25–30 minutes. Keep warm.

5. Serve each diner half a rack of ribs. To cut the ribs for each serving, hold the half rack with tongs and cut between the bones with a large sharp knife. Serve the reheated sauce on the side.

SERVES 6

NUTRITIONAL ANALYSIS PER SERVING
Calories 904 (Kilojoules 3,797); Protein 46 g; Carbohydrates 46 g; Total Fat 60 g; Saturated Fat 22 g; Cholesterol 220 mg; Sodium 1,320 mg; Dietary Fiber 1 g

Pulled Pork with Mint Julep Barbecue Sauce

1 bone-in pork shoulder, 5 lb (2.5 kg)

2 teaspoons red pepper flakes

1 tablespoon *each* salt and freshly ground black pepper

1 tablespoon yellow mustard seeds

1 cup (8 fl oz/250 ml) apple cider

1 cup (8 fl oz/250 ml) cider vinegar

4 yellow onions, thinly sliced

4 cloves garlic, chopped

1 green bell pepper (capsicum), seeded and finely chopped

12 sesame seed–topped sandwich buns, split and warmed

12 dill pickle spears

SAUCE
¼ cup (2 oz/60 g) unsalted butter

3 yellow onions, thinly sliced

2 tablespoons peeled and chopped fresh ginger

2 cups (16 fl oz/500 ml) tomato purée

¾ cup (9 oz/280 g) dark molasses

⅓ cup (3 oz/90 g) coarse-grain Dijon mustard

½ cup (4 fl oz/125 ml) bourbon

½ cup (4 fl oz/125 ml) cider vinegar

2 tablespoons Worcestershire sauce

1 lemon, sliced

salt and ground black pepper to taste

⅓ cup (½ oz/15 g) chopped fresh mint

1 teaspoon Tabasco or other hot-pepper sauce

In the Carolinas, barbecue sauce is a subject of fierce debate. East Carolinians prefer a spicy vinegar-based blend, West Carolinians swear by a slightly sweet tomato-based sauce, and South Carolinians favor mustard-based mixes. This sauce combines them all with a bit of bourbon and fresh mint added.

1. Preheat the oven to 300°F (150°C). Lightly coat a large baking pan with vegetable oil. Rub the pork shoulder with the red pepper flakes, salt, black pepper, and mustard seeds and place in the baking pan. Pour the cider and vinegar over and around the pork. Scatter the onions, garlic, and bell pepper over and around the pork. Cover with aluminum foil.

2. Roast for 3 hours. Uncover and continue to roast until an instant-read thermometer inserted into the thickest part of the pork registers 180°F (82°C), about 1 hour.

3. While the pork is roasting, make the sauce: In a saucepan over medium heat, melt the butter. Add the onions and ginger and sauté until soft, about 5 minutes. Stir in the tomato purée, molasses, mustard, bourbon, vinegar, Worcestershire, lemon, salt, and black pepper. Reduce the heat to very low and simmer uncovered, stirring occasionally, until very thick, about 2 hours. Discard the lemon. Stir in the mint and Tabasco.

4. Remove the pork from the oven and transfer to a plate. Let stand for 1 hour. Reserve the roasted vegetables. Using 2 forks, shred the pork by steadying the meat with 1 fork and pulling it away with the other, discarding any fat. Place the shredded pork in a bowl. With a slotted spoon, transfer the roasted vegetables to the bowl with the pork.

5. Mix the sauce with the shredded pork. Stuff each bun with some of the pork and serve immediately, with the pickle spears on the side.

MAKES 12 SANDWICHES

NUTRITIONAL ANALYSIS PER SANDWICH
Calories 602 (Kilojoules 2,528); Protein 30 g; Carbohydrates 55 g; Total Fat 29 g; Saturated Fat 11 g; Cholesterol 114 mg; Sodium 1,494 mg; Dietary Fiber 4 g

Broiled Poussins with Arugula Salad

MARINADE

3 tablespoons extra-virgin olive oil

1 teaspoon Dijon mustard

1 teaspoon fennel seeds, coarsely crushed in a mortar or spice grinder

1 teaspoon black peppercorns, coarsely crushed in a mortar or spice grinder

¼ teaspoon red pepper flakes

1 clove garlic, minced

2 poussins or Cornish hens, about 1¼ lb (625 g) each

salt to taste

¼ lb (125 g) baby arugula (rocket) or spinach, tough stems removed

¼ lb (125 g) cherry tomatoes, halved, or quartered if large

2 lemon quarters

In summer, the vegetables for this salad are best at local farmers' markets, such as the Ferry Plaza market in San Francisco. There, shoppers are likely to find not just cherry tomatoes, but also the tiny red currant tomatoes, yellow pear tomatoes, and the bright orange, cherry-sized Sun Gold tomatoes—all beautiful additions here.

1. To make the marinade, in a small bowl, whisk together the oil, mustard, fennel seeds, black pepper, red pepper flakes, and garlic. Set aside.

2. Rinse the birds and pat dry. Place each hen, breast side down, on a work surface. With kitchen scissors or poultry shears, cut from the neck to the tail along both sides of the backbone; lift out the backbone. Turn breast side up and, using the heel of your hand, press down on the breastbone to flatten it. Cut off the wing tips and discard. Put the hens in a dish just large enough to hold them and coat with the marinade. Let stand for 1 hour at room temperature, turning once.

3. Preheat the broiler (grill) and position a rack 8–10 inches (20–25 cm) from the heat source. Preheat the broiler pan until very hot.

4. Season the hens well with salt on both sides. Put the hens on the broiler pan, skin side down. Broil (grill) until browned and sizzling, about 12 minutes. Remove from the broiler and collect any drippings in the broiler pan. Turn the hens, baste with the drippings, and return to the broiler. Broil, skin side up, until the skin is well browned and the juices run clear, about 8 minutes longer. Remove from the broiler.

5. Divide the greens evenly between 2 plates. Place the hens directly on the greens. Drizzle the exposed greens on each plate with about 2 teaspoons drippings from the broiler pan. Scatter the tomatoes over the greens. Squeeze the lemon quarters over all. Serve immediately.

SERVES 2

NUTRITIONAL ANALYSIS PER SERVING
Calories 774 (Kilojoules 3,251); Protein 55 g; Carbohydrates 6 g; Total Fat 58 g; Saturated Fat 14 g; Cholesterol 312 mg; Sodium 214 mg; Dietary Fiber 2 g

Pork Chops with Apples & Cranberries

4 tablespoons (2 oz/60 g) unsalted butter

2 shallots, thinly sliced

2 tart green apples such as Newtown Pippin or Granny Smith, peeled, halved, cored, and cut lengthwise into slices ¼ inch (6 mm) thick

½ cup (2 oz/60 g) fresh or frozen cranberries

4 loin pork chops, each about ½ lb (250 g) and 1 inch (2.5 cm) thick

½ teaspoon coarse salt

½ teaspoon freshly ground pepper

¾ cup (6 fl oz/180 ml) hard cider or apple juice

½ teaspoon chopped fresh sage

Cranberries are commercially raised along the Oregon and Washington coasts, in areas where wild cranberries once flourished. If fresh or frozen berries aren't available for this dish, substitute dried cranberries, adding them to the sauce as it is reducing.

1. In a large frying pan over high heat, melt 2 tablespoons of the butter. Add the shallots and apples and cook, stirring frequently, until the apples are browned and slightly softened, about 5 minutes. Stir in the cranberries and cook until warmed through, about 1 minute. Transfer to a platter and keep warm.

2. Add 1 tablespoon of the remaining butter to the same pan over medium-high heat. Sprinkle the chops on both sides with the salt and pepper and add to the pan. Brown on the first side for 1 minute, then turn and brown on the second side for 1 minute. Cover and reduce the heat to low. Cook for 2 minutes, then turn the chops over and cook until done at the center but still pale pink, about 2 minutes longer. Transfer the chops to a platter, cover, and keep warm.

3. Return the apple mixture to the pan and add the cider or juice and the sage. Bring to a boil over high heat and deglaze the pan, stirring to scrape up any browned bits on the pan bottom. Cook until the liquid is reduced by half, 2–3 minutes, then swirl in the remaining 1 tablespoon butter.

4. Pour the sauce over the chops and serve immediately.

SERVES 4

NUTRITIONAL ANALYSIS PER SERVING
Calories 521 (Kilojoules 2,188); Protein 35 g; Carbohydrates 18 g; Total Fat 34 g; Saturated Fat 15 g; Cholesterol 143 mg; Sodium 275 mg; Dietary Fiber 2 g

Apples & Pears

Annual apple tastings are commonly held throughout the Pacific Northwest. Northwesterners are known to boisterously debate the merits of each apple, sampling many varieties, from the Cox's Orange Pippin to the Liberty, Mutsu, and a Dutch apple with an operatic name and a brilliant flavor: the Karmijn de Sonnaville.

Washington's apple industry got its start in 1826, from seeds planted at Fort Vancouver, Washington. Today, more than half of the nation's eating apples come from orchards planted in the eastern foothills of the Cascade Mountains. Red and Golden Delicious apples predominate, but growers are expanding to include Galas, Braeburns, Gravensteins, and tart Granny Smiths and Newtown Pippins. Starring in both sweet and savory dishes, they also partner perfectly with Oregon blue or cheddar cheeses.

Not surprisingly, pears flourish in the Northwest as well, growing in the Medford and mid-Columbian regions of Oregon and the Yakima and Wenatchee valleys of Washington. The crop includes the Bartlett (Williams') and Red Bartlett, Anjou and Red Anjou, Bosc, Comice, and the smaller Seckel and Forelle.

Of course, pears are delightful both fresh and cooked. Crushed and distilled, however, they become a magnificent brandy or eau-de-vie. Clear Creek Distillery of Portland, Oregon, makes a lovely pear eau-de-vie, with a whole Hood River Bartlett floating inside each graceful bottle.

West Coast apples and pears bring crisp, sweet, and tart fall flavors to such dishes as salads, stews, and desserts.

Grilled Lamb with Zinfandel Marinade

1 boneless leg of lamb, about 4 lb
   (2 kg), butterflied

salt and freshly ground pepper to taste

MARINADE
½ cup (4 fl oz/125 ml) olive oil

½ cup (4 fl oz/125 ml) Zinfandel or
   other dry red wine

6 cloves garlic, minced

1 tablespoon Dijon mustard

1½ tablespoons minced fresh
   rosemary

When a barbecue calls for an impressive centerpiece, a butter-flied leg of lamb is a popular choice. Ask your butcher to bone the leg for you, then marinate it briefly in a mixture of Zinfandel, mustard, and rosemary. To drink? Zinfandel, of course.

1. Trim all visible fat from the lamb, and then trim away the thin external membrane.

2. To make the marinade, in a bowl, whisk together the olive oil, wine, garlic, mustard, and rosemary. Put the lamb in a shallow nonaluminum container large enough to hold it comfortably. Add the marinade and turn the lamb to coat both sides with the marinade. Cover and refrigerate for 4 hours, turning the lamb in the marinade once or twice during that time.

3. Prepare a medium-hot fire in a charcoal grill with a cover.

4. Meanwhile, bring the lamb to room temperature. When the coals are ready, put half of them on either side of the grill pan. Make a drip pan from heavy-duty aluminum foil and position it between the coals.

5. Remove the lamb from the marinade and season well with salt and pepper. Preheat the grill rack. Put the lamb on the rack directly over the drip pan, external side down. Cover the grill, leaving the vents partially open, and cook until an instant-read thermometer inserted in the thickest part of the leg registers 125°F (52°C) for medium-rare. The cooking time will depend on the heat of your fire and the size of the lamb leg, but a 4-lb (2-kg) butterflied leg should take 35–40 minutes. Transfer to a cutting board, cover loosely with aluminum foil, and let rest for 15 minutes before carving.

6. Carve the lamb against the grain and arrange on a warmed platter. Serve immediately.

SERVES 8–10

NUTRITIONAL ANALYSIS PER SERVING
Calories 345 (Kilojoules 1,449); Protein 43 g; Carbohydrates 0 g; Total Fat 18 g;
Saturated Fat 5 g; Cholesterol 135 mg; Sodium 123 mg; Dietary Fiber 0 g

Turkey Croquettes

1 small yellow onion, chopped

1 celery stalk with leaves, chopped

3 tablespoons unsalted butter

1 cup (5 oz/155 g) all-purpose (plain) flour

1 cup (8 fl oz/250 ml) milk or chicken stock

2 cups (12 oz/375 g) chopped, skinless cooked turkey

1 teaspoon fresh lemon juice

½ teaspoon salt

¼ teaspoon sweet paprika

2 eggs, lightly beaten with a few drops of water

1 cup (4 oz/125 g) fine dried bread crumbs

vegetable oil for deep-frying

These croquettes are too delectable to wait for Thanksgiving leftovers. Instead, poach some fresh turkey (or chicken) whenever you crave them. Serve with cranberry sauce, if you like.

1. In a food processor, combine the onion and celery and pulse to chop finely. In a saucepan over medium-low heat, melt the butter. Add the chopped vegetables and cook, stirring often, until starting to soften, about 5 minutes. Stir in 3 tablespoons of the flour and cook, stirring, for 1 minute. Whisk in the milk or stock and simmer, stirring often, until the sauce is quite thick and smooth, 6–8 minutes. Remove from the heat.

2. Put the turkey into the food processor and pulse to chop finely. Add the turkey to the sauce and add the lemon juice, salt, and paprika. Pour the turkey mixture into a shallow baking dish, press a piece of plastic wrap directly onto the surface, and refrigerate until firm, 2–3 hours.

3. Preheat the oven to 200°F (95°C). Put the eggs and bread crumbs into 2 separate shallow bowls. Put the remaining flour on a work surface. Using a ¼-cup (2–fl oz/60-ml) measure, scoop up some of the turkey mixture and drop it onto the flour. Dip your fingers in the flour and shape the mixture into a patty, a rectangle, or even a small pyramid (the classic shape). Dip the croquette first into the egg and then roll in the bread crumbs to coat evenly. Place on a sheet of waxed paper. Repeat until all the turkey mixture is used up. You should have 8 croquettes.

4. Pour oil to a depth of about 2 inches (5 cm) into a heavy saucepan and heat to 375°F (190°C) on a deep-frying thermometer. Lower 4 croquettes into the oil and fry, turning as necessary, until browned on all sides, about 3 minutes total. Using a slotted spoon, transfer to paper towels to drain, then place in the oven while you fry the remaining croquettes.

5. Arrange the croquettes on a warmed platter and serve piping hot.

MAKES 8 CROQUETTES; SERVES 4

NUTRITIONAL ANALYSIS PER SERVING
Calories 686 (Kilojoules 2,881); Protein 46 g; Carbohydrates 54 g; Total Fat 31 g; Saturated Fat 11 g; Cholesterol 225 mg; Sodium 691 mg; Dietary Fiber 3 g

Blue Plate Meat Loaf

½ cup (1 oz/30 g) fresh bread crumbs

½ cup (4 fl oz/125 ml) buttermilk

1 lb (500 g) ground (minced) beef

½ lb (250 g) bulk pork sausage meat

½ lb (250 g) ground (minced) turkey
   or veal

1 egg, lightly beaten

1 small yellow onion, minced

¼ cup (⅓ oz/10 g) minced fresh
   flat-leaf (Italian) parsley

½ teaspoon freshly ground pepper

¼ teaspoon salt

3 slices hickory-smoked bacon
   (optional)

Thick slices of meat loaf, a pillow of mashed potatoes smothered with rich, dark gravy, and green beans is a blue-plate special to tempt the traveler off any winding highway. While opinions on meat loaf run deep, the best loaves are moist and honestly seasoned. No fussy ingredients such as smoked peppers or capers, please. This loaf is shaped on the baking sheet (not pressed into a loaf pan), so that all sides brown and the fat runs off the meat instead of being trapped in by the pan.

1. Preheat the oven to 350°F (180°C).

2. In a small bowl, soak the bread crumbs in the buttermilk until the buttermilk is absorbed, about 3 minutes.

3. In a bowl, combine the soaked bread crumbs, beef, sausage, turkey or veal, egg, onion, and parsley. Gently mix together with your hands. Add the pepper and salt and mix again.

4. Turn the mixture onto a rimmed baking sheet and shape it into a loaf about 9 by 3 inches (23 by 7.5 cm). If using the bacon, lay the strips across the loaf lengthwise.

5. Bake, basting occasionally with the pan juices, until the meat loaf is lightly browned and firm and an instant-read thermometer inserted into its center registers 160°F (71°C), 45–55 minutes.

6. Using a serrated knife, cut the loaf into slices 1½ inches (4 cm) thick. Transfer to individual plates and serve.

SERVES 4–6

NUTRITIONAL ANALYSIS PER SERVING
Calories 487 (Kilojoules 2,045); Protein 31 g; Carbohydrates 7 g; Total Fat 37 g;
Saturated Fat 14 g; Cholesterol 162 mg; Sodium 560 mg; Dietary Fiber 1 g

Pan-Roasted Duck with Dried-Cherry Sauce

4 boneless, skinless duck breast
   halves

salt and freshly ground pepper to taste

1 tablespoon olive oil

4 tablespoons (2 oz/60 g) unsalted
   butter

1 large shallot, minced

¾ cup (6 fl oz/180 ml) Port

⅓ cup (1½ oz/45 g) dried pitted
   cherries

2 cups (16 fl oz/500 ml) duck or
   chicken stock, boiled until reduced
   to 1 cup (8 fl oz/250 ml)

2 teaspoons cherry preserves
   or 1 teaspoon sugar

2 teaspoons balsamic vinegar

Roast duck is a fine partner for California's esteemed Pinot Noirs. In this recipe, a dried-cherry sauce makes the food and wine marriage even better because so many Pinot Noirs have cherry nuances. If you must buy two ducks to get the four breast halves required here, save the legs for braising and use the carcasses to make stock.

1. Preheat the oven to 375°F (190°C).

2. Season the duck breasts on both sides with salt and pepper. Heat a large ovenproof frying pan over high heat until hot. Add the olive oil and swirl to coat the pan. When the oil is hot, add the duck breasts, skin side down. Reduce the heat to medium-high and cook until nicely browned, 1½–2 minutes. Then, turn and cook until the second side is lightly browned, 1½–2 minutes. Transfer the pan to the oven and roast until an instant-read thermometer inserted into the thickest part of the breast registers 125°F (52°C), about 5 minutes, or until done to your liking. Transfer the breasts to a platter and let rest while you make the sauce.

3. Pour off any fat remaining in the frying pan. Add 1 tablespoon of the butter and return to medium-low heat. When the butter melts, add the shallot and sauté until softened, about 2 minutes. Add the Port and cherries, raise the heat to high, and simmer until the pan is almost dry. Add the reduced stock, cherry preserves or sugar, balsamic vinegar, and any duck juices that have collected on the platter. Boil until the sauce is reduced to about ⅔ cup (5 fl oz/160 ml) and is almost syrupy. Remove from the heat and add the remaining 3 tablespoons butter. Swirl the pan until the butter melts.

4. Slice the duck breasts on the diagonal and transfer to warmed dinner plates. Top with the sauce, dividing it evenly. Serve immediately.

SERVES 4

NUTRITIONAL ANALYSIS PER SERVING
Calories 376 (Kilojoules 1,579); Protein 35 g; Carbohydrates 21 g; Total Fat 16 g;
Saturated Fat 8 g; Cholesterol 210 mg; Sodium 686 mg; Dietary Fiber 0 g

Seared Beef & Asian Greens

1 lb (500 g) well-trimmed beef sirloin
or London broil

2 tablespoons Thai or Vietnamese
fish sauce

2 tablespoons peanut oil

1 tablespoon soy sauce

½ teaspoon Asian sesame oil

2 large cloves garlic, minced

several grinds of pepper

½ lb (250 g) Asian stir-fry greens
such as baby mustard and tatsoi

24 fresh Asian basil leaves, torn into
small pieces

½ red onion, thinly sliced

salt to taste

DRESSING
3 tablespoons peanut oil

2 tablespoons fresh lime juice

1 large shallot, minced

1 serrano chile, seeded and minced

½ teaspoon sugar

Many California markets now carry a blend of pungent baby greens suitable for stir-frying or for warm salads such as this one. Here, thin strips of lean beef are marinated with Asian seasonings, then quickly seared and tossed with the leafy greens. If you can't find Asian stir-fry greens, substitute a mixture of spinach and watercress.

1. Place the meat in the freezer for about 30 minutes to make it easier to slice. Then thinly slice against the grain into strips about 2 inches (5 cm) long and 1 inch (2.5 cm) wide and place in a large bowl. Add the fish sauce, 1 tablespoon of the peanut oil, soy sauce, sesame oil, garlic, and pepper and toss to coat evenly. Let stand for about 30 minutes at room temperature.

2. To make the dressing, in a small bowl, whisk together the 3 tablespoons peanut oil, lime juice, shallot, chile, and sugar. Let stand for 30 minutes to allow the shallot flavor to mellow.

3. Just before you are ready to cook the meat, put the stir-fry greens, basil, and onion in a large serving bowl. Add the dressing and toss to coat evenly.

4. Heat a 12-inch (30-cm) frying pan over high heat. When the pan is hot, add the remaining 1 tablespoon peanut oil and swirl to coat the pan. When the oil is very hot, add the meat and stir and toss until it loses most of its red color, 30–45 seconds; the meat should still be rare.

5. Add the contents of the pan to the bowl with the greens and toss well. Season with salt and pepper and serve immediately.

SERVES 4

NUTRITIONAL ANALYSIS PER SERVING
Calories 357 (Kilojoules 1,499); Protein 28 g; Carbohydrates 9 g; Total Fat 23 g;
Saturated Fat 5 g; Cholesterol 69 mg; Sodium 638 mg; Dietary Fiber 1 g

Farmhouse Roast Chicken with Pan Gravy

CHICKEN

1 roasting chicken, 3–5 lb (1.5–2.5 kg)

3 tablespoons unsalted butter,
    at room temperature

½ teaspoon coarse salt

¼ teaspoon freshly ground pepper

2 fresh tarragon sprigs

5 fresh flat-leaf (Italian) parsley sprigs

GRAVY

2 tablespoons all-purpose (plain) flour

3 cups (24 fl oz/750 ml) chicken stock

2 tablespoons chopped fresh flat-leaf
    (Italian) parsley

1 tablespoon chopped fresh tarragon

2 tablespoons brandy (optional)

salt and freshly ground pepper to taste

You don't have to live on a farm in the Midwest, and it doesn't have to be Sunday, to enjoy this old-fashioned chicken that in the past was the typical centerpiece of the big midday family meal following church services.

1. Preheat the oven to 450°F (230°C). Remove the giblets from the chicken's cavity and reserve for another use. Rinse the chicken inside and out and pat dry with paper towels. Rub the outside of the chicken with butter, then gently loosen the skin and slide some butter under it to coat evenly. Sprinkle the outside and the cavity with the salt and pepper, and place the tarragon and parsley in the cavity. Tie the legs together for a nicer presentation, if you like. Put the chicken, breast side up, on a V-shaped rack set in a roasting pan just larger than the rack.

2. Roast for 15–20 minutes. Reduce the heat to 375°F (190°C) and continue roasting until an instant-read thermometer inserted into the thickest part of the thigh away from the bone registers 170°F (71°C) or the juices run clear when the thigh is pierced with a fork, about 45 minutes for a 3-lb (1.5-kg) chicken. For larger birds, add 10 minutes for each additional pound (500 g). Transfer the chicken to a warmed platter and tent with aluminum foil to keep warm. Remove the rack from the pan.

3. To make the gravy, pour the pan juices into a saucepan and skim off the fat, reserving about 2 tablespoons. Spoon the 2 tablespoons fat back into the roasting pan, sprinkle the bottom of the pan with the flour, set on the stove top over low heat, and scrape the pan bottom to loosen the bits of dark drippings. Cook over low heat, stirring constantly, until smooth, about 5 minutes. Gradually stir in the pan juices, stock, parsley, and tarragon. Cook, stirring occasionally, until the mixture thickens, about 5 minutes. Add the brandy, if using, and season with salt and pepper.

4. Carve the chicken and arrange on the platter. Pour the gravy into a warmed bowl and pass at the table.

SERVES 4–6

NUTRITIONAL ANALYSIS PER SERVING
Calories 555 (Kilojoules 2,331); Protein 47 g; Carbohydrates 3 g; Total Fat 38 g;
Saturated Fat 13 g; Cholesterol 165 mg; Sodium 885 mg; Dietary Fiber 0 g

Kansas City–Style BBQ

DRY RUB

⅓ cup (3 oz/90 g) firmly packed brown sugar

¼ cup (1¼ oz/37 g) sweet paprika

3 tablespoons freshly ground pepper

2 tablespoons chili powder

1 tablespoon coarse salt

1 beef brisket, 5 lb (2.5 kg), trimmed of excess fat

SAUCE

1 tablespoon vegetable oil

1 small yellow onion, chopped

3 cloves garlic, minced

1½ cups (12 fl oz/375 ml) ketchup

2 tablespoons brown sugar

2 tablespoons Worcestershire sauce

2 teaspoons prepared horseradish

2 teaspoons cider vinegar

1 bay leaf

1 teaspoon chili powder

1 teaspoon freshly ground pepper

2 or 3 drops Tabasco or other hot-pepper sauce

During the Depression, Henry Perry, the father of Kansas City–style barbecue, prepared great slabs of beef in an outdoor pit, sold them in sandwiches wrapped in newspaper, and made the city—and its barbecue—world famous.

1. To make the dry rub, in a small bowl, stir together the brown sugar, paprika, pepper, chili powder, and salt. Rub the brisket all over with the dry rub. Cover with plastic wrap and refrigerate overnight.

2. Prepare an indirect-heat fire in a covered grill. When the coals are white with ash, place chunks of hickory or fruit wood (apple or cherry) on top. (If using a gas grill, preheat to low, then place the wood on top.)

3. Place the meat, fat side up, on the center of the grill rack, cover, and barely open the vents. Cook the meat for 10 minutes, then turn and cook for another 10 minutes to seal the outside of the meat. Turn again, replace the lid, and continue to cook the meat at about 225°F (110°C), turning two or three times, until an instant-read thermometer inserted into the thickest part registers 165°F (74°C) or until tender, about 3 hours.

4. Remove the meat from the grill, wrap tightly in aluminum foil, return to the grill, and continue cooking at about 200°F (95°C) until the meat is very tender, 2–3 hours longer. Remove the meat from the grill and let rest in the foil for about 10 minutes.

5. To make the sauce, in a saucepan over low heat, warm the vegetable oil. Add the onion and sauté until translucent, 7–8 minutes, then add the garlic and sauté until the garlic softens, 2–3 minutes longer. Add the ketchup, brown sugar, Worcestershire sauce, horseradish, vinegar, bay leaf, chili powder, pepper, and Tabasco sauce and simmer, uncovered, until slightly thickened, 7–10 minutes.

6. Thinly slice the meat and arrange on a warmed platter. Pour the sauce into a warmed bowl and pass at the table.

SERVES 8–12

NUTRITIONAL ANALYSIS PER SERVING
Calories 403 (Kilojoules 1,693); Protein 36 g; Carbohydrates 27 g; Total Fat 17 g; Saturated Fat 6 g; Cholesterol 108 mg; Sodium 1,008 mg; Dietary Fiber 2 g

Chicken & Portobello Pot Pie

8 tablespoons (4 oz/125 g) unsalted butter

½ lb (250 g) fresh portobello or cremini mushrooms, brushed clean and cut into ½-inch (12-mm) dice

salt and freshly ground pepper to taste

1 large yellow onion, chopped

1 celery stalk with leaves, diced

2 carrots, peeled and diced

1½ lb (750 g) boneless, skinless chicken thighs or breasts, trimmed of excess fat and cut into bite-sized pieces

2 cloves garlic, minced

1 tablespoon chopped fresh rosemary, thyme, or tarragon, or 1 teaspoon dried herb of choice

¼ cup (1½ oz/45 g) all-purpose (plain) flour

1 cup (8 fl oz/250 ml) chicken stock

1 cup (8 fl oz/250 ml) light (single) cream or milk, plus more for glazing pastry

1 cup (5 oz/155 g) shelled fresh or frozen English peas (optional)

2 teaspoons sherry or Madeira wine or fresh lemon juice

½ recipe pie pastry (opposite) or 1 sheet frozen puff pastry (½ lb/ 250 g), thawed in the refrigerator if frozen

Deep-dish, single-crust savory meat pies have long been a favorite winter dish throughout the New England region.

1. Preheat the oven to 400°F (200°C).

2. In a large frying pan over high heat, melt 2 tablespoons of the butter. Add the mushrooms, season with salt and pepper, and sauté until they release their juices and brown, 5–7 minutes. Transfer to a large bowl.

3. Reduce the heat to medium and add another 2 tablespoons butter. When it melts, add the onion, celery, and carrots and cook, stirring often, until barely tender, 5–8 minutes. Add the chicken, garlic, and herb of choice and continue to cook, stirring often, until the chicken is barely cooked through, 3–4 minutes. Transfer to the bowl holding the mushrooms.

4. Return the pan to the heat and melt the remaining 4 tablespoons (2 oz/60 g) butter over medium heat. Whisk in the flour and cook, stirring, for 1 minute. Whisk in the chicken stock and the 1 cup (8 fl oz/ 250 ml) cream or milk and simmer, whisking often to prevent scorching, until a smooth and rather thick sauce forms, about 10 minutes.

5. Add the sauce and the peas, if using, to the chicken and vegetables. Add the sherry, wine, or lemon juice and season with salt and pepper. Spoon the filling into a 2-qt (2-l) baking dish or deep-dish pie dish.

6. On a lightly floured work surface, roll out the pastry 1½ inches (4 cm) larger than the top of the baking dish or pie dish. Trim ½ inch (12 mm) from the edges so that they are straight. Carefully transfer the pastry to the dish, allowing it to fall evenly over the filling. Fold the edge under and crimp to seal. Brush the top with cream or milk and cut 4 steam vents. Place on a baking sheet to catch any spills.

7. Bake until the crust is well browned and the filling is bubbling visibly through the vents, about 40 minutes. Let sit for 10 minutes before serving.

SERVES 6

NUTRITIONAL ANALYSIS PER SERVING
Calories 861 (Kilojoules 3,616); Protein 33 g; Carbohydrates 62 g; Total Fat 53 g;
Saturated Fat 28 g; Cholesterol 203 mg; Sodium 496 mg; Dietary Fiber 4 g

American Pie

One of the truest expressions of New England cooking is pie. The first British settlers easily adapted their pie-eating habits to New World ingredients and created an array of American pies, including oyster, clam, pumpkin, grape, and spiced cranberry. New England bakers tend to use an all-purpose pie crust with little or no sweetener for both sweet and savory pies. Here's a good one.

PIE PASTRY

(FOR ONE 9-INCH/23-CM DOUBLE-CRUST PIE)

2½ cups (12½ oz/390 g) all-purpose (plain) flour

½ teaspoon salt

½ cup (4 oz/125 g) chilled unsalted butter, cut into small pieces

¼ cup (2 oz/60 g) solid vegetable shortening, chilled

1 teaspoon white vinegar

6–7 tablespoons (3–3½ fl oz/90–105 ml) ice water

In a food processor, combine the flour and salt and pulse briefly to mix. Add the butter and shortening, and pulse several times, until the dough is crumbly. Pour in the vinegar and 6 tablespoons of the water, and pulse just until the dough begins to come together, adding the remaining water if the mixture is too dry. Transfer the dough to a clean work surface, divide into 2 pieces, one slightly larger than the other (the larger one will be the bottom crust), and flatten each into a thick disk. Wrap separately in plastic wrap and refrigerate for at least 1 hour or for as long as 2 days.

A pie pastry that swings both sweet and savory is an integral part of New England's culinary repertoire.

Beer-Braised Short Ribs

2 tablespoons canola oil

3–4 lb (1.5–2 kg) beef short ribs, from chuck or rib sections, trimmed of excess fat

1 teaspoon coarse salt

1 teaspoon freshly ground pepper

¼ cup (1½ oz/45 g) all-purpose (plain) flour

2 leeks, white and pale green parts only, chopped

2 cloves garlic, minced

2 tablespoons peeled and chopped fresh ginger

1 tablespoon firmly packed light brown sugar

4 large parsnips, about 1¼ lb (625 g) total weight, peeled and cut into 1-inch (2.5-cm) lengths

8 carrots, peeled and cut into 1-inch (2.5-cm) lengths

2 bay leaves

1 bottle (12 fl oz/375 ml) Hefeweizen or brown ale

1 cup (8 fl oz/250 ml) beef stock

2 tablespoons chopped fresh flat-leaf (Italian) parsley

These ribs are braised in Hefeweizen, a cloudy unfiltered beer made from wheat malt by many microbreweries in the Pacific Northwest. The beer blends well with the fresh ginger and brown sugar that flavor the stew. Pour more Hefeweizen to drink at the table—slip a lemon wedge in each glass— and serve buttered caraway noodles on the side.

1. Preheat the oven to 350°F (180°C).

2. In a Dutch oven or large, heavy, deep, ovenproof frying pan, warm the canola oil until very hot. Meanwhile, sprinkle the ribs with the salt and pepper. Spread the flour on a plate and turn the ribs in the flour, coating evenly and shaking off any excess. In batches, add the ribs to the hot oil and brown on all sides, 6–7 minutes for each batch. Transfer to a plate.

3. Pour off all but 2 tablespoons of the fat and return the Dutch oven to medium-high heat. Add the leeks, garlic, ginger, and brown sugar and cook, stirring frequently, until the leeks are soft, 2–3 minutes. Stir in the parsnips, carrots, and bay leaves and return the meat to the Dutch oven. Pour in the beer and beef stock, and bring to a boil over high heat. Cover, transfer to the oven, and bake until the ribs are very tender, about 2 hours.

4. Using a slotted spoon, transfer the meat and vegetables to a deep platter. Cover and keep warm. Using a large spoon, skim off any fat from the surface of the cooking liquid and discard the bay leaves. Bring to a boil over high heat and simmer until the liquid is slightly reduced, 3–4 minutes.

5. Spoon the sauce over the meat and vegetables, sprinkle with the parsley, and serve.

SERVES 6

NUTRITIONAL ANALYSIS PER SERVING
Calories 682 (Kilojoules 2,864); Protein 28 g; Carbohydrates 39 g; Total Fat 46 g; Saturated Fat 18 g; Cholesterol 106 mg; Sodium 520 mg; Dietary Fiber 8 g

Chiles Rellenos with Carne Adobada

CARNE ADOBADA

¼ cup (2 fl oz/60 ml) peanut oil

2 lb (1 kg) pork shoulder or butt, cut into ¾-inch (2-cm) cubes

1 large white onion, diced

2 large cloves garlic, minced

3 cups (24 fl oz/750 ml) chicken stock, or as needed

1 teaspoon *each* cumin and coriander seeds, toasted and ground *(page 314)*

1 teaspoon dried Mexican oregano

½ cup (1½ oz/45 g) ground Chimayó chile

pinch of kosher salt, or to taste

CHILES RELLENOS

6 large New Mexico green chiles, roasted and peeled *(page 311)*

⅓ cup (3 fl oz/80 ml) gold tequila

6 tablespoons (2 oz/60 g) golden raisins (sultanas)

½ lb (250 g) fresh goat cheese

6 tablespoons (2 oz/60 g) piñon nuts or other pine nuts, toasted

kosher salt to taste

vegetable oil for deep-frying

½ cup (2½ oz/75 g) unbleached all-purpose (plain) flour

2 eggs, lightly beaten with 2 table-spoons water

Cornmeal Coating *(page 315)*

steamed white rice, crema, and Fresh Tomato Salsa *(page 315)* (optional)

1. To make the *carne adobada,* in a large, heavy pot over medium-high heat, warm the oil. Working in batches, add the pork and brown well on all sides, 4–5 minutes. Transfer to a plate. Add the onion to the pot and sauté until golden, about 5 minutes. Add the garlic and cook for 1 minute until fragrant. Pour in 1 cup (8 fl oz/250 ml) of the stock and deglaze the pot, stirring to scrape up the browned bits on the bottom.

2. Add the cumin, coriander, oregano, ground chile, and salt to the pot and mix well. Add the remaining 2 cups (16 fl oz/500 ml) stock, stirring until smooth. Return the pork cubes to the pot and bring to a boil. Reduce the heat to low, cover, and simmer until the pork is tender, about 1 hour. Add stock as needed to keep the meat covered at all times.

3. To make the chiles rellenos, slit each green chile lengthwise, leaving the stem and end intact, and remove the ribs and seeds. Pour the tequila into a small frying pan, add the raisins, and bring to a boil. Reduce the heat, simmer briefly, then set aside for 10 minutes. In a small bowl, mix together the cheese, nuts, raisins and any unabsorbed tequila, and salt.

4. Line a baking sheet with paper towels. Fill each chile with 2–3 table-spoons of the cheese mixture and pinch closed. Place on the prepared baking sheet, cover, and refrigerate for at least 2 hours or up to overnight.

5. Pour vegetable oil to a depth of 3 inches (7.5 cm) into a deep, heavy saucepan and heat to 365°F (185°C). Meanwhile, coat each chile evenly with the flour, shaking off the excess, then dip in the egg mixture, and finally in the cornmeal coating, pressing lightly to adhere.

6. Slip 2 chiles into the hot oil and fry until golden, about 3 minutes. Drain on paper towels; keep warm. Repeat with the remaining chiles.

7. Place the chiles on individual plates and top with some of the pork and sauce. Serve with steamed white rice, crema, and salsa, if you like.

SERVES 6

NUTRITIONAL ANALYSIS PER SERVING
Calories 987 (Kilojoules 4,145); Protein 46 g; Carbohydrates 64 g; Total Fat 60 g; Saturated Fat 19 g; Cholesterol 196 mg; Sodium 1,522 mg; Dietary Fiber 8 g

Chicken, Blue Cheese & Arugula Salad

6 tablespoons (3 fl oz/90 ml) extra-virgin olive oil

2 teaspoons tarragon vinegar or white wine vinegar

2 teaspoons fresh lemon juice

¾ teaspoon coarse salt

¾ teaspoon freshly ground pepper

4 slices artisan walnut bread or other artisan bread, each about ½ inch (12 mm) thick

1 clove garlic, halved

4 boneless, skinless chicken breast halves, each about 5 oz (155 g)

2 large bunches arugula (rocket), tough stems removed

1 cup (5 oz/155 g) crumbled Oregon blue or other blue cheese

2 cups (4 oz/125 g) berries such as raspberries, marionberries, or blackberries

2 tablespoons chopped fresh tarragon

2 tablespoons chopped fresh basil

This casual main-dish salad exemplifies a favorite way to eat: everything—salad, meat, cheese, bread, berries—served on a single plate. To complete this perfect summer meal, pour a glass of chilled Washington State Riesling.

1. In a large bowl, whisk together 3 tablespoons of the olive oil, the vinegar, the lemon juice, and ¼ teaspoon each of the salt and pepper. Set aside.

2. Toast the bread slices in a toaster or in a preheated broiler (grill) until golden brown on both sides. Rub one side of each slice with the garlic and then brush with 1 tablespoon of the olive oil. Set aside.

3. In a large frying pan over medium-high heat, warm the remaining 2 tablespoons olive oil. Sprinkle the chicken with the remaining ½ teaspoon each salt and pepper and add to the hot oil. Cook, turning once, until the juices run clear when pierced at the thickest point, 10–12 minutes total. Remove from the heat and transfer to a cutting board.

4. Toss the arugula leaves with the dressing to coat. Divide the arugula among individual plates. Cut each chicken breast half into 3 or 4 lengthwise slices and fan out the slices on top of the arugula. Cut the toasted bread slices in half and place next to the chicken. Sprinkle the blue cheese, berries, tarragon, and basil over the top of the salads. Serve at once.

SERVES 4

NUTRITIONAL ANALYSIS PER SERVING
Calories 635 (Kilojoules 2,667); Protein 47 g; Carbohydrates 35 g; Total Fat 36 g; Saturated Fat 10 g; Cholesterol 109 mg; Sodium 1,178 mg; Dietary Fiber 5 g

Vegetables

Texas Potato Salad

DRESSING

⅓ cup (3 fl oz/80 ml) cider vinegar

⅓ cup (3 fl oz/80 ml) safflower oil
   or vegetable oil

¼ cup (2 fl oz/60 ml) mayonnaise

1 small white onion, diced

2 small cloves garlic, minced

1 tablespoon juice from sweet gherkins

1 tablespoon yellow mustard

1 tablespoon sugar

1 teaspoon kosher salt

2 lb (1 kg) new potatoes, unpeeled

kosher salt and freshly ground pepper
   to taste

3 hard-boiled eggs, peeled and coarsely
   chopped

4 small sweet gherkins, finely diced

⅓ cup (2 oz/60 g) diced roasted red
   bell pepper (capsicum) *(page 311)*

1 celery stalk, finely diced (optional)

5 green (spring) onions, including
   tender green tops, thinly sliced
   on the diagonal

3 tablespoons chopped fresh flat-leaf
   (Italian) parsley

It comes as no surprise to even the most casual observer that Texans like their potatoes. A classic salad such as this one, with its mixture of mild and tangy, soft and crunchy ingredients, makes a perfect foil for more assertively seasoned main courses cooked on the backyard grill.

1. To make the dressing, in a blender, combine the vinegar, oil, mayonnaise, onion, garlic, gherkin juice, mustard, sugar, and salt. Blend until thoroughly emulsified. Taste and adjust the seasoning. Set aside.

2. In a saucepan, combine the potatoes with water to cover by 2–3 inches (5–7.5 cm). Bring to a boil and boil until tender, 25–35 minutes. Drain well and when just cool enough to handle, cut into slices ¼ inch (6 mm) thick or into 1-inch (2.5-cm) chunks. Place in a bowl and, while the potatoes are still warm, pour about one-third of the dressing over them. Season with salt and pepper and toss gently.

3. Add the hard-boiled eggs, gherkins, roasted bell pepper, celery (if using), green onions, and parsley to the potatoes. Add the remaining dressing and toss to coat evenly. Serve at room temperature, or cover and refrigerate to chill slightly before serving.

SERVES 6

NUTRITIONAL ANALYSIS PER SERVING
Calories 373 (Kilojoules 1,566); Protein 7 g; Carbohydrates 38 g; Total Fat 22 g;
Saturated Fat 3 g; Cholesterol 112 mg; Sodium 505 mg; Dietary Fiber 3 g

Gai Lan with Crispy Garlic

2 tablespoons canola oil

3 cloves garlic, thinly sliced

¼ teaspoon red pepper flakes

1 large bunch gai lan, 1½ lb (750 g), tough stem ends trimmed

3 tablespoons rice wine or dry white wine

2 tablespoons tamari

Most Northwest farmers' markets offer lots of different Asian vegetables, many of which are excellent for stir-frying. Gai lan (Chinese broccoli) is delicious cooked this way, but you can substitute bok choy, broccoli, or broccoli rabe as well. Make sure to cook the garlic just until golden; if it burns, you may not enjoy its taste.

1. Place a large frying pan or wok over high heat. When the pan is hot, add the canola oil and swirl the pan to coat the bottom. When the oil is very hot but not smoking, add the garlic and red pepper flakes and cook, stirring constantly, until the garlic is golden, about 1 minute. Using a slotted spoon, transfer the garlic to paper towels to drain.

2. Add the gai lan and 2 tablespoons of the wine and cook, tossing and stirring to prevent scorching, until tender, about 5 minutes. Add the tamari and the remaining 1 tablespoon wine and stir until the liquid reduces slightly, about 1 minute longer.

3. Transfer the gai lan to a warmed platter, sprinkle with the reserved garlic, and serve immediately.

SERVES 4

NUTRITIONAL ANALYSIS PER SERVING
Calories 112 (Kilojoules 470); Protein 5 g; Carbohydrates 8 g; Total Fat 7 g; Saturated Fat 1 g; Cholesterol 0 mg; Sodium 582 mg; Dietary Fiber 3 g

Heirloom Tomatoes with Balsamic Vinaigrette

3 tablespoons extra-virgin olive oil

1 tablespoon balsamic vinegar

1 large shallot, minced

salt and freshly ground pepper to taste

1–1¼ lb (500–625 g) heirloom tomatoes, preferably a variety of colors and sizes

One of the most encouraging developments on California's family farms is the interest in "heirloom" produce—fruit and vegetable varieties from an earlier time. Many of these varieties have lost favor commercially because they don't ship or store well, but they often have superior flavor. At California's farmers' markets, it's not uncommon to find two dozen different heirloom tomatoes in a multitude of colors and sizes.

1. In a small bowl, whisk together the olive oil, vinegar, shallot, salt, and pepper. Let stand for approximately 30 minutes to allow the shallot flavor to mellow.

2. Core the tomatoes. Halve them vertically if large, then slice thinly or cut into thin wedges. Halve cherry tomatoes or baby pear tomatoes, if you like. Arrange the sliced tomatoes on a platter, mixing the colors attractively. Top with the small tomatoes. Spoon the vinaigrette over the tomatoes and serve.

SERVES 4

NUTRITIONAL ANALYSIS PER SERVING
Calories 117 (Kilojoules 491); Protein 1 g; Carbohydrates 6 g; Total Fat 11 g; Saturated Fat 2 g; Cholesterol 0 mg; Sodium 11 mg; Dietary Fiber 2 g

Spinach Soufflé

1 lb (500 g) spinach, stems removed

½ cup (2 oz/60 g) chopped yellow onion

1 tablespoon water

5 tablespoons (2½ oz/75 g) unsalted butter

4 tablespoons (1 oz/30 g) grated Parmesan cheese

¼ cup (1½ oz/45 g) all-purpose (plain) flour

1½ cups (12 fl oz/375 ml) milk, heated

6 eggs, separated

2 pinches of salt

pinch of freshly ground black pepper

pinch of cayenne pepper

This recipe makes showy and easy use of the plentiful eggs produced on Midwest farms. Use organic eggs if possible, as the true flavor of a good egg shines in this simple dish.

1. In a saucepan, combine the spinach, onion, and water. Cover, place over medium-low heat, and cook until the spinach is bright green and tender, about 4 minutes. Drain the spinach mixture, pressing out any liquid. Chop and set aside.

2. Preheat the oven to 400°F (200°C). Butter a 2-qt (2-l) soufflé dish or four 2-cup (16–fl oz/500-ml) individual soufflé dishes. Sprinkle the inside of the dish(es) with about 1 tablespoon of the cheese, tilting to coat the bottom and sides evenly.

3. In a saucepan over medium heat, melt the butter. When it foams, add the flour and reduce the heat to medium-low. Cook, stirring, until the mixture darkens a bit, about 3 minutes. Whisk in the milk a little at a time, whisking vigorously after each addition to prevent lumps. When all of the milk has been added, cook over low heat, whisking, until thick, 1–2 minutes longer. Remove from the heat.

4. In a small bowl, beat together the egg yolks, a pinch of salt, the black pepper, cayenne, and the remaining 3 tablespoons cheese. Stir into the milk mixture. Add the spinach mixture and stir to combine.

5. In a bowl, beat the egg whites with a pinch of salt until they hold stiff peaks. Stir a couple of spoonfuls of the beaten egg whites into the egg yolk–milk mixture to lighten it. Using a rubber spatula, gently fold in the remaining whites. Transfer the batter to the prepared dish(es).

6. Bake until the soufflé has risen and is browned on top, 30–40 minutes or 15–18 minutes if using individual soufflé dishes. Use a knife to check the interior; it should be a little moist. If still wet, bake for another 5 minutes. Serve immediately.

SERVES 4–6

NUTRITIONAL ANALYSIS PER SERVING
Calories 306 (Kilojoules 1,285); Protein 15 g; Carbohydrates 13 g; Total Fat 22 g; Saturated Fat 12 g; Cholesterol 301 mg; Sodium 271 mg; Dietary Fiber 2 g

Collard Greens with Benne Seeds & Chile Oil

2 lb (1 kg) collard greens, mustard greens, turnip greens, or broccoli rabe, tough stems and wilted leaves discarded

2 tablespoons olive oil

6 cloves garlic, thinly sliced

2 dried hot chiles, broken in half crosswise

¼ cup (¾ oz/20 g) sesame seeds

1 tablespoon chopped fresh rosemary

2 tablespoons honey

salt and freshly ground pepper to taste

2 tablespoons cider vinegar

1 tablespoon hot chile oil

The unexpected flavors of this dish exemplify contemporary Southern cuisine at its best. The greens are not cooked for hours as in grandmothers' day, and the toasty flavors of the benne (sesame) seeds pair nicely with the bitterness of the vegetable. If you prefer, use hot-pepper vinegar instead of the cider vinegar and chile oil.

1. Cut the greens into 1-inch (2.5-cm) pieces. Bring a large saucepan three-fourths full of lightly salted water to a boil over high heat. Add the greens and stir to immerse completely in the water. Return to a boil, reduce the temperature to medium, and cook until tender-crisp, about 10 minutes. Drain and place under cold running water to stop the cooking. Transfer to a large kitchen towel, wrap well, and squeeze out as much excess water as possible.

2. In a large frying pan with deep sides, warm the olive oil over medium heat. Add the garlic, chiles, sesame seeds, and rosemary and cook, stirring, until the sesame seeds begin to lightly brown, about 1 minute. Stir in the greens and honey. Sauté, stirring occasionally, until the greens are well coated with the other ingredients and heated through, about 3 minutes. Season with salt and pepper.

3. Transfer to a large bowl and drizzle with the vinegar and chile oil just before serving.

SERVES 6

NUTRITIONAL ANALYSIS PER SERVING
Calories 139 (Kilojoules 584); Protein 2 g; Carbohydrates 15 g; Total Fat 9 g;
Saturated Fat 1 g; Cholesterol 0 mg; Sodium 19 mg; Dietary Fiber 4 g

Pan-Glazed Parsnips with Sherry

1 lb (500 g) parsnips, peeled

½ cup (4 fl oz/125 ml) chicken stock
  or water

2 tablespoons unsalted butter

2 tablespoons dry sherry or Madeira

2 teaspoons peeled and minced fresh
  ginger

1 teaspoon chopped fresh thyme,
  or ¼ teaspoon dried thyme

salt to taste

few drops of fresh lemon juice

freshly ground pepper to taste

The town of Westfield, Massachusetts, is the self-appointed Parsnip Capital of the World, and in fact these sweet and flavorful root vegetables are favored throughout the region. Real connoisseurs prefer spring-dug parsnips, which grow sweeter after a winter in the frozen ground.

1. Cut the parsnips in half lengthwise, then cut the halves in half again if they are very thick. Cut the pieces in half crosswise so you have finger-length sticks that are more or less the same thickness. If the cores are distinctly darker and denser than the rest of the root, remove them with a paring knife. These tough cores result from long storage and will remain fibrous even after cooking. Freshly dug parsnips will have tender cores that do not need to be removed.

2. Lay the parsnips in a frying pan large enough to accommodate them in a single layer. Add the stock or water, butter, sherry or Madeira, ginger, and thyme. Season with salt. Partially cover the pan and place over medium heat. Bring to a simmer and cook until the parsnips are tender enough to be easily pierced with the tip of a knife, 7–9 minutes.

3. Uncover the pan, raise the heat to high, and continue to cook, uncovered, until the juices are reduced to a glaze, 4–6 minutes. Season with the lemon juice and a few grinds of pepper. Taste and adjust the seasoning as desired

4. Transfer the parsnips to a warmed serving dish and serve immediately.

SERVES 3 OR 4

NUTRITIONAL ANALYSIS PER SERVING
Calories 189 (Kilojoules 794); Protein 2 g; Carbohydrates 24 g; Total Fat 8 g;
Saturated Fat 5 g; Cholesterol 21 mg; Sodium 182 mg; Dietary Fiber 6 g

Chinese Long Beans with Sesame Seeds

1½ tablespoons sesame seeds

1 lb (500 g) Chinese long beans, trimmed and cut into 3–4-inch (7.5–10-cm) lengths

1½ tablespoons peanut oil

2 tablespoons peeled and finely minced fresh ginger

1 large clove garlic, minced

1 serrano chile, seeded and minced

salt to taste

1 teaspoon Asian sesame oil

⅓ cup (½ oz/15 g) chopped fresh cilantro (fresh coriander)

Often called yard-long beans—with some hyperbole—these slender green beans can easily reach half a yard (45 cm) in length. In Chinatown markets from Los Angeles to San Francisco, you will inevitably find them for sale arranged in neat skeins. They take well to strong seasonings.

1. In a small, dry frying pan over medium heat, toast the sesame seeds, stirring often, until fragrant and lightly colored, about 5 minutes. Pour onto a small plate.

2. Bring a large saucepan three-fourths full of salted water to a boil over high heat. Add the beans and cook until just tender, about 5 minutes. Drain in a sieve and rinse with cold running water to stop the cooking. Drain thoroughly, then pat dry.

3. Place a 12-inch (30-cm) frying pan over medium-high heat. When it is hot, add the peanut oil and swirl to coat the pan. When the oil is hot, add the ginger, garlic, and chile and cook, stirring constantly, for about 30 seconds to release the fragrance of the ginger and garlic. Add the green beans and salt and toss to coat with the seasonings. Cook until the beans are hot throughout. Stir in the sesame seeds, reserving some for garnish. Remove from the heat and add the sesame oil and cilantro. Toss well.

4. Transfer the beans to a large warmed platter. Top with the reserved sesame seeds and serve immediately.

SERVES 4

NUTRITIONAL ANALYSIS PER SERVING
Calories 110 (Kilojoules 462); Protein 3 g; Carbohydrates 9 g; Total Fat 8 g;
Saturated Fat 1 g; Cholesterol 0 mg; Sodium 8 mg; Dietary Fiber 2 g

Fried Green Tomatoes with Goat Cheese

6 slices bacon, coarsely chopped

1 cup (5 oz/155 g) all-purpose (plain) flour

1 cup (5 oz/155 g) yellow cornmeal

1 teaspoon salt

1 teaspoon freshly ground pepper

4 green tomatoes, sliced ½ inch (12 mm) thick

about ½ cup (4 fl oz/120 ml) peanut oil

¼ lb (125 g) soft fresh goat cheese

1 large, very ripe red tomato, seeded and finely diced

The hit movie of the same name brought this Southern side dish to national prominence a few years back. But in the frugal South, fried green tomatoes have been enjoyed for generations. With artisan cheese makers popping up all over the region, this version adds a contemporary goat cheese layer to the traditional recipe.

1. In a large frying pan, preferably cast iron, fry the bacon over medium-high heat until crisp, about 5 minutes. Using a slotted spoon, transfer the bacon to paper towels to drain and set aside. Pour off about half of the drippings and discard.

2. In a pie dish or shallow bowl, stir together the flour, cornmeal, salt, and pepper. Coat each tomato slice on both sides with the seasoned flour and place on a wire rack.

3. Add about ¼ cup (2 fl oz/60 ml) of the peanut oil to the reserved drippings in the pan and place over medium-high heat. When hot, add the green tomato slices, in batches, and cook, turning once, until golden brown and crisp, about 1 minute on each side. Using a slotted spatula, transfer to paper towels to drain. Repeat with the remaining slices, adding more peanut oil as needed.

4. Carefully spread about 1 teaspoon of the goat cheese on each tomato slice. Arrange the slices, overlapping them, on a round serving plate and top with the diced red tomato and the bacon. Serve at once.

SERVES 4

NUTRITIONAL ANALYSIS PER SERVING
Calories 657 (Kilojoules 2,759); Protein 17 g; Carbohydrates 64 g; Total Fat 37 g; Saturated Fat 12 g; Cholesterol 28 mg; Sodium 902 mg; Dietary Fiber 4 g

Fresh Corn Pudding

8 ears of corn, husks and silk removed

1 can (15 fl oz/470 ml) evaporated milk

4 eggs, lightly beaten

¼ cup (2 oz/60 g) unsalted butter

1 white onion, chopped

2 cloves garlic, minced

1½ cups (5 oz/150 g) crushed rich cracker crumbs

1 cup (4 oz/120 g) shredded sharp cheddar cheese

sugar to taste, if needed

kosher salt and freshly ground pepper to taste

From July through September, bins at the Santa Fe farmers' market are piled high with fresh sweet corn, and shoppers can't seem to get enough of it. For a change of pace, turn the cut kernels into a simple pudding to serve alongside beef or lamb.

1. Preheat the oven to 350°F (180°C). Butter a 2-qt (2-l) baking dish.

2. Working with 1 ear of corn at a time, steady the stalk end on a cutting board and strip off the kernels with a knife. You should have about 4 cups (1½ lb/750 g).

3. In a blender, combine 3 cups (18 oz/560 g) of the corn kernels and the evaporated milk and purée until smooth. Pass the purée through a medium-mesh sieve placed over a bowl. Stir the eggs into the purée.

4. In a frying pan over medium-high, melt the butter. Add the onion and garlic and sauté until softened, about 3 minutes. Add the sautéed mixture to the puréed corn and stir to combine. Stir in the reserved 1 cup (6 oz/190 g) corn kernels, 1 cup (3 oz/90 g) of the cracker crumbs, and ½ cup (2 oz/60 g) of the cheese. Season with the sugar, if needed, salt, and pepper. Pour the mixture into the prepared baking dish and sprinkle with the remaining ½ cup (2 oz/60 g) cheese and ½ cup (2 oz/60 g) cracker crumbs.

5. Bake the corn pudding until set and golden, 45–50 minutes. Remove from the oven and let stand for 5 minutes. Spoon onto warmed individual plates to serve.

SERVES 6

NUTRITIONAL ANALYSIS PER SERVING
Calories 510 (Kilojoules 2,146); Protein 20 g; Carbohydrates 45 g; Total Fat 30 g; Saturated Fat 15 g; Cholesterol 207 mg; Sodium 432 mg; Dietary Fiber 5 g

Grilled Asparagus with Parmesan

2 bunches asparagus, 2–2½ lb
(1–1.25 kg) total weight

ice water as needed

2 tablespoons extra-virgin olive oil

kosher salt

¼ cup (1 oz/30 g) grated Parmesan
cheese

Put just olive oil and kosher salt on the asparagus spears,
then add a shower of Parmesan cheese.

1. Prepare a hot fire in a charcoal grill. If possible, position the grill
rack so that the asparagus will be only 3 inches (7.5 cm) from the coals.

2. Holding an asparagus spear at the stem end and in the middle, bend
the spear gently. It will break naturally at the point at which it becomes
tough. Discard the tough ends. Repeat with the remaining spears. You
should have about 1¼ lb (625 g) trimmed spears.

3. Bring a wide, shallow saucepan three-fourths full of salted water
to a boil over high heat. Add the asparagus and boil until they are just
beginning to become tender, 2–4 minutes, depending on size; they should
still be somewhat crisp. Drain and immerse in ice water to stop the cooking. When cool, drain well and pat dry in a kitchen towel.

4. Put the spears on a baking sheet with all the tips pointing in the
same direction. Drizzle with the olive oil and sprinkle with kosher salt.
Turn to coat evenly with the oil and salt.

5. Place the asparagus on the preheated grill rack directly over the
coals in a single layer, all the tips pointing in the same direction. Take
care to place them across the bars so they don't fall into the fire. Cook
until they blister, 1–2 minutes, then carefully turn with tongs and grill on
the other side until blistered, 1–2 minutes longer.

6. Transfer to a platter and sprinkle with the Parmesan cheese. Serve
immediately.

SERVES 4

NUTRITIONAL ANALYSIS PER SERVING
Calories 133 (Kilojoules 559); Protein 9 g; Carbohydrates 8 g; Total Fat 9 g;
Saturated Fat 2 g; Cholesterol 5 mg; Sodium 118 mg; Dietary Fiber 2 g

The Organic Movement

Concerned about pesticide residues on food, about the safety of their farm workers and families, and about the spiraling use of increasingly ineffective chemicals, fifty California farmers founded California Certified Organic Farmers (CCOF) in 1973. Today, CCOF has about thirteen hundred farmer members whose agricultural practices meet the group's standards. What's more, the California Department of Food and Agriculture reports that about two thousand of the state's farms are registered organic, although not all of them have sought third-party certification.

In the context of California's enormous farm economy, organic production is minuscule—about 1–2 percent of total cash sales. But among California consumers, at least, demand appears to be strong. More grocery stores are offering at least a few organic items, and many farmers' markets offer a wide choice of organically grown fruits and vegetables. At the same time, a growing number of California chefs are seeking out organic produce, featuring it on their menus, increasing the public's awareness of organic alternatives, and speaking out in support of the industry.

Organic farmers don't just avoid using chemicals. To meet CCOF standards, they implement practices to restore the health of their soil and the biodiversity of their farms. Organic farmers strive for a balanced ecosystem, where beneficial insects eat destructive ones, waste is recycled, and well-nourished plants can resist disease.

California led the way in establishing the organic produce movement. Today, many states have thriving organic industries. Indeed, the USDA instituted federal guidelines in 2002.

Beets & Beans with Hazelnuts

3 large red or golden beets, about
1½ lb (750 g) total weight

1 tablespoon water

2 tablespoons hazelnuts (filberts)

¼ lb (125 g) sugar snap peas,
trimmed

¼ lb (125 g) green beans, trimmed
and cut into 2-inch (5-cm) lengths

2 teaspoons olive oil

½ teaspoon coarse salt

½ teaspoon freshly ground pepper

1 tablespoon hazelnut oil or walnut oil

2 teaspoons sherry vinegar

Hazelnuts blend beautifully with the sweet, earthy taste of beets. Toss in green beans, sugar snaps, and a tangy sherry vinaigrette, and you have a wonderful warm salad. If available, use a combination of red, Chioggia, and golden beets.

1. Preheat the oven to 400°F (200°C).

2. Trim off the greens from each beet, leaving ½ inch (12 mm) of the stem intact. Reserve the greens for another use. Scrub the beets but do not peel. Place in a baking dish and add the water. Cover tightly with aluminum foil and bake until very tender, 45–60 minutes. Remove from the oven and let cool a bit.

3. While the beets are baking, spread the hazelnuts on a baking sheet and toast in the same oven until the skins have blackened and the nuts are lightly browned, about 15 minutes. Transfer the still-warm nuts to a kitchen towel and rub briskly to remove the skins (don't worry if a few flecks remain). Chop coarsely and set aside.

4. Raise the oven temperature to 450°F (230°C).

5. In a bowl, combine the sugar snap peas and the green beans. Add the olive oil and ¼ teaspoon each of the salt and pepper. Toss to coat the beans and peas well and then turn out onto a baking sheet, spreading them in a single layer. Roast until tender, about 10 minutes.

6. While the beans are roasting, slip the skins off the beets. Quarter the beets through their stem ends, then slice the quarters crosswise into slices ¼ inch (6 mm) thick. Place in a bowl. When the snap peas and green beans are ready, add them to the bowl.

7. In a small bowl, whisk together the hazelnut or walnut oil, vinegar, and the remaining ¼ teaspoon each salt and pepper. Pour over the vegetables and sprinkle with the hazelnuts. Toss well and serve at once.

SERVES 4

NUTRITIONAL ANALYSIS PER SERVING
Calories 123 (Kilojoules 517); Protein 3 g; Carbohydrates 11 g; Total Fat 8 g;
Saturated Fat 1 g; Cholesterol 0 mg; Sodium 234 mg; Dietary Fiber 2 g

Posole with Winter Vegetables

2 cups (1 lb/500 g) dried posole, soaked overnight in water and drained, or 1 lb (500 g) thawed frozen posole

2 white onions, coarsely chopped

2 large cloves garlic, chopped

1 tablespoon dried Mexican oregano

1 tablespoon chile caribe or 2 teaspoons red pepper flakes

½ cup (4 fl oz/125 ml) olive oil

2 small carrots, peeled and chopped

2 small parsnips, peeled and chopped

1 fennel bulb, stems and feathery tops trimmed, coarsely chopped

2 butternut squashes, about 1½ lb (750 g) each, halved, seeded, peeled, and cut into ½-inch (12-mm) cubes

1 can (28 oz/875 g) diced tomatoes with juice

8 cups (64 fl oz/2 l) chicken stock, plus more as needed

½ cup (4 fl oz/125 ml) dry white wine

2 teaspoons each cumin and coriander seeds, toasted and ground *(page 314)*

large pinch of saffron threads

kosher salt to taste

¾–1 cup (6–8 fl oz/180–250 ml) crema or crème fraîche

¼ small head green cabbage, finely shredded

½ cup (¾ oz/20 g) coarsely chopped fresh cilantro (fresh coriander)

3 limes, cut into wedges

Throughout the Southwest, posole is served as a main-dish stew and as a side dish with burritos, enchiladas, and other tortilla-wrapped items. The same term refers to the main ingredient, kernels of field or dent corn that have been treated with slaked lime to soften their hulls. If you can't find dried or frozen posole, substitute similar canned white hominy.

1. In a large saucepan, combine the soaked posole, onions, garlic, oregano, and chile caribe or red pepper flakes with water to cover by 3 inches (7.5 cm). Bring to a boil over high heat, cover partially, reduce the heat to medium-low, and simmer until the posole has softened, about 1 hour.

2. In a large saucepan over medium heat, warm the olive oil. Add the carrots, parsnips, and fennel and sauté until slightly softened, about 5 minutes. Add the squashes and continue to cook, stirring, for 2 minutes. Add the tomatoes, 8 cups (64 fl oz/2 l) stock, wine, cumin, coriander, saffron, and salt, raise the heat to high, and bring to a boil. Add the posole and its cooking liquid, reduce the heat to medium-low, and simmer uncovered, stirring frequently, until the vegetables are tender, about 1 hour. If the stew seems too thick, add more stock to thin to desired consistency. Taste and adjust the seasoning.

3. Ladle into warmed bowls and garnish each serving with the crema or crème fraîche, cabbage, and cilantro. Serve the posole immediately. Pass the lime wedges at the table.

SERVES 10–12

NUTRITIONAL ANALYSIS PER SERVING
Calories 437 (Kilojoules 1,835); Protein 9 g; Carbohydrates 58 g; Total Fat 21 g; Saturated Fat 6 g; Cholesterol 16 mg; Sodium 905 mg; Dietary Fiber 7 g

Walla Walla Onion Rings

vegetable oil for deep-frying

1 large Walla Walla or other sweet
onion, sliced ¼ inch (6 mm) thick

⅔ cup (5 fl oz/160 ml) water

⅔ cup (3½ oz/105 g) all-purpose
(plain) flour

1½ cups (3½ oz/105 g) panko

grated zest of 1 lime

1 teaspoon coarse salt

2 tablespoons chopped fresh cilantro
(fresh coriander)

lime wedges

The Japanese bread crumbs known as panko make the coating for these onion rings astonishingly light and crunchy. For entertaining, coat and fry the rings ahead of time and reheat them just before serving in a 350°F (180°C) oven for 10 minutes. The crunch will return.

1. Pour vegetable oil into a deep, heavy saucepan to a depth of 2 inches (5 cm) and heat to 375°F (190°C) on a deep-frying thermometer. Preheat the oven to 250°F (120°C). Line a baking sheet with paper towels.

2. Separate the onion slices into rings. In a bowl, whisk together the water and flour until smooth. Spread the panko on a plate.

3. When the oil reaches the correct temperature, dip the onion rings, 4 or 5 at a time, into the batter. Lift out, let the excess batter drip off, and then dip the rings in the panko, coating evenly. Slip the rings into the oil and fry, flipping them once until golden brown, 1–2 minutes. Transfer to the lined baking sheet and place in the oven. Repeat until all the rings are cooked.

4. Transfer the rings to a platter and sprinkle with the lime zest, salt, and cilantro. Serve immediately with the lime wedges.

SERVES 4

NUTRITIONAL ANALYSIS PER SERVING
Calories 343 (Kilojoules 1,441); Protein 8 g; Carbohydrates 45 g; Total Fat 15 g;
Saturated Fat 2 g; Cholesterol 0 mg; Sodium 454 mg; Dietary Fiber 3 g

Smashed Winter Root Vegetables

1 large russet or Yukon gold potato, about 1 lb (500 g), peeled and cut into 1-inch (2.5-cm) chunks

2 lb (1 kg) root vegetables such as rutabaga, celeriac, parsnip, or carrot (a single vegetable or a mixture), peeled and cut into 1-inch (2.5-cm) chunks

1 teaspoon salt, plus salt to taste

3 tablespoons vegetable oil

3 shallots, about 3 oz (90 g) total weight, sliced into thin rounds

½ teaspoon sugar

¼ cup (2 oz/60 g) unsalted butter, cut into 4 equal pieces

pinch of freshly grated nutmeg

freshly ground pepper to taste

Because of the short growing season in the Northeast, many homes continue to rely on their root cellars to provide fresh vegetables throughout the winter. Whether made from a single type of vegetable or a combination of two or three, this side dish is a favorite accompaniment to roasts and stews.

1. In a saucepan, combine the potato and root vegetable(s), the 1 teaspoon salt, and water to cover. Place over high heat and bring to a boil. Immediately reduce the heat to medium and simmer rapidly, uncovered, until the vegetables are tender enough to mash on the side of the pot with a wooden spoon, 20–30 minutes.

2. Meanwhile, in a frying pan over high heat, warm the vegetable oil. Separate the shallot slices into rings and add to the oil. Fry, stirring often, until golden brown, 4–7 minutes. Add the sugar and a good pinch of salt, and cook for 1 minute longer. The shallots should be crisp and well colored. Using a slotted spoon, transfer the shallots to paper towels to drain, arranging them in a single layer.

3. When the vegetables are tender, drain them, reserving 1 cup (8 fl oz/ 250 ml) of the cooking liquid. Return the vegetables to the saucepan and, using a potato masher or large wooden spoon, mash them, adding the butter pieces as you work. Add enough of the reserved cooking liquid to make a soft consistency. Season with the nutmeg, salt, and pepper.

4. Transfer the vegetables to a warmed serving dish and sprinkle with the crisp shallots. Serve immediately.

SERVES 6

NUTRITIONAL ANALYSIS PER SERVING
Calories 241 (Kilojoules 1,012); Protein 3 g; Carbohydrates 25 g; Total Fat 15 g;
Saturated Fat 6 g; Cholesterol 21 mg; Sodium 324 mg; Dietary Fiber 4 g

Tomato & Summer Squash Gratin

1 lb (500 g) tomatoes, cut into slices ¼ inch (6 mm) thick

coarse salt to taste

3 tablespoons olive oil

2 cloves garlic, minced

1 zucchini (courgette), trimmed and cut into slices ¼ inch (6 mm) thick

1 yellow summer squash, trimmed and cut into slices ¼ inch (6 mm) thick

1 small yellow onion, very thinly sliced

freshly ground pepper to taste

1 teaspoon chopped fresh thyme

½ cup (2 oz/60 g) shredded sharp cheddar cheese

¼ cup (1 oz/30 g) grated Parmesan cheese

Gratins are favorite Yankee supper dishes all year round. Add a simple steak, pork chop, or chicken breast to this summertime version, and you've got a satisfying meal. Feel free to use other fresh herbs—basil, tarragon, marjoram, dill—in place of the thyme.

1. Sprinkle each tomato slice on both sides with coarse salt and arrange in a single layer in a colander or on a rack over a sink or bowl. Let drain for 35–45 minutes, then pat dry with paper towels.

2. Preheat the oven to 350°F (180°C). Brush the bottom and sides of a medium-sized oval gratin dish or a 7-by-11-inch (18-by-28-cm) baking dish with ½ tablespoon of the olive oil.

3. Scatter one-half of the garlic over the bottom of the prepared dish. Arrange a neat layer of the tomato, zucchini, yellow squash, and onion slices in the bottom of the dish, alternating the vegetables and overlapping the slices. Sprinkle the layer with coarse salt and pepper and with some of the garlic and thyme. (Be judicious with the salt, as the tomatoes are already salted.) Make additional layers in the same manner until all the vegetables have been used and the dish is full. Sprinkle the surface with coarse salt, pepper, any remaining garlic and thyme, and then with the cheddar and Parmesan cheeses. Drizzle the remaining 2½ tablespoons olive oil evenly over the top.

4. Bake until nicely browned and most of the juices released by the vegetables have evaporated, 40–60 minutes. Remove from the oven and let stand for 5–10 minutes before serving.

SERVES 4

NUTRITIONAL ANALYSIS PER SERVING
Calories 230 (Kilojoules 966); Protein 9 g; Carbohydrates 12 g; Total Fat 17 g; Saturated Fat 6 g; Cholesterol 20 mg; Sodium 233 mg; Dietary Fiber 3 g

Fresh Succotash Salad

about 8 ears of corn, husks and
silk removed, or about 3 cups
(18 oz/560 g) frozen kernels

1 cup (7 oz/220 g) fresh or frozen
shelled soybeans

2 cups (12 oz/375 g) cherry
tomatoes, stemmed and halved

1 red bell pepper (capsicum), seeded
and cut into ¼-inch (6-mm) dice

3 green (spring) onions, including
3 inches (7.5 cm) of green tops,
thinly sliced

2 tablespoons fresh lime juice

½ teaspoon Dijon mustard

1 small clove garlic, minced

½ teaspoon sugar

¼ teaspoon curry powder

¼ cup (2 fl oz/60 ml) olive oil

2 tablespoons chopped fresh cilantro
(fresh coriander)

2 tablespoons chopped fresh basil

1 tablespoon chopped fresh mint

salt and freshly ground pepper to taste

In this version of succotash, lima beans are replaced with young soybeans, which are pale, vibrant green, and sweeter than limas. The Midwest grows one-third of the world's soybean supply. Fresh soybeans are sold in their green pods and, for this recipe, will need to be shelled and briefly cooked. If fresh soybeans are unavailable, substitute frozen ones, or use fresh or frozen baby lima beans. If you use frozen vegetables, reduce the blanching time to 30 seconds.

1. If using fresh corn, rest an ear on its stalk end in a shallow bowl and cut down along the ear with a sharp knife, stripping off the kernels and rotating the ear with each cut. Repeat with as many ears as necessary until you have 3 cups (18 oz/560 g) kernels.

2. Bring a large saucepan three-fourths full of water to a boil. Add the soybeans and corn kernels and blanch for 1 minute. Drain immediately and plunge into ice water to stop their cooking. Drain well.

3. In a large bowl, toss together the soybeans, corn kernels, tomatoes, bell pepper, and green onions.

4. In a small bowl, whisk together the lime juice, mustard, garlic, sugar, and curry powder. Whisk in the olive oil. Pour over the vegetables and toss to coat evenly.

5. Add the cilantro, basil, and mint and season with salt and pepper. Toss again and serve immediately.

SERVES 4–6

NUTRITIONAL ANALYSIS PER SERVING
Calories 370 (Kilojoules 1,554); Protein 18 g; Carbohydrates 38 g; Total Fat 20 g;
Saturated Fat 3 g; Cholesterol 0 mg; Sodium 38 mg; Dietary Fiber 10 g

Mushroom & Onion Strudel

STRUDEL

3 lb (1.5 kg) mixed fresh mushrooms such as oyster, shiitake, portobello, morel, and cremini, brushed clean or rinsed if laden with grit and cut into 1-inch (2.5-cm) pieces

2 sweet yellow or white onions, cut into 1-inch (2.5-cm) pieces

about ¼ cup (2 fl oz/60 ml) olive oil

2 teaspoons coarse salt

grated zest of 1 orange

juice of 1 orange

¼ cup (⅓ oz/10 g) chopped fresh flat-leaf (Italian) parsley

2 tablespoons chopped fresh rosemary

2 cloves garlic, coarsely chopped

1 teaspoon freshly ground pepper

8 sheets filo dough, thawed in the refrigerator if frozen

¼ cup (2 oz/60 g) unsalted butter, melted and cooled

SAUCE

2 tablespoons olive oil

2 yellow onions, chopped

2 cloves garlic

4 red bell peppers (capsicums), seeded and sliced

1 red or green jalapeño chile, seeded and sliced (optional)

2 tablespoons tomato paste

1 tablespoon balsamic vinegar

salt and freshly ground pepper to taste

This savory vegetable strudel makes a stunning first course or simple dinner.

1. To make the strudel, preheat the oven to 400°F (200°C). In a large bowl, toss the mushrooms and onions with olive oil to coat generously. Sprinkle with the salt. Spread the vegetables, the pieces not touching, in roasting pans. Roast until the mushrooms are tender and begin to brown and the onions are golden, 20–30 minutes. Transfer to a bowl and toss in the orange zest and juice, parsley, rosemary, garlic, and pepper.

2. Reduce the heat to 350°F (180°C). Lightly butter a baking sheet or line with parchment (baking) paper. Lay 2 sheets of the filo dough on a large piece of waxed paper. (Cover the other sheets with a damp cloth to prevent drying.) Brush the top sheet with some butter, top with a single sheet, and brush it with butter. Continue adding sheets, brushing each one with butter, until all 8 sheets are used. Mound the filling lengthwise down the center of the filo, leaving 2 inches (5 cm) uncovered on all sides. Fold in a long side, overlapping the filling by 1 inch (2.5 cm). Fold in the short ends, then roll up to enclose the filling completely. Place seam side down on the prepared baking sheet. Brush the top and sides with the remaining butter. Bake until browned and crisp, about 40 minutes.

3. Meanwhile, make the sauce: In a frying pan over medium heat, warm the olive oil. Add the onions and garlic and sauté until translucent, about 3 minutes. Add the bell peppers and the chile, if using, and cook until very soft, 7–10 minutes. Purée in a blender until smooth, press through a sieve, stir in the tomato paste, vinegar, salt, and pepper, and reheat.

4. Let the strudel stand for 3 minutes, then cut on the diagonal into slices 3 inches (7.5 cm) thick. Serve with the warm sauce.

SERVES 6–8 AS A FIRST COURSE, OR 4–6 AS A MAIN COURSE

NUTRITIONAL ANALYSIS PER FIRST-COURSE SERVING
Calories 342 (Kilojoules 1,436); Protein 8 g; Carbohydrates 35 g; Total Fat 21 g; Saturated Fat 6 g; Cholesterol 18 mg; Sodium 579 mg; Dietary Fiber 5 g

Golden Squash Purée with Garlic & Onions

ROASTED GARLIC

3 heads garlic

3 tablespoons olive oil

kosher salt and freshly ground pepper
　　to taste

2 tablespoons water

SQUASH PURÉE

3 lb (1.5 kg) winter squashes such as
　　butternut or small Hubbard, halved
　　lengthwise and seeded

3 tablespoons extra-virgin olive oil

kosher salt and freshly ground pepper
　　to taste

CARAMELIZED ONIONS

3 small red onions, cut through the
　　root end into 6 wedges

3 tablespoons balsamic vinegar

3 tablespoons extra-virgin olive oil

kosher salt and freshly ground pepper
　　to taste

¼ cup (2 oz/60 g) unsalted butter

1. Preheat the oven to 400°F (200°C). To prepare the roasted garlic, cut off the top third of each garlic head and discard. Stand the garlic heads upright in the center of an 8-inch (20-cm) square of aluminum foil. Drizzle with the olive oil, season with salt and pepper, and sprinkle with the water. Loosely seal the foil closed. Place on the oven rack and roast until soft and slightly caramelized, about 1½ hours. Set aside. (This will make about 6 tablespoons/2 oz/60 g roasted garlic.)

2. Reduce the oven temperature to 375°F (190°C). Line a baking sheet with aluminum foil. Place the squash halves, cut side up, on the prepared baking sheet. Drizzle with the olive oil and season with salt and pepper. Place in the oven and bake until the squashes are soft when pierced, about 1½ hours. Set aside to cool.

3. Raise the oven temperature to 400°F (200°C). Line another baking sheet with aluminum foil. To prepare the onions, in a bowl, toss the onion wedges with the vinegar, oil, salt, and pepper. Pour the onions and the liquid onto the prepared baking sheet. Roast until caramelized and the edges are crisp, 12–15 minutes. Remove from the oven and let cool. With small scissors, snip off the root end holding the layers of onion together on each wedge. Set the onion pieces aside.

4. Using a large spoon, scoop the flesh from the squash halves. Put half of the flesh in a food processor and purée until very smooth. Transfer to a bowl. Repeat with the remaining squash.

5. In a saucepan over medium heat, melt the butter. Add the squash purée and then squeeze the roasted garlic from its papery sheaths into the purée. Add the caramelized onion pieces and stir gently to incorporate all of the ingredients and heat through.

6. Transfer to a warmed bowl and serve at once.

SERVES 6

NUTRITIONAL ANALYSIS PER SERVING
Calories 375 (Kilojoules 1,575); Protein 5 g; Carbohydrates 30 g; Total Fat 29 g;
Saturated Fat 8 g; Cholesterol 21 mg; Sodium 21 mg; Dietary Fiber 5 g

Nopales with Jicama & Pumpkin Seeds

8 or 9 large nopal cactus paddles, about 1½ lb (750 g) total weight

¼ cup (2 fl oz/60 ml) olive oil

kosher salt and freshly ground pepper to taste

⅓ cup (1½ oz/45 g) hulled pumpkin seeds

3 large navel oranges

1 jicama, about 1 lb (500 g), peeled and julienned

1 small red onion, slivered

¼ cup (⅓ oz/10 g) coarsely chopped fresh cilantro (fresh coriander)

3 tablespoons toasted pumpkin seed oil

DRESSING
3 or 4 pickled jalapeño chiles, stems removed, plus 2 tablespoons of the juice

pinch of sugar

kosher salt to taste

⅓ cup (3 fl oz/80 ml) safflower oil

Exotic though they may seem, *nopales,* the pads of the prickly pear cactus, have an appealing color and flavor reminiscent of green beans. When preparing them, handle with care, using a thick towel or padded glove to protect your hands.

1. Position a rack in the upper third of the oven and preheat to 400°F (200°C). Line a baking sheet with aluminum foil.

2. Working with 1 cactus paddle at a time, and using a large knife, cut off the entire outside edge of the paddle, including the end where it was cut from the plant. Then, cut off the thorny nodes. Cut the paddles horizontally into strips ½ inch (12 mm) wide. In a bowl, combine the strips, olive oil, salt, and pepper. Spread on the prepared baking sheet.

3. Roast until the strips are "dry" and the edges are slightly crisp, 20–25 minutes. Set aside to cool.

4. To make the dressing, in a blender, combine the chiles and juice, sugar, salt, and safflower oil. Purée until smooth. Set aside.

5. To toast the pumpkin seeds, in a small frying pan over medium-high heat, toast the seeds, stirring, until they begin to pop and are plump and lightly golden, about 3 minutes. Pour onto a plate to cool.

6. Working with 1 orange at a time, cut a slice off the top and bottom to expose the flesh. Stand the orange upright and thickly cut off the peel in strips to expose the flesh. Holding the orange over a large bowl, cut along either side of each section, letting it drop into the bowl.

7. In a bowl, combine the cactus strips, orange sections, jicama, onion, and cilantro and mix gently. Pour the dressing over the mixture and toss to combine. Divide among individual plates. Sprinkle with the pumpkin seeds and drizzle with the pumpkin seed oil. Serve immediately.

SERVES 6

NUTRITIONAL ANALYSIS PER SERVING
Calories 357 (Kilojoules 1,499); Protein 3 g; Carbohydrates 24 g; Total Fat 29 g; Saturated Fat 4 g; Cholesterol 0 mg; Sodium 153 mg; Dietary Fiber 6 g

Nopal Cactus

Cacti of all kinds dot the deserts of the Southwest, flourishing where other life withers under a relentless sun. When they bloom in the spring, they punctuate the landscape with colorful flowers. But even the eye-catching blossoms fail to convince most outlanders to eat any part of these prickly plants.

The Pueblo Indians have always known better. Long before others came to settle in the Southwest, these original residents were harvesting the big, flat paddles, or joints, and plump, oval fruits of the nopal, or prickly pear, cactus. They cooked and ate the fleshy joints and dried the fruits, which could then be ground and used as a sweetener.

Today, Southwest cooks use the paddles, or *nopales,* as a vegetable in salsas, stews, and salads; cooked with eggs; and grilled. Locals claim that nopales taste like a cross between green beans and okra with a touch of asparagus and a light citrus note. Like okra, they can become mucilaginous over heat unless cooked only a short time or blanched before using.

The egg-shaped fruit, with flesh ranging from white, pink, and yellow to orange and red, goes by many names: prickly pear, cactus pear, Indian fig, Barbary fig, and the Spanish *tuna.* Cooks use it as they do other fruits, principally in sweet and savory sauces, in compotes, and to make marmalade and jam. Prickly pears are also wonderful eaten out of hand, but care must be taken—thick gloves and judicious handling—to avoid their tiny spines.

The fruit of the nopal catus is a rite of spring in the desert South-west and a boon to the resourceful cooks of the region.

Fresh Stirred Corn with Chives

8 ears of corn, husks and silk removed

¼ teaspoon coarse salt, plus salt
   to taste

2 tablespoons chopped fresh chives

freshly ground pepper to taste

1 tablespoon unsalted butter (optional)

Baked corn pudding enriched with cream and eggs is a popular New England holiday indulgence. In the summer, however, when sweet corn is at its peak, there's nothing better than this simple preparation. It goes with everything from grilled hamburgers to roast lamb.

1. With the tip of a sharp knife, score the kernels of an ear of corn by drawing the tip of the knife down the center of each row. Then stand the ear upright on a plate or in a shallow bowl and scrape a spoon down each row, applying enough pressure to remove all of the pulp and juices, leaving behind the kernel skins. Repeat with the remaining ears. You should have about 3 cups (18 oz/560 g) of very milky corn.

2. Put the corn in a saucepan, preferably nonstick, and place over medium heat. Add the ¼ teaspoon salt and bring to a simmer. Cook, stirring often with a wooden spoon, until about one-third of the liquid has evaporated and the corn is the consistency of thick porridge, 8–10 minutes. The corn will bubble and sputter, but it should not boil vigorously. If you are not using a nonstick pan, a brown crust will form on the bottom and sides of the pan. Do not try to scrape this off to mix it with the corn. Instead, simply stir the corn without breaking up the crust. This crust will protect the corn from burning while infusing it with a toasty flavor.

3. Stir in the chives, pepper, and the butter, if using. Taste and adjust the seasoning.

4. Spoon into a warmed bowl and serve immediately.

SERVES 4

NUTRITIONAL ANALYSIS PER SERVING
Calories 248 (Kilojoules 1,042); Protein 9 g; Carbohydrates 55 g; Total Fat 3 g;
Saturated Fat 1 g; Cholesterol 0 mg; Sodium 134 mg; Dietary Fiber 9 g

Beans & Grains

Pappardelle with Spring Vegetables

½ lb (250 g) fiddlehead ferns

1½ tablespoons unsalted butter
or olive oil

6 oz (185 g) fresh morel or chanterelle
mushrooms, brushed clean

salt and freshly ground pepper
to taste

1 shallot, minced

1½ cups (12 fl oz/375 ml) chicken
stock

½ lb (250 g) asparagus, tough ends
removed and spears cut on the
diagonal into 1½-inch (4-cm)
lengths

½ cup (4 fl oz/125 ml) heavy (double)
cream

few drops of fresh lemon juice

2 tablespoons chopped fresh chives,
plus extra for garnish

¾ lb (375 g) fresh pappardelle or
fettuccine

This is pasta primavera, New England style. If available, use fiddleheads, the tightly coiled fern shoots that pop up in the woods in the early spring. If you can't find them in your market, simply double the amount of asparagus.

1. Trim the tails (or stems) on the fiddleheads to about ½ inch (12 mm). Rinse the fiddleheads in a large basin or sink filled with water, sloshing them around to remove the bits of brown chaff that cling to the coils. Drain well.

2. Bring a large pot three-fourths full of water to a boil. Add the fiddleheads and blanch for 1–2 minutes. Drain and rinse under cold water to stop the cooking. Drain again.

3. Refill the pot three-fourths full of water and bring to a boil.

4. While the water is heating, in a large frying pan over medium heat, warm the butter or olive oil. Add the mushrooms and sauté, stirring often, until they soften but do not brown, about 5 minutes. Season with salt and pepper. Add the shallot and fiddleheads and cook for 1 minute. Add the stock and bring to a simmer. Stir in the asparagus and the cream and cook until the asparagus is tender, about 5 minutes. Add the lemon juice and the 2 tablespoons chives. Taste and adjust the seasoning.

5. Meanwhile, generously salt the boiling water and add the pasta. Stir well and cook until al dente, 2–3 minutes. Rinse a large bowl with hot water to heat it. Dry and set aside. Drain the pasta and transfer it to the warmed bowl. Pour the sauce onto the pasta and toss to coat.

6. Divide the pasta among warmed pasta bowls and garnish with chives. Serve immediately.

SERVES 4

NUTRITIONAL ANALYSIS PER SERVING
Calories 430 (Kilojoules 1,806); Protein 15 g; Carbohydrates 54 g; Total Fat 18 g;
Saturated Fat 10 g; Cholesterol 115 mg; Sodium 413 mg; Dietary Fiber 3 g

Grits & Greens Soufflé

½ lb (250 g) mixed assorted greens such as turnip, collard, mustard, or Swiss chard, tough stems removed

¼ cup (2 oz/60 g) unsalted butter

½ Vidalia or other sweet onion, chopped

1 clove garlic, chopped

¼ cup (2 fl oz/60 ml) chicken stock

1¾ cups (14 fl oz/430 ml) milk

½ cup (4 fl oz/125 ml) heavy (double) cream

¾ cup (4½ oz/140 g) quick-cooking grits

3 green (spring) onions, white and pale green parts only, chopped

1½ teaspoons fresh thyme leaves

salt and freshly ground pepper to taste

½ cup (2 oz/60 g) shredded cheddar cheese

3 eggs, separated

½ cup (2 oz/60 g) grated Parmesan cheese

Grits and greens pair naturally in the South, like red Georgia clay on a five-year-old's knees or sticky fingers and ice cream at a church social. This soufflé will not rise as tall as a traditional one, but it will still puff up and lighten in texture.

1. Preheat the oven to 350°F (180°C). Lightly butter a 9-by-13-inch (23-by-33-cm) baking or gratin dish.

2. Stack 5 or 6 leaves of the greens on top of one another and roll up tightly. Cut on a diagonal into thin strips. Repeat with the remaining greens.

3. In a large frying pan over medium-high heat, melt the butter. Add the greens, sweet onion, and garlic and cook, stirring occasionally, until the greens are wilted, about 10 minutes. Add the stock, reduce the heat to medium, cover partially, and cook until the greens are tender, about 20 minutes longer. Remove from the heat and let cool. Pour into a sieve and drain well, pressing out any excess liquid. Transfer to a large bowl. Reserve the cooking liquid for another use.

4. In a saucepan over medium heat, combine the milk and cream and bring to a simmer. Slowly whisk in the grits, green onions, thyme leaves, salt, and pepper. Cook, stirring frequently to prevent the grits from sticking, until thick and creamy, about 5 minutes. Remove from the heat and stir in the cheddar cheese. Add to the greens and stir to combine well.

5. In a small bowl, lightly beat the egg yolks with a fork, then quickly stir into the grits mixture. In a large bowl, using an electric mixer set on high speed, beat the egg whites until stiff peaks form. Stir one-fourth of the egg whites into the grits mixture to lighten it, then, using a rubber spatula, gently fold the lightened grits into the remaining egg whites. Pour the mixture into the prepared dish. Top with the Parmesan cheese.

6. Bake until puffed and golden, about 40 minutes. Serve at once.

SERVES 6

NUTRITIONAL ANALYSIS PER SERVING
Calories 401 (Kilojoules 1,684); Protein 15 g; Carbohydrates 26 g; Total Fat 27 g; Saturated Fat 16 g; Cholesterol 183 mg; Sodium 369 mg; Dietary Fiber 2 g

Baked Beans with Molasses

2 rounded cups (1 lb/500 g) navy beans or other dried white beans

½ cup (5½ oz/170 g) molasses

¼ cup (3 oz/90 g) maple syrup or ¼ cup (2 oz/60 g) firmly packed brown sugar

2 tablespoons dark rum (optional)

2 teaspoons dry mustard

1½ teaspoons coarse salt

1 teaspoon freshly ground pepper

3 cups (24 fl oz/750 ml) water

6 oz (185 g) lean salt pork

1 bay leaf

1 yellow onion

2 or 3 whole cloves

Boston earned its sobriquet Beantown because of the Puritans, who made a pot of beans every Saturday to last through Sunday, their day of rest. Serve these robust beans with brown bread and coleslaw for supper or as a welcome side dish at any barbecue.

1. Pick over the beans and discard any stones or misshapen beans. Rinse the beans, place in a large bowl, and add water to cover by 3 inches (7.5 cm). Let soak for at least 8 hours or as long as overnight. Drain well.

2. Preheat the oven to 275°F (135°C).

3. In a saucepan, stir together the molasses, maple syrup or brown sugar, rum (if using), mustard, coarse salt, pepper, and water. Place over medium heat and bring to a simmer, stirring to combine the ingredients. Immediately remove from the heat and set aside.

4. Trim off the rind from the salt pork, keeping it in one piece, and cut the pork into ½-inch (12-mm) cubes. Put the rind in the bottom of a 2½–3-qt (2.5–3-l) Dutch oven or earthenware bean pot. Attach the bay leaf to the whole onion, using the cloves as tacks. Add it to the pot. Then add the beans and the salt pork. Pour the molasses mixture evenly over the top. The beans should be completely immersed in the liquid; if not, add enough water to cover. Place the lid on the pot, securing a tight fit.

5. Bake for 5 hours, checking every hour to see that the top is still moist. If it is not, add a little more water. After 5 hours, increase the oven temperature to 300°F (150°C), remove the lid, and lift out and discard the onion and bay leaf. Continue to bake, uncovered, stirring gently every 15 minutes or so, until the beans are very tender, about 1 hour longer.

6. Discard the pork rind and serve the beans hot directly from the pot. Leftovers can be refrigerated for up to a week and reheated to serve.

SERVES 6 AS A MAIN COURSE, OR 10–12 AS A SIDE DISH

NUTRITIONAL ANALYSIS PER SERVING
Calories 552 (Kilojoules 2,318); Protein 19 g; Carbohydrates 76 g; Total Fat 20 g; Saturated Fat 7 g; Cholesterol 20 mg; Sodium 727 mg; Dietary Fiber 8 g

One-Pot Meals

From the communal iron pot of boiled smoked meats, salted fish, and hardtack biscuits that nourished the earliest settlers during their arduous transatlantic crossing to today's weeknight macaroni-and-cheese casserole, Yankee cooking has a rich heritage of one-pot meals. In contrast to the Southern tradition of abundant side dishes, the archetypal New England meal is a comforting stew, chowder, braise, pot roast, or casserole. Born of thrift and Puritan ethics, these simple, hearty dishes require no fussing and are provincially referred to as "made" dishes. They economize on both fuel and effort, as they can be left to simmer slowly on the back of a stove (originally the woodstove, now quite often a low oven) for hours, leaving the cook free to complete other chores. This is also an ideal way to coax tough cuts of meat, poultry, and even seafood such as chowder clams to tenderness.

Possibly the most renowned one-pot meal of all time is Boston baked beans. Simply made with navy beans, salt pork, molasses or brown sugar, and onions, baked beans are typically cooked in the oven for hours in a bean pot, a stoneware vessel with a small top and bulging sides

designed to minimize evaporation and retain heat after the beans are cooked.

Another favorite category of "made" dishes is savory meat pies, including shepherd's pie, turkey pot pie, Hartley's pork pie from Fall River, Massachusetts, and French-Canadian *tourtière* (pastry-wrapped pork pâté).

The traditional design of this earthenware bean pot protects the beans from scorching and keeps them moist and tasty during their long, slow bake.

Spaetzle with Thyme–Brown Butter

2 cups (10 oz/315 g) all-purpose (plain) flour

2 eggs

½ cup (4 fl oz/125 ml) heavy (double) cream

¼ cup (2 fl oz/60 ml) milk

2 tablespoons finely chopped fresh flat-leaf (Italian) parsley

1½ teaspoons finely chopped fresh thyme

¼ teaspoon salt

¼ teaspoon freshly ground pepper

⅛ teaspoon freshly grated nutmeg

½ cup (4 oz/125 g) unsalted butter

The word *spaetzle* means "little sparrow" in German, describing these tiny dumplings, traditionally served with roast meat and gravy. They are also delicious tossed with butter and herbs and dusted with a little grated cheese. While skilled cooks work the sticky dough between their fingers into a pot of boiling water, it is simpler to press it through a potato ricer or a colander, because the dough becomes easier to manipulate as it warms over the boiling liquid.

1. In a bowl, stir together the flour, eggs, cream, milk, 1 tablespoon of the parsley, 1 teaspoon of the thyme, salt, pepper, and nutmeg. Beat until the dough is smooth and elastic.

2. Fill a large pot three-fourths full of water and bring to a boil. Reduce the heat to a steady simmer.

3. Scoop out about ¼ cup (2 oz/60 g) of the dough and press it through a colander or ricer directly into the simmering water. Simmer until the dough pieces remain floating on the surface, about 2 minutes. Lift out with a slotted spoon, draining well, put into a serving dish, cover, and place in a low oven to keep warm. Repeat with the remaining dough. The spaetzle may be kept warm in a low oven for 10–15 minutes before serving.

4. In a small saucepan over medium-low heat, melt the butter with the remaining ½ teaspoon thyme. Cook, shaking the pan occasionally, just until the butter turns from yellow to medium brown, about 7 minutes. (Be careful. If cooked too long, the butter may burn, but if not cooked long enough, it will lack the nutty flavor characteristic of brown butter.)

5. Drizzle the spaetzle with the thyme–brown butter, sprinkle with the remaining 1 tablespoon parsley, and toss to mix. Transfer to a warmed serving bowl and serve immediately.

SERVES 4–6

NUTRITIONAL ANALYSIS PER SERVING
Calories 490 (Kilojoules 2,058); Protein 9 g; Carbohydrates 45 g; Total Fat 30 g; Saturated Fat 18 g; Cholesterol 169 mg; Sodium 159 mg; Dietary Fiber 2 g

Sesame Noodles

2 tablespoons peanut oil

1 teaspoon red pepper flakes

2 large cloves garlic, minced

2 tablespoons peeled and minced fresh ginger

3 tablespoons Asian sesame oil

2 tablespoons soy sauce

1½ tablespoons balsamic vinegar

1½ tablespoons sugar

2 teaspoons salt

1 lb (500 g) thin fresh Chinese egg noodles

12 green (spring) onions, white and pale green parts only, thinly sliced

2 tablespoons sesame seeds

⅓ cup (½ oz/15 g) coarsely chopped fresh cilantro (fresh coriander)

These room-temperature noodles are an excellent party or potluck dish because you can—in fact, should—make them one to two hours ahead. Resting longer won't hurt them. Serve as a warm-weather dinner with room-temperature roast chicken or make them the centerpiece of a picnic lunch.

1. In a small frying pan over medium heat, warm the peanut oil. Add the red pepper flakes and cook, stirring, until the oil develops some red color and the pepper flakes are fragrant. Add the garlic and ginger and cook, stirring, until fragrant and slightly soft, about 1 minute. Remove from the heat.

2. In a small bowl, whisk together the sesame oil, soy sauce, balsamic vinegar, sugar, and salt. Whisk in the garlic-ginger mixture.

3. Bring a large pot three-fourths full of salted water to a boil over high heat. Add the noodles, stir well, and cook until al dente, 2–3 minutes. Drain and rinse under cold running water until cold. Drain thoroughly, then transfer to a large bowl. Add the sauce and toss to coat the noodles evenly. Add the green onions, reserving about 2 tablespoons for garnish. Toss to mix. Cover and let stand at room temperature for 1–2 hours, tossing occasionally so the noodles absorb the seasonings evenly.

4. Just before serving, in a small, dry frying pan over medium heat, toast the sesame seeds, stirring often, until fragrant and lightly colored, about 5 minutes. Pour onto a plate to cool.

5. Add the sesame seeds and cilantro to the noodles, reserving about 2 tablespoons of the cilantro for garnish. Transfer the noodles to a large platter. Garnish with the reserved green onions and cilantro and serve.

SERVES 4

NUTRITIONAL ANALYSIS PER SERVING
Calories 548 (Kilojoules 2,302); Protein 15 g; Carbohydrates 74 g; Total Fat 22 g; Saturated Fat 3 g; Cholesterol 83 mg; Sodium 2,106 mg; Dietary Fiber 4 g

Sweet Potato & Cracked Pepper Biscuits

1 large yellow sweet potato, about 10 oz (315 g)

½ cup (4 fl oz/125 ml) buttermilk

3 cups (15 oz/465 g) soft winter-wheat self-rising flour such as White Lily brand

1 tablespoon firmly packed light brown sugar

1 teaspoon freshly cracked pepper

½ teaspoon salt

¼ cup (2 oz/60 g) chilled unsalted butter, cut into small cubes, plus 2 tablespoons melted

2 tablespoons solid vegetable shortening, chilled

The rite of passage from amateur Southern cook to accomplished baker is achieved with a perfect batch of biscuits. The secret to making these light, flaky breads is passed down from generation to generation.

1. Preheat the oven to 400°F (200°C). Prick the sweet potato several times with a fork and place directly on the center rack of the oven. Bake until very soft when pierced, about 1 hour. Let cool, peel, place in a bowl, and mash with a fork until very smooth. Whisk in the buttermilk.

2. Raise the oven temperature to 450°F (230°C) and preheat for at least 15 minutes. Lightly grease a large baking sheet.

3. In a bowl, combine 2 cups (10 oz/315 g) of the flour, the brown sugar, pepper, and salt. Using a pastry blender, 2 knives, or your fingers, cut in the butter cubes and shortening until the mixture resembles a coarse meal. Shake the bowl occasionally so that the larger pieces come to the top and can be worked to a consistent size, about that of peas. Make a well in the center and add the sweet potato mixture to it. Stir with a fork to moisten evenly. Do not overwork it. Sprinkle about ¼ cup (1½ oz/45 g) of the remaining flour over the top, turn the dough over, and sprinkle with another ¼ cup (1½ oz/45 g) of the flour.

4. Flour your hands well, pinch off a piece of dough about the size of an egg, dip the wet part of the dough into the remaining ½ cup (2 oz/60 g) flour, and knead gently into a ball. The dough should not be too sticky or too wet. Flatten slightly and place on the prepared baking sheet. Repeat with the remaining dough, placing the biscuits so they just barely touch. Brush the tops lightly with the melted butter.

5. Bake until golden brown, 18–20 minutes. Transfer to a wire rack and let cool for 5 minutes. Serve immediately.

MAKES 12 BISCUITS

NUTRITIONAL ANALYSIS PER BISCUIT
Calories 210 (Kilojoules 882); Protein 4 g; Carbohydrates 33 g; Total Fat 7 g; Saturated Fat 3 g; Cholesterol 11 mg; Sodium 560 mg; Dietary Fiber 1 g

Macaroni & Cheese with Onions

4 thick slices bacon, about ¼ lb (125 g) total weight

3 tablespoons unsalted butter

1 small Walla Walla or other sweet onion, finely chopped

1½ cups (3 oz/90 g) fresh bread crumbs

1½ teaspoons chopped fresh thyme

¾ teaspoon coarse salt, plus salt to taste

¾ teaspoon freshly ground pepper

1 lb (500 g) large elbow macaroni

2 tablespoons all-purpose (plain) flour

2 cups (16 fl oz/500 ml) low-fat or skim milk

4 cups (1 lb/500 g) shredded sharp cheddar cheese

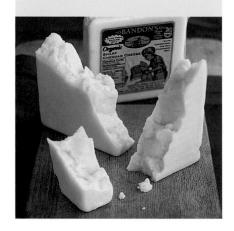

This rich dish is pure comfort food, perfect for a cold, wet June day when the season's first Walla Walla onions appear in the market. Look for Oregon's Bandon organic cheddar, but any of the fine Tillamook or Cougar Gold cheddars will work, too.

1. Preheat the oven to 350°F (180°C). Grease a 1½-qt (1.5-l) baking dish with butter.

2. In a frying pan over medium-high heat, fry the bacon until crisp, 6–8 minutes. Using a fork, transfer to paper towels to drain, then chop coarsely. Discard all but 1 tablespoon of the drippings from the pan.

3. Return the pan to medium-high heat and add 1 tablespoon of the butter. When it melts, stir in the onion and cook, stirring often, until golden, 3–4 minutes. Stir in the bread crumbs, bacon, thyme, and ¼ teaspoon each of the salt and pepper. Remove from the heat.

4. Meanwhile, bring a large saucepan three-fourths full of water to a boil. Add salt to taste and the macaroni, stir well, and cook until al dente, 8–10 minutes. Drain well and pour into the prepared baking dish.

5. In a small saucepan over medium heat, melt the remaining 2 tablespoons butter. When it melts, whisk in the flour and continue to whisk for 1 minute. Gradually whisk in the milk until smooth. Simmer, stirring occasionally, until lightly thickened, 2–3 minutes. Whisk in the cheese until melted and smooth. Add the remaining ½ teaspoon each salt and pepper and pour over the macaroni. Sprinkle evenly with the bread-crumb mixture.

6. Bake the macaroni until the topping is lightly browned and the mixture is bubbling, 35–40 minutes. Serve hot directly from the dish.

SERVES 6

NUTRITIONAL ANALYSIS PER SERVING
Calories 779 (Kilojoules 3,272); Protein 35 g; Carbohydrates 72 g; Total Fat 38 g; Saturated Fat 22 g; Cholesterol 107 mg; Sodium 867 mg; Dietary Fiber 3 g

Walla Walla Onions

From June through August, the sweet, creamy globes known as Walla Walla onions grace the marketplace. Similar in taste to the Vidalia, Maui, and Texas 1015 Supersweet varieties, Walla Walla onions are high in moisture and low in sulfur (only about half the amount of most onions). This combination gives this juicy onion its illusion of pure sweetness.

Although Walla Wallas have been grown in the United States for nearly a century, the seed originated on the French island of Corsica. Introduced by a Frenchman, Peter Pieri, to the southeast Washington town of Walla Walla, it was quickly embraced by the local Italian American farmers. John Arbini hand-selected his stock and developed an onion of remarkable sweetness, the Yellow Globe. Although the name didn't stick, his stock did and later became known as the Walla Walla Sweet.

In May 1995, a federally protected growing area, similar to the French *appellation d'origin contrôlée* system for wines, was designated to protect Walla Walla onions. Therefore, Walla Wallas can be marketed as such only if they are grown in the Walla Walla Valley of southeast

Washington and northeast Oregon. When these delicate seasonal beauties appear, use them quickly, as their shelf life is short. They are wonderful raw, deep-fried, or roasted, or used in relishes and chutneys. Although some enthusiasts insist that the onion can be eaten like an apple, others find this a bit extreme.

Each year, the finest onions are selected from the Walla Walla crop and used as seed the following year to ensure exceptional sweetness, jumbo size, and round shape.

Sour Cream & Chive Spoon Bread

2 cups (16 fl oz/500 ml) milk

½ cup (4 fl oz/125 ml) water

2 tablespoons unsalted butter

1 teaspoon salt

½ teaspoon freshly ground pepper

1 cup (5 oz/155 g) yellow cornmeal

⅔ cup (5 oz/160 g) sour cream

4 eggs

1½ cups (6 oz/185 g) shredded
   cheddar cheese

⅓ cup (½ oz/15 g) chopped fresh
   chives

A question has vexed Southerners for generations: "Is spoon bread a bread or a side dish?" Let's just say it is a winning combination of both. Spoon bread resembles a grits casserole, but it has a lighter, softer, more custardy texture and is made with cornmeal. It is delicious served alongside country ham or fried chicken.

1. Preheat the oven to 350°F (180°C). Lightly butter a 1½-qt (1.5-l) soufflé dish.

2. In a saucepan over medium-high heat, combine the milk, water, butter, salt, and pepper. Bring to a boil over high heat and slowly whisk in the cornmeal. When the mixture returns to a boil, reduce the heat to medium and continue whisking until the mixture thickens and pulls away from the sides of the pan, about 3 minutes. Remove from the heat and whisk in the sour cream.

3. In a bowl, using a handheld electric mixer set at high speed, beat the eggs until thick and a pale lemon yellow, about 5 minutes. Gradually stir about one-fourth of the hot cornmeal mixture into the beaten eggs, then fold the eggs into the remaining cornmeal mixture, stirring constantly. Fold in the cheese and chives. Pour into the prepared soufflé dish.

4. Bake until a toothpick inserted into the center comes out clean, about 35 minutes. Serve immediately.

SERVES 6

NUTRITIONAL ANALYSIS PER SERVING
Calories 396 (Kilojoules 1,663); Protein 17 g; Carbohydrates 24 g; Total Fat 26 g;
Saturated Fat 15 g; Cholesterol 206 mg; Sodium 661 mg; Dietary Fiber 1 g

Wild Rice Pilaf with Ramps & Mushrooms

1 tablespoon unsalted butter

4 ramps or 1 small leek, white part only, chopped

1 lb (500 g) mixed fresh mushrooms such as white button, shiitake, morel, and wood ear, brushed clean or rinsed if laden with grit

1 cup (6 oz/185 g) wild rice, rinsed and drained

¼ cup (⅓ oz/10 g) chopped fresh flat-leaf (Italian) parsley

salt and freshly ground pepper to taste

Although cultivated wild rice is widely available, use the hand-harvested lake rice if you can find it, as it has a particularly light and delicate flavor. Ramps, which grow wild throughout the Midwest, have an intense garlic-onion flavor. Look for them in the springtime at farmers' markets or specialty-foods stores.

1. In a saucepan over medium heat, melt the butter. Add the ramps or leek and the mushrooms and sauté until the leek or ramps are translucent and the mushrooms begin to brown, about 8 minutes.

2. Add the wild rice, parsley, salt, pepper, and water to cover by 1 inch (2.5 cm). Bring to a boil, reduce the heat to low, cover, and cook until the wild rice is tender, about 45 minutes. Drain off any excess water. The cooking time will vary with different batches of rice. The wild rice is ready when the grains puff up and the inner, lighter part is visible. Overcooking increases the volume but turns the rice mushy.

3. Transfer to a warmed serving dish and serve.

SERVES 6

NUTRITIONAL ANALYSIS PER SERVING
Calories 146 (Kilojoules 613); Protein 6 g; Carbohydrates 27 g; Total Fat 2 g; Saturated Fat 1 g; Cholesterol 5 mg; Sodium 7 mg; Dietary Fiber 3 g

Wild Harvest

Heartlanders are serious foragers of all kinds of wild foods. In Michigan and Minnesota, morel gatherers are obsessively protective of their hunting grounds and insist that guests be blindfolded before setting out. In mid- to late May, the honeycombed mushrooms poke up through dead leaves and out from under oak stumps. They taste of loam and the damp woods. To clean them, split the stems and rinse under running water to dislodge the grit.

Ramps, sometimes called wild leeks, are prized by many of today's restaurant chefs for their assertive flavor. Resembling green (spring) onions with lilylike leaves, they sprout in fields and on the borders of forests. Split them as you would a leek and rinse under running water to clean.

Wild asparagus push their heads up through the cool earth in early May. They are wonderful combined in a quick sauté. Fiddleheads are pale green baby ferns shaped like the scroll of a violin.

Hickory nuts flourish from central Wisconsin through Missouri. They have an extraordinarily hard shell, the cracking of which requires a hammer swung with considerable force. Although wonderfully rich and buttery, hickory nuts have never been

harvested commercially because of their steel-tough shells.

Wild huckleberries, which resemble tiny blueberries, are found growing on thick, low bushes in the northern Heartland. They have small, hard seeds, thick skins, and a tart flavor. They are usually cooked into jams and jellies.

Wild hickory nuts, morels, apples, and huckleberries (clockwise from bottom left) are just part of the rich bounty that announces the arrival of autumn in the American Heartland.

Lentils with Browned Onions

2 large Walla Walla or other sweet onions

1½ cups (10½ oz/330 g) brown or green lentils

4 fresh thyme sprigs

⅓ cup (3 fl oz/80 ml) extra-virgin olive oil

¾ teaspoon coarse salt

¾ teaspoon freshly ground pepper

The Palouse region of eastern Washington and northern Idaho is famous for its dried peas and lentils. Every September, residents of Pullman, Washington, celebrate the lentil harvest with the National Lentil Festival. Here's one delicious and simple way to enjoy the versatile legume.

1. Cut the onions in half lengthwise. Cut the halves crosswise into slices ¼ inch (6 mm) thick.

2. Pick over the lentils, discarding any misshapen ones or stones, rinse well, and place in a large saucepan. Add water to cover by 2 inches (5 cm) and add the thyme sprigs. Bring to a boil over high heat, reduce the heat to medium-low, and simmer gently until very tender, about 25 minutes.

3. Meanwhile, cook the onions: In a large frying pan over medium-high heat, warm the olive oil. Add the onions and cook, stirring frequently, until dark brown, about 15 minutes. Stir in ¼ teaspoon each of the salt and pepper. Remove from the heat, cover, and keep warm.

4. Remove the lentils from the heat and remove and discard the thyme sprigs. Drain the lentils well, return them to the saucepan, and stir in the remaining ½ teaspoon each salt and pepper and half of the onions. Transfer the lentil mixture to a serving platter. Top with the remaining onions and serve immediately.

SERVES 4

NUTRITIONAL ANALYSIS PER SERVING
Calories 458 (Kilojoules 1,924); Protein 23 g; Carbohydrates 53 g; Total Fat 19 g; Saturated Fat 3 g; Cholesterol 0 mg; Sodium 296 mg; Dietary Fiber 11 g

Native American Fry Bread

3 cups (15 oz/470 g) unbleached all-purpose (plain) flour

1 tablespoon baking powder

1 teaspoon kosher salt

3 tablespoons lard or vegetable shortening, at room temperature

about 1 cup (8 fl oz/250 ml) warm water or milk

vegetable oil for frying

Reminiscent of sopaipillas (page 286), this deep-fried bread is a staple among the Navajos and other Native Americans of the Southwest. The simple recipe goes nicely with stews, torn into pieces to sop up the juices. Eat the fry bread within an hour of making it for the best flavor and texture.

1. In a food processor, combine the flour, baking powder, and salt. Pulse a few times to mix. Add the lard or shortening and pulse to incorporate well. With the motor running, slowly pour in the warm water or milk through the feed tube, adding only enough liquid and processing only long enough for the dough to come together into a ball.

2. Transfer the dough to a lightly floured work surface and knead until smooth and elastic, about 10 minutes. Shape into a ball, cover with plastic wrap, and let rest for 20 minutes.

3. Divide the dough into 6 equal portions. On the lightly floured surface, roll out each portion into a round about ¼ inch (6 mm) thick. In a heavy saucepan or a deep, heavy frying pan, pour in vegetable oil to a depth of 3–4 inches (7.5–10 cm) and heat to 365°F (185°C) on a deep-frying thermometer. Add a dough round and fry, turning once, until puffed and golden, about 1 minute on each side. Using tongs, transfer to paper towels to drain; keep warm. Repeat with the remaining rounds, frying them one at a time. Serve warm.

SERVES 6

NUTRITIONAL ANALYSIS PER SERVING
Calories 407 (Kilojoules 1,709); Protein 8 g; Carbohydrates 57 g; Total Fat 16 g; Saturated Fat 4 g; Cholesterol 6 mg; Sodium 491 mg; Dietary Fiber 2 g

Spaghetti with Dungeness Crab Sauce

1 whole Dungeness crab, cooked
   and cooled

2 tablespoons extra-virgin olive oil

2 cloves garlic, thinly sliced

pinch of red pepper flakes

1 can (28 oz/875 g) whole tomatoes
   with juice

1 can (14 oz/440 g) chopped plum
   (Roma) tomatoes with juice

½ teaspoon coarse salt

1 lb (500 g) spaghetti

2 tablespoons chopped fresh basil

In the Northwest, cooked Dungeness crabs are available year-round in every fish store and supermarket, making this an easy dish to prepare. If you like, ask the fishmonger to clean the crab for you. Just be sure to save the shell along with the crabmeat, as you'll need both for the sauce.

1. Remove the crab carapace, the bony shield covering the back, and rinse. Crack and clean the crab, removing the meat to a bowl and reserving the shells. Refrigerate the meat.

2. Break up the carapace and collect all the shell pieces in a 12-inch (30-cm) square of cheesecloth (muslin). Tie the ends together with kitchen string and set aside.

3. In a large saucepan over medium-high heat, warm the olive oil. Add the garlic and red pepper flakes and sauté until the garlic is golden, about 1 minute. Add the cheesecloth packet of crab shells, the whole and chopped tomatoes with their juice, breaking up the tomatoes with a wooden spoon, and the salt. Bring to a boil, reduce the heat to medium, and simmer, uncovered, until lightly thickened, about 40 minutes. Lift out the packet of crab shells (let any juices drain back into the pan) and discard.

4. Meanwhile, bring another large saucepan three-fourths full of salted water to a rolling boil. Add the spaghetti, stir well, and boil until half cooked, 4–6 minutes. Drain well and return the spaghetti to the same pan.

5. Pour the tomato sauce over the spaghetti and continue cooking over medium-high heat, stirring frequently, until al dente, 3–5 minutes longer. Add the crabmeat, stir well, and remove from the heat.

6. Divide the pasta among warmed individual dishes and sprinkle with the basil. Serve immediately.

SERVES 4

NUTRITIONAL ANALYSIS PER SERVING
Calories 579 (Kilojoules 2,432); Protein 25 g; Carbohydrates 98 g; Total Fat 9 g;
Saturated Fat 1 g; Cholesterol 24 mg; Sodium 797 mg; Dietary Fiber 5 g

Skillet Corn Bread with Crisp Sage Leaves

3 ears of yellow corn, husks and silk removed

¼ cup (2 fl oz/60 ml) vegetable oil

16 whole fresh sage leaves

2 cups (10 oz/315 g) ground yellow cornmeal

½ cup (2½ oz/75 g) all-purpose (plain) flour

1 tablespoon sugar

1 tablespoon baking powder

1 teaspoon salt

½ teaspoon baking soda (bicarbonate of soda)

2 cups (16 fl oz/500 ml) buttermilk

2 eggs, lightly beaten

2 tablespoons unsalted butter, melted

Corn bread in any form boasts a loyal following in the South. You can buy plain cornmeal or self-rising (leavening already added) cornmeal or a complete corn bread mix (just add water). Yellow and white cornmeal can be used interchangeably.

1. Resting an ear of corn on its stalk end in a shallow bowl, cut down along the ear with a sharp knife, stripping off the kernels and rotating the ear with each cut. Then run the flat side of the blade along the ear to remove any "milk." Repeat with the remaining ears. You should have about 2 cups (12 oz/375 g) kernels in all.

2. Preheat the oven to 450°F (230°C). Pour the vegetable oil into a 10-inch (25-cm) well-seasoned cast-iron frying pan and place in the oven. Heat until sizzling hot, about 5 minutes. Remove from the oven and lay the sage leaves evenly in the frying pan. Return the frying pan to the oven for 5 minutes to crisp the sage leaves.

3. Meanwhile, in a bowl, sift together the cornmeal, flour, sugar, baking powder, salt, and baking soda. Stir in the buttermilk, eggs, and butter just until mixed. Add the corn kernels and stir to blend. Do not overmix.

4. Spoon the batter over the crisp sage leaves, return to the oven, and reduce the temperature to 400°F (200°C). Bake until golden brown and a toothpick inserted into the center comes out clean, about 25 minutes. Transfer to a wire rack to cool for 5 minutes, then invert and carefully cut into 8 wedges. Serve immediately.

MAKES 8 WEDGES

NUTRITIONAL ANALYSIS PER WEDGE
Calories 326 (Kilojoules 1,369); Protein 8 g; Carbohydrates 48 g; Total Fat 12 g; Saturated Fat 3 g; Cholesterol 37 mg; Sodium 633 mg; Dietary Fiber 3 g

Corn, The Amazing Grain

Corn, native to the Western Hemisphere, is a paragon of versatility, thus placing it at the center of the Southern pantry. Southerners grow both the yellow and white varieties.

One of the most common side dishes on the Southern table is hominy grits, most often simply called grits. This soft, savory cornmeal mush is made from hominy— ground corn kernels that have been treated with lye and dried. Grits can be stone- or steel-ground, and are usually slowly simmered in water, milk, or cream, though a quick-cooking version is also available. Long a down-home specialty, they now appear on more upscale menus as well.

Cornmeal is ground from dried corn kernels, and may be white or yellow, depending on the color of the corn. Available in a variety of grinds and either stone- or steel-ground, it is used for many Southern breads, including corn bread; corn pone; corn muffins; hush puppies; hoecakes, sometimes called Johnny cakes; and spoon bread.

Finally, there is bourbon, the only corn-based distilled spirit to originate in the United States. It began in Bourbon County, Kentucky as a corn whiskey called moonshine or the rough-and-tumble white lightning. By the 1800s, distillers discovered that wooden casks developed a smoother, mellower spirit. Today, bourbon is a connoisseur's delight, and Southerners use this celebrated spirit in everything from mint juleps to barbecue sauces to apple pies.

Southern cooks rely on corn like no others. Hominy grits, cornmeal, and Bourbon are all staples of the Southern pantry.

Risotto with Fresh Corn & Basil Oil

2 or 3 ears of yellow corn, husks and silk removed

2 tablespoons unsalted butter

1 cup (3 oz/90 g) thinly sliced leeks, white and pale green parts only

2 cups (16 fl oz/500 ml) chicken stock

3 cups (24 fl oz/750 ml) water

1½ cups (10½ oz/330 g) Arborio rice

salt and freshly ground pepper to taste

2 tablespoons thinly sliced fresh chives

4 tablespoons (2 fl oz/60 ml) store-bought basil oil

Californians are so enamored of risotto that they have taken it in new directions, adding ingredients that would make most Italians shudder. But even Italians, who rarely eat sweet corn, would appreciate this variation. Offer it as a starter before a shrimp (prawn) or salmon main course or serve it in smaller portions as a side dish.

1. Holding each ear of corn by its pointed end, and steadying its stalk end on a cutting board, cut down along the ear with a sharp knife to strip off the kernels, turning the ear with each cut. You should have 1½ cups (9 oz/280 g) corn kernels. Set aside.

2. In a saucepan over medium heat, melt the butter. Add the leeks and stir to coat with the butter. Cover, reduce the heat to medium-low, and cook until wilted and soft, about 5 minutes. Check occasionally to make sure they are not burning.

3. Meanwhile, pour the stock and water into a saucepan and place over medium heat. Adjust the heat to keep the mixture hot but not simmering.

4. Raise the heat under the leeks to medium, add the rice, and cook, stirring constantly, until the rice is hot throughout, about 3 minutes. Begin adding the hot liquid ½ cup (4 fl oz/125 ml) at a time, stirring constantly and adding more liquid only when the previous addition has been absorbed. After 10 minutes, stir in the corn. It should take about 20 minutes for the rice to absorb all the liquid and become al dente. The risotto should be creamy, neither soupy nor stiff. If you need more liquid, use boiling water. Season with salt and pepper.

5. Remove from the heat and stir in the chives and 2 tablespoons of the basil oil. Divide the risotto among warmed bowls. Top with the remaining 2 tablespoons basil oil, dividing evenly. Serve immediately.

SERVES 4

NUTRITIONAL ANALYSIS PER SERVING
Calories 501 (Kilojoules 2,104); Protein 8 g; Carbohydrates 70 g; Total Fat 22 g; Saturated Fat 6 g; Cholesterol 16 mg; Sodium 515 mg; Dietary Fiber 7 g

Fettuccine with Mushrooms & Truffle Oil

1½ lb (750 g) fresh wild mushrooms of one kind, such as chanterelles, oyster mushrooms, or morels, brushed clean and thinly sliced

6 tablespoons (3 oz/90 g) unsalted butter

salt and freshly ground pepper to taste

about ¾ cup (6 fl oz/180 ml) veal stock or best-quality canned beef broth, if needed to moisten the mushrooms, plus 1½ cups (12 fl oz/375 ml)

4 cloves garlic, minced

¼ cup (⅓ oz/10 g) minced fresh flat-leaf (Italian) parsley

1 lb (500 g) fresh fettuccine

1 tablespoon black or white truffle oil

California chefs have fallen for truffle oil, sprinkling this earthy, concentrated essence on everything from carpaccio to mashed potatoes. The oil is expensive, but it doesn't take much to impart a powerful truffle fragrance.

1. Preheat the oven to the lowest setting. Put a large bowl in the oven.

2. Heat a 12-inch (30-cm) frying pan over high heat until very hot and add the mushrooms. They will soon begin to release moisture and will not stick. Cut 4 tablespoons (2 oz/60 g) of the butter into small pieces and add to the pan. Season the mushrooms highly with salt and pepper. Sauté over high or medium-high heat until all the mushroom juices have evaporated and the mushrooms begin to sizzle and brown, about 15 minutes. Reduce the heat if the mushrooms threaten to burn. If they do not release much moisture and cook dry before they are tender, add a little of the stock or broth. Continue cooking until tender, adding more stock or broth, a little at a time, if necessary. Add the garlic and sauté for 2 minutes to release its fragrance. Stir in the parsley. Transfer the mushrooms to the warmed bowl and return the bowl to the warm oven.

3. Add the 1½ cups (12 fl oz/375 ml) stock or broth to the frying pan and deglaze over medium-high heat, scraping up any browned bits on the pan bottom with a wooden spoon. Simmer until the stock is reduced by half. Adjust the heat so the stock stays warm without reducing further.

4. Bring a large pot three-fourths full of salted water to a boil. Add the pasta to the boiling water, stir well, and cook until al dente, 1–2 minutes. Drain and immediately transfer to the pan with the stock. Add the remaining 2 tablespoons butter and the truffle oil and toss well.

5. Add the fettuccine to the mushrooms and toss again. Serve immediately on warmed individual plates.

SERVES 4

NUTRITIONAL ANALYSIS PER SERVING
Calories 566 (Kilojoules 2,377); Protein 18 g; Carbohydrates 72 g; Total Fat 24 g; Saturated Fat 12 g; Cholesterol 131 mg; Sodium 882 mg; Dietary Fiber 5 g

White Pizza with Sardines

DOUGH

1 teaspoon active dry yeast

¾ cup (6 fl oz/180 ml) warm
water (105°F/40°C)

1½–2 cups (7½–10 oz/235–315 g)
all-purpose (plain) flour

1½ teaspoons coarse salt

1 tablespoon extra-virgin olive oil

TOPPING

2 tablespoons extra-virgin olive oil

2 or 3 cloves garlic, minced

1 tablespoon chopped fresh oregano,
or 1 teaspoon dried oregano

1 teaspoon grated lemon zest

½ red onion, sliced into thin rings

1 tin (3¾ oz/110 g) sardines, drained
and cut into 1-inch (2.5-cm) pieces

⅓ cup (1½ oz/45 g) grated
Parmesan cheese

2 tablespoons chopped fresh flat-leaf
(Italian) parsley

freshly ground pepper to taste

This version of *pizza bianca* honors the busy sardine canneries that once proliferated along the Maine coast.

1. To make the dough, in a large bowl, sprinkle the yeast over the warm water. Using a wooden spoon, stir in 1½ cups (7½ oz/235 g) of the flour, the coarse salt, and the olive oil. When the dough becomes too stiff to stir, transfer it to a floured work surface and knead until smooth and elastic, 6–10 minutes, adding up to ½ cup (2½ oz/80 g) more flour as needed to reduce the stickiness. (Alternatively, use a stand mixer, stirring with a spoon as directed, then kneading on low speed with a dough hook.) Form the dough into a ball and place in an oiled bowl. Turn the ball to coat on all sides with the oil, then cover the bowl with plastic wrap and let stand in a warm place until the dough is doubled in size, 2–2½ hours.

2. Meanwhile, begin making the topping: In a small bowl, stir together the olive oil, garlic, oregano, and lemon zest. Let stand for 2 hours.

3. If you have a pizza stone, put it on the bottom rack in the oven. Preheat the oven to 475°F (245°C). Allow the pizza stone to heat for at least 45 minutes before baking.

4. Punch down the dough in the bowl and let it rest for 30 minutes. Then turn it out onto a well-floured work surface and roll it out into a round 12–14 inches (30–35 cm) in diameter and about ¼ inch (6 mm) thick. Do not make a lip on the pizza. Let it rest for 15 minutes.

5. Transfer the round to a baker's peel or rimless baking sheet if using a pizza stone, or to a baking sheet if not using a stone. Brush the olive oil mixture over the dough. Scatter the onion rings and sardine pieces evenly on top, then sprinkle with the cheese. Slide the pizza onto the stone, if using, or place the baking sheet on the bottom rack in the oven. Bake the pizza until the bottom of the crust is brown, about 12 minutes. Remove from the oven and top with the parsley and pepper. Serve hot.

SERVES 8

NUTRITIONAL ANALYSIS PER SERVING
Calories 226 (Kilojoules 949); Protein 9 g; Carbohydrates 27 g; Total Fat 9 g;
Saturated Fat 2 g; Cholesterol 21 mg; Sodium 436 mg; Dietary Fiber 1 g

Texas Bowl o' Red

3 lb (1.5 kg) boneless beef chuck

2 tablespoons vegetable oil

1 large white onion, coarsely chopped

3 cloves garlic, minced

2–3 tablespoons ground New Mexico chile

2 bay leaves

1 tablespoon coriander seeds, toasted and ground *(page 314)*

2 teaspoons cumin seeds, toasted and ground *(page 314)*

2 teaspoons freshly ground canela or 1 teaspoon ground cinnamon

2 teaspoons dried Mexican oregano

1 can (28 oz/875 g) plum (Roma) tomatoes with juice, puréed

1 oz (30 g) bittersweet chocolate

pinch of sugar

1 tablespoon *masa harina* stirred into ¼ cup (2 fl oz/60 ml) water (optional)

kosher salt and freshly ground pepper to taste

sour cream

Taking its traditional cowboy nickname from the dried red chiles that give it color and fire, authentic Texas chili has as many variations as there are cooks who claim to make the best bowl in the state. Add more or less ground chile to make this classic beef-and-no-beans version as hot or as mild as you like.

1. Trim any excess fat from the beef, then cut into ½-inch (12-mm) cubes. In a large saucepan over medium-high heat, warm the vegetable oil. Add the onion and sauté until softened, 3–4 minutes. Add the garlic and sauté for 1–2 minutes longer. Raise the heat to high and, in batches, add the beef and brown well on all sides, 8–10 minutes. Reduce the heat to medium and stir in the ground chile, bay leaves, coriander, cumin, canela or cinnamon, oregano, and the puréed tomatoes. Bring to a boil, reduce the heat to medium, and simmer uncovered, stirring frequently, until thickened, about 1 hour.

2. Add the chocolate, sugar, and the diluted *masa harina,* if you wish to thicken the stew slightly, and stir to combine. Cook for 15–20 minutes to blend the flavors. Taste and adjust the seasoning with salt and pepper.

3. Ladle into warmed bowls, garnish with a dollop of sour cream, and serve immediately.

SERVES 6

NUTRITIONAL ANALYSIS PER SERVING
Calories 707 (Kilojoules 2,969); Protein 42 g; Carbohydrates 15 g; Total Fat 54 g; Saturated Fat 21 g; Cholesterol 163 mg; Sodium 406 mg; Dietary Fiber 4 g

Texas Chili

Most people consider politics and religion subjects too volatile to discuss in polite company. But when compared to a debate about "authentic" chili, both topics seem tame. Chili? Most Mexicans disdain it, every Texan claims it, and some folks are hard put even to agree on whether or not it contains meat and chiles.

Meat? The only choice is Texas beef, but then upstart chili cooks use pork, lamb, and even duck. Chiles? Everything is possible, whole and ground. Texans insist on red chiles, of course, thus the nickname for the dish, bowl o' red. Beans? Not for any self-respecting Texan, but others add them without a second thought. Tomatoes? Maybe and maybe not.

Although most folks will never agree on what ingredients go into an authentic chili, they have transferred some of the energy once devoted to those fierce exchanges to competing in chili cook-offs. The oldest group to sponsor these contests remains the Chili Appreciation Society International. It has sanctioned more than 450 cook-offs throughout North America, and winners go on to compete at the Terlingua International Chili Championship in Texas.

Begun in 1967, the International Chili Society, whose members proudly sport the nickname chiliheads, holds more than 300 cook-offs worldwide, with more than one million people tasting, cooking, and judging. Each year a world championship is held, with such colorfully named winners as Nevada Annie and Tarantula Jack.

A dollop of sour cream cools the heat of Texas bowl o' red.

Sally Lunn Herbed Rolls

5 teaspoons (2 packages) active dry yeast

⅓ cup (3 oz/90 g) sugar

1 cup (8 fl oz/250 ml) warm milk (110°F/43°C)

4 eggs

2 teaspoons salt

4 cups (1¼ lb/625 g) bread (hard-wheat) flour

½ cup (4 oz/125 g) unsalted butter, melted

½ cup (¾ oz/20 g) mixed chopped fresh herbs such as parsley, sage, rosemary, and thyme

1 egg beaten with 1 tablespoon milk

18 fresh flat-leaf (Italian) parsley or sage leaves

The French *soleil, lune,* "sun, moon," provides the name for this old English recipe because the top of each roll bakes up as golden as the sun, while the bottom is said to be as pale as a harvest moon. Sally Lunn rolls have been a part of Southern heritage for so long, Southerners claim them as their own.

1. In a small bowl, combine the yeast, sugar, and warm milk. Let stand until frothy, about 10 minutes.

2. In the bowl of a stand mixer fitted with the paddle attachment, beat together the eggs and salt until fluffy and a pale lemon yellow, about 5 minutes. Add the yeast mixture and beat until smooth, about 1 minute. Add the flour to the egg mixture in three batches alternately with the melted butter, beginning and ending with the flour. Beat in the chopped herbs. Cover with plastic wrap and let rise in a warm place until doubled in size, about 2 hours.

3. Preheat the oven to 350°F (180°C). Lightly butter 18 standard muffin cups.

4. Punch down the dough with a wooden spoon. Scoop out and divide the batter among the prepared muffin cups. Lightly butter a sheet of plastic wrap and place, buttered side down, over the muffins. Let rise again until doubled in size, about 45 minutes.

5. Uncover the rolls and lightly brush the tops with the egg-milk mixture. Lay 1 whole herb leaf on the center of each roll. Bake until a toothpick inserted into the center of a roll comes out clean, about 25 minutes. Transfer to a wire rack and let cool for 5 minutes. Turn out of the pan onto the rack and let cool completely before serving.

MAKES 18 ROLLS

NUTRITIONAL ANALYSIS PER ROLL
Calories 219 (Kilojoules 920); Protein 6 g; Carbohydrates 29 g; Total Fat 8 g; Saturated Fat 5 g; Cholesterol 77 mg; Sodium 296 mg; Dietary Fiber 1 g

Polenta with Mushrooms & Hazelnuts

¼ cup (1¼ oz/37 g) hazelnuts (filberts)

2 tablespoons extra-virgin olive oil

1 lb (500 g) fresh cremini mushrooms, brushed clean and quartered

1 lb (500 g) fresh wild mushrooms such as chanterelle or oyster, rinsed quickly or brushed clean, and cut into ½-inch (12-mm) pieces

1 can (28 oz/875 g) plum (Roma) tomatoes, seeded and chopped, with juice reserved

2 cloves garlic, minced

½ teaspoon *each* coarse salt and freshly ground pepper

1 cup (5 oz/155 g) crumbled fresh goat cheese

2 tablespoons chopped fresh flat-leaf (Italian) parsley

POLENTA

4 cups (32 fl oz/1 l) water

3 cups (24 fl oz/750 ml) low-fat milk

2 teaspoons coarse salt

2 cups (10 oz/315 g) imported instant polenta

Northwest hazelnuts find their way into many local dishes, whether sweet or savory. Here, their warm, luscious flavor blends beautifully with this woodsy wild mushroom ragout. The same ragout also is delicious served over pasta.

1. Preheat the oven to 350°F (180°C). Spread the hazelnuts on a baking sheet and toast until the skins have blackened and the nuts are lightly browned, about 15 minutes. Transfer the still-warm nuts to a kitchen towel and rub briskly to remove the skins (don't worry if some flecks remain). Chop coarsely and set aside.

2. In a large frying pan over high heat, warm the olive oil. Add all of the mushrooms and cook, stirring occasionally, until they have browned and are starting to soften, about 5 minutes. Add the tomatoes and ½ cup (4 fl oz/ 125 ml) of the reserved tomato juice, garlic, salt, and pepper and cook, stirring, until the mushrooms are very tender, about 10 minutes longer.

3. To make the polenta, combine the water, milk, and salt in a heavy saucepan and bring to a boil over medium-high heat. Add the polenta slowly while whisking constantly in one direction. Switch to a wooden spoon and continue stirring until the polenta is thickened, 1–2 minutes.

4. Divide the polenta among warmed individual plates and top with the mushrooms. Sprinkle with the goat cheese, hazelnuts, and parsley. Serve immediately.

SERVES 4

NUTRITIONAL ANALYSIS PER SERVING
Calories 647 (Kilojoules 2,718); Protein 27 g; Carbohydrates 82 g; Total Fat 26 g; Saturated Fat 10 g; Cholesterol 35 mg; Sodium 1,524 mg; Dietary Fiber 12 g

Oregon Hazelnuts

When is a hazelnut a filbert and a filbert a hazelnut? Both names refer to the same nut, although much confusion cloaks the two monikers. Originally used in the United Kingdom, the name hazelnut arrived in this country with its earliest settlers. The name filbert, however, seems to be of French origin, although no one knows for sure. In 1989, Oregon formally declared its preference with the designation of the hazelnut as the Official State Nut.

In fact, Oregon's Willamette Valley grows 99 percent of the national crop. With the planting of the New World's first tree in 1858 in Scottsburg, Oregon, the Northwest hazelnut industry was born. Today, a dozen varieties grow in the Pacific Northwest, with the nuts sold whole or shelled, roasted or raw, in addition to being pressed into oil.

The hazelnut is a versatile nut, easily playing a role in just about any meal. Each fall, the Essential Bread Bakery in Seattle bakes a loaf studded with ripe local pears, dried figs, and a healthy helping of hazelnuts. At Zefiro Restaurant in Portland, roasted quail are dusted with a coating of finely ground hazelnuts and served with greens and a sauce of port and blackberries. The Bay Cafe on Lopez Island, Washington, prepares halibut encrusted in chopped hazelnuts. And at Fran's Chocolates in Seattle, a hazelnut paste from Dundee, Oregon, is transformed into *gianduia,* an Italian confection combining the rich paste with Venezuelan chocolate.

The luscious mild flavor of hazelnuts is compatible with a wide variety of foods and flavors, both sweet and savory.

Penne with Morels & Spring Vegetables

¼ cup (2 fl oz/60 ml) extra-virgin olive oil

2 oz (60 g) fresh morel or other flavorful wild or cultivated mushrooms (about 6 large), rinsed quickly or wiped clean, and halved if large

1 leek, including tender pale greens, finely julienned

2 oz (60 g) prosciutto, diced

¼ teaspoon red pepper flakes

1 bunch Swiss chard, about ¾ lb (375 g), leaves finely shredded and stems cut into 1-inch (2.5-cm) pieces

table salt to taste

1 lb (500 g) asparagus, tough ends removed and cut into 1½-inch (4-cm) lengths

1 cup (5 oz/155 g) fresh or frozen baby lima beans

½ teaspoon coarse salt

1 lb (500 g) penne

grated zest of 1 lemon (2 teaspoons)

½ cup (2 oz/60 g) grated or shaved pecorino romano cheese

Morels, with their earthy mushroom flavor, make this pasta special. They grow all over the Northwest in the spring, but as with any wild mushroom, you should refrain from picking them unless you are, or are with, an expert forager.

1. In a large frying pan over medium-high heat, warm the olive oil. Add the mushrooms, leek, prosciutto, and red pepper flakes and cook, stirring occasionally, until the leek is soft, about 2 minutes. Stir in the chard leaves, cover, and cook, stirring occasionally, until the chard wilts, 3–4 minutes.

2. Meanwhile, bring a large saucepan three-fourths full of water to a rolling boil. Add table salt to taste and the chard stems and boil until tender, about 3 minutes. Scoop the stems out with a wire skimmer and add to the frying pan. Add the asparagus to the boiling water and cook until tender, 2–3 minutes. The timing will depend upon the thickness of the spears. Scoop out the asparagus and add to the frying pan. Add the lima beans to the boiling water and cook until tender, about 4 minutes. Scoop out and add to the frying pan. Season the vegetables with the coarse salt and set aside; keep warm.

3. Add the penne to the boiling water and cook until al dente, about 10 minutes. Drain, reserving ½ cup (4 fl oz/125 ml) of the pasta water. Place the pasta and the reserved water in a large warmed serving bowl.

4. Pour the contents of the frying pan over the pasta, add the lemon zest and cheese, and toss well. Serve immediately.

SERVES 6

NUTRITIONAL ANALYSIS PER SERVING
Calories 490 (Kilojoules 2,058); Protein 21 g; Carbohydrates 70 g; Total Fat 15 g; Saturated Fat 4 g; Cholesterol 17 mg; Sodium 554 mg; Dietary Fiber 5 g

Desserts

Rhubarb-Strawberry-Ginger Pie

Pie Pastry *(page 161)*

4 cups (1 lb/500 g) strawberries, stems removed and berries thickly sliced

1 lb (500 g) rhubarb, trimmed and cut into ¾-inch (2-cm) pieces

1 teaspoon peeled and grated fresh ginger

1 teaspoon grated orange zest

1 cup (8 oz/250 g) sugar

¼ cup (1 oz/30 g) cornstarch (cornflour)

1 egg white, lightly beaten with a few drops of water until slightly foamy

1 tablespoon unsalted butter, cut into small pieces (optional)

Make this pie, the first fruit pie of the summer, when the rhubarb stalks are young and slender and the berries are irresistibly ripe. For a special treat, serve it with vanilla ice cream.

1. Prepare the pastry dough and chill as directed.

2. Position a rack in the lower third of the oven and preheat the oven to 425°F (220°C).

3. On a lightly floured work surface, roll out the larger pastry disk into a 13-inch (33-cm) round about ⅛ inch (3 mm) thick. Drape the round over the rolling pin and carefully transfer it to a 9-inch (23-cm) pie dish, easing it into the bottom and sides. Trim the overhang to ½ inch (12 mm). Roll out the remaining pastry disk in the same way and carefully transfer it to a baking sheet. Place both crusts in the refrigerator.

4. In a large bowl, combine the strawberries, rhubarb, ginger, and orange zest. Toss to mix well. In a small bowl, stir together the sugar and cornstarch until the mixture is free of lumps. Add the sugar mixture to the fruit mixture and toss to combine.

5. Remove the pie dish from the refrigerator and brush the bottom and sides of the pie crust with the egg white. Spoon the fruit mixture evenly into the dish. Dot the surface with the butter, if using. Place the top crust over the fruit and trim the edges to leave a ¾-inch (2-cm) overhang. Fold the edge of the top crust under the edge of the bottom crust, then crimp the edges attractively to seal. Using a sharp knife, cut a few vents in the top crust. Set the pie on a baking sheet to catch any spills.

6. Bake the pie until the crust is golden and the filling is bubbling visibly through the vents, about 40 minutes. Transfer the pie to a wire rack and let cool for at least 1 hour before serving.

SERVES 8

NUTRITIONAL ANALYSIS PER SERVING
Calories 483 (Kilojoules 2,029); Protein 6 g; Carbohydrates 73 g; Total Fat 19 g; Saturated Fat 9 g; Cholesterol 31 mg; Sodium 157 mg; Dietary Fiber 3 g

Caramel Apples with Hazelnuts

1 cup (5 oz/155 g) hazelnuts (filberts)

½ teaspoon salt, plus pinch of salt

6 small green or red apples

½ cup (4 oz/125 g) granulated sugar

½ cup (3½ oz/105 g) firmly packed
light brown sugar

½ cup (5 oz/155 g) light corn syrup

2 cups (16 fl oz/500 ml) heavy
(double) cream

Caramel apples are standard fare at Northwest festivals in the fall. Here's an upscale version made with hazelnuts that's guaranteed to delight both children and adults. If you have any caramel left over after you've coated all the apples, pour it onto a greased baking sheet, let cool, and then cut into squares to make caramel candies.

1. Preheat the oven to 350°F (180°C). Spread the hazelnuts on a baking sheet and toast until the skins are blackened and the nuts are lightly browned, about 15 minutes. Transfer the still-warm nuts to a kitchen towel and rub briskly to remove the skins (don't worry if some flecks remain). Chop coarsely and pour into a small bowl. Mix in the ½ teaspoon salt.

2. Push a popsicle stick into the stem end of each apple, burying it about 1½ inches (4 cm) deep, and set aside. Have ready 6 paper muffin-cup liners.

3. In a deep, narrow, heavy saucepan, combine the granulated and brown sugars, corn syrup, pinch of salt, and cream. Bring to a boil over medium-high heat and cook, stirring constantly, until the mixture registers 250°F (120°C) on a candy thermometer. Remove the saucepan from the heat. Working quickly, dip each apple into the caramel, coating evenly and letting the excess drip off. Then dip the end of each apple into the nuts. Place the apples, stick side up, in the muffin-cup liners. Let cool completely before serving.

SERVES 6

NUTRITIONAL ANALYSIS PER SERVING
Calories 695 (Kilojoules 2,919); Protein 5 g; Carbohydrates 77 g; Total Fat 45 g;
Saturated Fat 19 g; Cholesterol 109 mg; Sodium 283 mg; Dietary Fiber 4 g

Walnut-Raisin Biscotti

½ cup (3 oz/90 g) raisins

½ cup (4 fl oz/125 ml) warm water

1½ cups (6 oz/185 g) walnut pieces

2 cups (10 oz/315 g) all-purpose (plain) flour

1 tablespoon aniseeds

1½ teaspoons baking powder

¼ teaspoon salt

½ cup (4 oz/125 g) unsalted butter, at room temperature

1 cup (8 oz/250 g) sugar

2 eggs

1 tablespoon brandy

2 teaspoons vanilla extract (essence)

Until Bonnie Tempesta, a young San Franciscan, began making biscotti commercially in 1983, few non–Italian Americans had ever heard of these twice-baked cookies. Now biscotti fill cookie jars in bakeries and cafés across the country.

1. In a bowl, combine the raisins and warm water and let stand until soft, about 1 hour. Drain and set aside.

2. Preheat the oven to 325°F (165°C). Spread the walnuts on a baking sheet and toast until fragrant and lightly colored, about 25 minutes. Let cool, then chop coarsely. Leave the oven on. Line a large, heavy baking sheet with parchment (baking) paper.

3. In a bowl, stir together the flour, aniseeds, baking powder, and salt. In a large bowl, using an electric mixer set on medium speed, beat together the butter and sugar until light and fluffy, about 3 minutes. Add the eggs one at a time, beating well after each addition. Beat in the brandy and vanilla. Reduce the speed to low and add the flour mixture gradually, beating just until blended. Beat in the walnuts and drained raisins.

4. Using two large spoons, transfer the dough to the prepared baking sheet. Divide it into 3 equal portions. Using the backs of the spoons or floured fingertips, shape each portion into a log about 14 inches (35 cm) long and 1½ inches (4 cm) in diameter. The dough will be sticky.

5. Bake until firm to the touch and lightly colored, about 40 minutes. Remove from the oven and let stand for 15 minutes, then transfer to a cutting board. Using a serrated knife, cut on the diagonal into slices ⅜ inch (1 cm) wide. Transfer to an unlined baking sheet, cut side down, and bake, in batches, until lightly colored and dry, 15–20 minutes. Transfer to a wire rack to cool. As they cool, they will become crisp. Store in a covered container.

MAKES ABOUT 7 DOZEN COOKIES

NUTRITIONAL ANALYSIS PER COOKIE
Calories 51 (Kilojoules 214); Protein 1 g; Carbohydrates 7 g; Total Fat 2 g; Saturated Fat 1 g; Cholesterol 8 mg; Sodium 18 mg; Dietary Fiber 0 g

Capirotada with Pistachios & Dried Fruits

6 cups (12 oz/375 g) day-old Italian
or French bread, cut into ¾–1-inch
(2–2.5-cm) cubes

1 cup (8 fl oz/250 ml) gold tequila
or sweet wine such as Marsala

⅓ cup (2 oz/60 g) dried currants

½ cup (2 oz/60 g) dried sour cherries

½ cup (3 oz/90 g) diced dried apricots

1½ cups (12 oz/375 g) sugar

2½ cups (20 fl oz/625 ml) water

¼ cup (2 oz/60 g) unsalted butter

1 vanilla bean, split lengthwise

1 canela or cinnamon stick

¼ teaspoon freshly grated nutmeg

pinch of ground allspice

¾ cup (3 oz/90 g) pistachios, piñon
nuts, or pecans, toasted

1 cup (4 oz/125 g) shredded Monterey
jack cheese

1 cup (4 oz/125 g) shredded mild
cheddar cheese

½ cup (4 fl oz/125 ml) crema or
crème fraîche

This typical bread pudding of the old Southwest substitutes cheese for the more familiar milk and eggs in such recipes. Pistachios, which are cultivated in New Mexico, Arizona, and west Texas, add a delightful crunch.

1. Preheat the oven to 350°F (180°C). Butter a 2-qt (2-l) baking dish.

2. Spread the bread cubes on a baking sheet and toast in the oven, turning to brown evenly, until lightly golden, 8–10 minutes. Set aside.

3. In a small saucepan over medium heat, combine the tequila or wine, currants, and sour cherries. Bring the mixture to a boil, reduce the heat to low, and simmer for 3 minutes. Remove from the heat and let stand for 10 minutes. Stir in the apricots and set aside.

4. In a heavy saucepan over medium-high heat, warm the sugar until it begins to melt around the edges of the pan. Then begin to mash it gently with a spoon, but do not stir. Continue to cook the sugar until it starts to turn deep amber, making sure that all of it is melted and it is clear. Immediately add the water in a slow, steady stream, being careful, as it will splatter. The caramel will harden, but then it will remelt as it heats through. When it is again liquid, add the butter, vanilla bean, canela or cinnamon, nutmeg, and allspice and simmer, stirring occasionally, for 10 minutes. Remove from the heat and let stand for 15 minutes. Pour through a fine-mesh sieve placed over a bowl.

5. Layer half of the bread cubes in the prepared baking dish. Sprinkle with half of the fruit mixture and any liquid left in the pan. Sprinkle with half of the nuts and half of the cheeses, and drizzle with half of the caramel syrup. Repeat the layers. Bake until lightly browned and bubbly, about 25 minutes. Spoon into individual bowls and top with the crema or crème fraîche. Serve immediately.

SERVES 8

NUTRITIONAL ANALYSIS PER SERVING
Calories 709 (Kilojoules 2,978); Protein 14 g; Carbohydrates 85 g; Total Fat 28 g;
Saturated Fat 14 g; Cholesterol 59 mg; Sodium 426 mg; Dietary Fiber 4 g

Angel-Light Beignets

⅔ cup (5 fl oz/160 ml) warm water (115°F/46°C)

¼ cup (2 oz/60 g) granulated sugar

¼ teaspoon salt

2½ teaspoons (1 package) active dry yeast

3½–4 cups (17½–20 oz/545–625 g) all-purpose (plain) flour

⅓ cup (3 fl oz/80 ml) heavy (double) cream

1 egg, lightly beaten

peanut oil for deep-frying

confectioners' (icing) sugar for dusting

Beignets (pronounced "ben-YAYS") are a traditional New Orleans deep-fried yeast pastry. In the heart of the French Quarter at the Café du Monde, every good day starts and often ends with a plate of these airy golden treats and a cup of chicory-infused café au lait.

1. In a 2-cup (16–fl oz/500-ml) measuring cup, combine the water, granulated sugar, salt, and yeast. Let stand until frothy, about 10 minutes.

2. Measure out 3½ cups (17½ oz/545 g) of the flour into a food processor. With the processor motor running, slowly add the yeast mixture, processing until fully absorbed. Add the cream and egg and process to form a soft dough. Add more flour, 1 tablespoon at a time, until the dough cleans the sides of the work bowl and is no longer sticky. Continue processing for 1 minute to knead. Place in a lightly oiled lock-top plastic bag, seal, and refrigerate overnight.

3. Transfer the dough to a lightly floured work surface and punch it down to eliminate air pockets. Using a floured rolling pin, roll out the dough into an 8-inch (20-cm) square about ¾ inch (2 cm) thick. With a sharp knife, square off the corners. Cut the dough into 16 2-inch (5-cm) squares, then cut the squares in half on the diagonal to form 32 triangles. Transfer to a lightly floured baking sheet and let rise, uncovered, until doubled in size, about 45 minutes.

4. Pour peanut oil to a depth of 4 inches (10 cm) into a heavy saucepan and heat to 375°F (190°C) on a deep-frying thermometer. Add the pieces of dough, a few at a time, and deep-fry, turning as needed, until golden, about 1 minute. Using a slotted spoon, transfer to paper towels to drain.

5. Sprinkle generously with confectioners' sugar and serve hot.

MAKES 32 BEIGNETS

NUTRITIONAL ANALYSIS PER BEIGNET
Calories 108 (Kilojoules 454); Protein 2 g; Carbohydrates 16 g; Total Fat 4 g;
Saturated Fat 1 g; Cholesterol 10 mg; Sodium 21 mg; Dietary Fiber 1 g

Gooseberry Fool

1 lb (500 g) gooseberries (about
   3 cups)

2 tablespoons water

¾–1 cup (6–8 oz/185–250 g) sugar,
   or to taste

1 cup (8 fl oz/250 ml) heavy (double)
   cream, well chilled

¼ teaspoon vanilla extract (essence)

Residents of both Old and New England share a love of the tart, translucent green gooseberries that thrive in their similar cool climes. Gooseberries are at their peak in midsummer, but you can make this sublime and simple dessert with other berries or stone fruits by simply adding a little lemon juice and cutting back on the sugar.

1. Remove the stem and blossom ends from the gooseberries with your thumb and forefinger or a sharp paring knife. Put the berries and water into a large, heavy saucepan and place over medium heat. As the berries heat, crush them with a potato masher or wooden spoon, then cook, stirring and mashing frequently, until the berries are quite juicy and somewhat puréed, about 10 minutes. Stir in the sugar to taste, using the lesser amount if you like your desserts a little tart. Continue to simmer for 1–2 minutes longer.

2. Remove the pan from the heat and transfer the berries to a bowl. Let cool, cover, and refrigerate until well chilled, at least 3 hours.

3. In a chilled bowl, whisk the cream until soft peaks form. Stir the vanilla into the chilled gooseberries and then fold the whipped cream into the gooseberries just until mixed.

4. Spoon the mixture into champagne flutes, wineglasses, or small sundae glasses. Serve immediately or cover and refrigerate for up to 1 day.

SERVES 4–6

NUTRITIONAL ANALYSIS PER SERVING
Calories 358 (Kilojoules 1,503); Protein 2 g; Carbohydrates 50 g; Total Fat 18 g;
Saturated Fat 11 g; Cholesterol 65 mg; Sodium 19 mg; Dietary Fiber 0 g

Old-Fashioned Vanilla Seed Pound Cake

2½ cups (10 oz/315 g) soft winter-wheat flour, such as White Lily brand, or cake (soft-wheat) flour

1¼ cups (10 oz/315 g) sugar

1 tablespoon baking powder

½ teaspoon salt

1 cup (8 oz/250 g) unsalted butter, at room temperature

⅓ cup (3 oz/90 g) sour cream

5 eggs, lightly beaten

2 teaspoons vanilla extract (essence)

1 vanilla bean, split lengthwise

Pound cake, originally made with a pound (500 g) each of butter, eggs, sugar, and flour, is a longtime Southern favorite. This cake is flavored and flecked with vanilla bean seeds. The addition of sour cream provides extra moistness.

1. Preheat the oven to 325°F (165°C). Lightly butter a 10-inch (25-cm) tube pan, then coat with flour, tapping out the excess. Line the bottom of the pan with waxed paper cut to fit precisely and butter and flour the paper.

2. In a large bowl, combine the flour, sugar, baking powder, and salt. With a handheld electric mixer set on low speed, mix to combine the dry ingredients. Add the butter and sour cream with half of the beaten eggs. Increase the speed to medium and beat for 1 minute, stopping once or twice to scrape down the sides of the bowl. Add the remaining eggs and the vanilla extract. Using the tip of a knife, scrape the seeds from the vanilla bean halves into the mixture. Beat for 30 seconds longer. Pour into the prepared pan.

3. Bake until a toothpick inserted into the center comes out clean, about 1¼ hours, covering the top loosely with aluminum foil if it begins to brown too quickly. Transfer to a wire rack and let cool for 10 minutes. Gently loosen the edges of the cake with a thin-bladed knife or icing spatula, invert onto the rack, and peel away the waxed paper. Carefully turn the cake upright and let cool completely before serving.

SERVES 10

NUTRITIONAL ANALYSIS PER SERVING
Calories 440 (Kilojoules 1,848); Protein 6 g; Carbohydrates 52 g; Total Fat 23 g; Saturated Fat 14 g; Cholesterol 161 mg; Sodium 307 mg; Dietary Fiber 0 g

Cherries in Port

2 tablespoons superfine (caster)
sugar

½ cup (4 fl oz/125 ml) Port

3 lemon zest strips, each 1 inch
(2.5 cm) wide and 2 inches (5 cm)
long

1¼ lb (625 g) ripe sweet cherries
with stems

Whidbeys Washington Port, a vintage-dated Port made
from Columbia Valley grapes, is perfect for this easily prepared dish. The cherries are lightly flavored and refreshing
after macerating for only one hour, although the longer
you leave them, the more deliciously soused they become.
Serve some fine Northwest chocolates on the side.

1. In a large bowl, stir together the sugar, Port, and lemon zest. Add
the cherries and toss well.

2. Cover and refrigerate for at least 1 hour or for up to 3 days, stirring
several times.

3. To serve, place the cherries in a serving bowl and let diners grab
them with their fingers. Have small bowls ready for the pits and stems.

SERVES 4

NUTRITIONAL ANALYSIS PER SERVING
Calories 163 (Kilojoules 685); Protein 2 g; Carbohydrates 31 g; Total Fat 1 g;
Saturated Fat 0 g; Cholesterol 0 mg; Sodium 3 mg; Dietary Fiber 2 g

Blueberry Tea Cake

2 cups (10 oz/315 g) all-purpose (plain) flour

1 teaspoon baking powder

½ teaspoon baking soda (bicarbonate of soda)

¼ teaspoon salt

¼ teaspoon ground cardamom

2 eggs

1½ cups (10½ oz/330 g) firmly packed light brown sugar

½ cup (4 oz/125 g) unsalted butter, melted and cooled

2 tablespoons dark rum

½ teaspoon grated lemon zest

1 cup (8 oz/250 g) plain yogurt

2 cups (8 oz/250 g) blueberries, picked over

confectioners' (icing) sugar

The idea for this moist yellow cake comes from Sam Hayward, chef-owner of Portland, Maine's Fore Street Restaurant, a lively spot known for its contemporary regional fare. Squares of this cake are wonderful for afternoon tea.

1. Preheat the oven to 350°F (180°C). Butter and flour an 8-inch (20-cm) square baking dish.

2. In a bowl, stir together the flour, baking powder, baking soda, salt, and cardamom. Set aside.

3. In a large bowl, using an electric mixer set on medium-high speed, beat together the eggs and brown sugar until thick and fluffy. Using a wooden spoon, stir in the cooled melted butter, rum, and lemon zest.

4. Add the flour mixture in three batches to the egg mixture alternately with the yogurt, beginning and ending with the flour. Mix just until smooth. (You can also use the mixer for this step, setting it at the lowest speed possible.) Gently fold in the blueberries. Spread the batter in the prepared baking dish.

5. Bake the cake until a toothpick inserted into the center comes out clean, 50–60 minutes. Transfer to a wire rack and let cool completely.

6. Using a sieve, dust the cooled cake with confectioners' sugar. Cut into squares and serve directly from the baking dish.

SERVES 9–12

NUTRITIONAL ANALYSIS PER SERVING
Calories 347 (Kilojoules 1,457); Protein 5 g; Carbohydrates 56 g; Total Fat 12 g; Saturated Fat 7 g; Cholesterol 71 mg; Sodium 207 mg; Dietary Fiber 1 g

Baked Figs with Honey Ice Cream

ICE CREAM

1½ cups (12 fl oz/375 ml) half-and-half (half cream)

1½ cups (12 fl oz/375 ml) heavy (double) cream

6 egg yolks

½ cup (6 oz/185 g) plus 2 tablespoons honey

1 tablespoon unsalted butter, cut into small pieces

12 large or 18 small ripe figs, halved lengthwise

1 tablespoon sugar

Many fig varieties produce two crops a year, one in early summer and another in late summer or early fall. California's farmers' markets are the best place to sample the harvests, as ripe figs are so fragile that they suffer when shipped far from the farm. Enjoy them out of hand, sliced and served with yogurt and honey, or baked, as described here.

1. To make the ice cream, in a saucepan over medium heat, combine the half-and-half and the heavy cream and heat until almost boiling. While the cream heats, in a large bowl, whisk together the egg yolks and honey until smooth. Gradually whisk in half of the hot cream, then return the mixture to the saucepan and cook over medium heat, stirring constantly, until the mixture visibly thickens and forms a custard, about 3 minutes. Do not let it boil, or it will curdle. Remove from the heat, let cool, and then refrigerate to chill thoroughly.

2. Freeze the custard in an ice-cream maker according to the manufacturer's directions. Store in the freezer until needed.

3. To bake the figs, preheat the oven to 425°F (220°C). Choose a baking dish large enough to hold the halved figs in a single layer. Dot the bottom of the dish with the butter.

4. Arrange the figs in the prepared dish, cut sides up, and sprinkle with the sugar. Bake until bubbling hot and tender, about 15 minutes.

5. Divide half of the figs among dessert goblets, balloon wineglasses, or compote dishes. Top each serving with some of the ice cream, the remaining figs, and any syrupy juices in the baking dish. You will have ice cream left over. Serve immediately.

SERVES 6

NUTRITIONAL ANALYSIS PER SERVING
Calories 570 (Kilojoules 2,394); Protein 7 g; Carbohydrates 60 g; Total Fat 36 g; Saturated Fat 21 g; Cholesterol 322 mg; Sodium 57 mg; Dietary Fiber 4 g

Fresh Figs

With the overwhelming majority of the crop destined for drying, fresh figs are a high-priced pleasure, even in California. Given that the state grows virtually the country's entire commercial crop and that ripe figs don't ship well, California is the best place to try them.

In fact, the state's history is intertwined with the fig. Spanish missionaries introduced the tree, first planting it at Mission San Diego in the late 1700s. Moving north, they planted the handsome trees at each new outpost that they established.

Today, California growers still widely cultivate what are now known as Mission figs, with their purple-black skins and sweet red flesh. The other commonly grown fig is the Calimyrna, a golden fig identical to the Turkish Smyrna but renamed by California growers after its introduction in the late 1800s. Patrons of farmers' markets may also find Kadotas, plump figs with yellowish green skin and amber flesh.

Mission fig trees produce two crops a year, an early harvest in June and another crop in late summer. Workers clamber up ladders to pick the tree-ripened fruits, wearing gloves to protect their hands from the irritating milky sap that oozes from the stem.

Figs must ripen on the tree since they don't ripen after harvest. You will find them at their best at farmers' markets or restaurants that buy from local growers. Pair them with prosciutto as an appetizer or with sugar and cream for dessert.

Figs from California are a delicacy to be simply prepared and enjoyed.

Toasted Piñon Shortbread

2 cups (10 oz/315 g) unbleached all-purpose (plain) flour

½ cup (4 oz/125 g) sugar

½ cup (2½ oz/75 g) piñon nuts or other pine nuts

2 teaspoons freshly ground canela or 1½ teaspoons ground cinnamon

pinch of kosher salt

1 cup (8 oz/250 g) chilled unsalted butter, cut into tablespoon-sized pieces

The piñon pine *Pinus edulis* grows profusely on the public lands of New Mexico, Arizona, and Colorado. Extracted from its cones, the plump nuts, called piñons, have a richer and more resinous flavor than that of imported pine nuts from the Mediterranean and are about half their size. They are enjoyed in all manner of sweets, including these simple, buttery cookies.

1. Preheat the oven to 300°F (150°C). Line a baking sheet with parchment (baking) paper.

2. In a food processor, combine the flour, sugar, nuts, canela or cinnamon, and salt. Pulse 10 times to combine the ingredients and to coarsely chop the nuts. Add the butter and process until the mixture just comes together into a ball. (The dough may be wrapped and refrigerated at this point for up to 2 days.)

3. On a lightly floured work surface, roll out the dough about ½ inch (12 mm) thick. Using a 2-inch (5-cm) round cookie cutter, cut out the cookies. Gather the scraps, reroll, and cut out more cookies until the dough is used up. Place the cutouts on the prepared baking sheet. Slip the baking sheet into the refrigerator or freezer to chill for 1 hour. (The cookies may be frozen at this point on the tray, then transferred to a lock-top plastic bag; they will keep frozen for up to 1 month.)

4. Bake the shortbread cookies, in batches, until slightly puffed and firm but not browned, about 45 minutes. Transfer the baking sheet to a rack and let cool for 10 minutes, then transfer the cookies to the rack and let cool completely.

MAKES ABOUT 30 COOKIES

NUTRITIONAL ANALYSIS PER COOKIE
Calories 118 (Kilojoules 496); Protein 2 g; Carbohydrates 12 g; Total Fat 7 g;
Saturated Fat 4 g; Cholesterol 17 mg; Sodium 4 mg; Dietary Fiber 1 g

Chocolate, Orange & Almond Cake

1 cup (5½ oz/170 g) plus 2 tablespoons whole blanched almonds

¾ cup (6 oz/185 g) sugar

6 eggs, separated

1 teaspoon vanilla extract (essence)

1 teaspoon grated orange zest

¾ cup (6 oz/185 g) unsalted butter

6 oz (185 g) bittersweet chocolate,
coarsely chopped

Apart from the flour used on the pan, this is a flourless cake with the moist, dense character that chocolate lovers crave. Ground almonds give it structure; orange zest enlivens the taste.

1. Preheat the oven to 375°F (190°C). Butter the bottom and sides of a 9-inch (23-cm) springform pan. Coat the bottom and sides with flour and tap out the excess.

2. In a food processor, combine the almonds with 1 tablespoon of the sugar and process until finely ground. Take care not to grind to a paste. Set aside.

3. Measure out 2 tablespoons of the sugar and set aside. In a bowl, using an electric mixer, beat together the egg yolks, the remaining sugar, the vanilla, and orange zest until pale and thick, 4–5 minutes.

4. In a small saucepan over low heat, melt the butter. Remove from the heat and add the chocolate. Let stand until the chocolate softens, 2–3 minutes, then stir until smooth.

5. In a large bowl, whisk the egg whites until soft peaks form. Gradually add the reserved 2 tablespoons sugar, whisking continuously until the whites are firm and glossy.

6. Add the chocolate mixture to the egg yolk mixture, then beat on medium-low speed until well blended, stopping to scrape down the sides of the bowl once or twice. Add the almonds and beat just until blended. Transfer the mixture to a large bowl. Using a rubber spatula, gently fold in the egg whites until just combined. Pour into the prepared pan.

7. Bake until the center is firm to the touch and the surface begins to crack, about 50 minutes. Transfer to a rack and let cool completely in the pan. To serve, remove the pan sides and slide the cake onto a serving plate.

SERVES 12

NUTRITIONAL ANALYSIS PER SERVING
Calories 356 (Kilojoules 1,495); Protein 7 g; Carbohydrates 26 g; Total Fat 27 g;
Saturated Fat 12 g; Cholesterol 139 mg; Sodium 35 mg; Dietary Fiber 2 g

Berry Fritters

1 cup (5 oz/155 g) all-purpose (plain) flour

2 tablespoons sugar, plus more for coating

1½ teaspoons baking powder

2 eggs, separated

⅔ cup (5 fl oz/160 ml) milk

finely grated zest of 1 lime

pinch of salt

1½ cups (6 oz/185 g) mixed berries such as blueberries, raspberries, and blackberries

canola oil for deep-frying

You can use a combination of berries for these fritters. It's important to keep the oil at 350°F (180°C) while frying; any lower and the fritters may end up with soggy centers. Slip a deep-frying thermometer into the oil to monitor its temperature from first batch to last.

1. Preheat the oven to 250°F (120°C).

2. In a large bowl, whisk together the flour, the 2 tablespoons sugar, and the baking powder. In a small bowl, lightly beat the egg yolks. Whisk them into the flour mixture along with the milk and lime zest, beating until smooth.

3. In another bowl, using an electric mixer, beat together the egg whites and salt until stiff peaks form. Using a rubber spatula, fold the egg whites into the batter just until no white streaks remain. Stir in the berries.

4. Spread additional sugar in a pie dish for coating the fritters after they are cooked. Pour canola oil into a deep frying pan to a depth of 2 inches (5 cm) and heat to 350°F (180°C) on a deep-frying thermometer. Working in batches, drop in the batter, 1 heaping tablespoon at a time. Cook until golden brown on the bottom, 2–3 minutes. Using a slotted spoon, turn the fritters and cook the other side until browned, about 2 minutes longer. With the slotted spoon, transfer to paper towels to drain briefly, then toss the fritters in the sugar until covered evenly. Transfer to a platter and place in the warm oven. Repeat with the remaining batter.

5. When all the fritters are cooked, serve piping hot.

SERVES 6

NUTRITIONAL ANALYSIS PER SERVING
Calories 229 (Kilojoules 962); Protein 6 g; Carbohydrates 30 g; Total Fat 10 g; Saturated Fat 2 g; Cholesterol 75 mg; Sodium 182 mg; Dietary Fiber 1 g

Dried-Fruit Compote with Mascarpone

2 cups (16 fl oz/500 ml) dry white wine

1 cup (8 oz/250 g) sugar

1 cup (8 fl oz/250 ml) water

1-inch (2.5-cm) piece vanilla bean, split lengthwise

1 whole clove

2 lemon zest strips

1 lb (500 g) dried fruits *(see note)*

1½ tablespoons brandy, or to taste

½ cup (4 oz/125 g) mascarpone cheese

For the prettiest results, use a mixture of dried fruits, aiming for a contrast of sizes and colors. Farmers' markets often have the best-quality fruit, dried by the growers themselves. Look for nectarines, peaches, apricots, pears, prunes, figs, cherries, and golden raisins (sultanas). Note that you will need to cook the fruits separately by type, as they require different cooking times.

1. In a saucepan, combine the wine, sugar, and water. Using a knife tip, scrape the seeds from the piece of vanilla bean into the saucepan, then add the pod as well. Add the clove and lemon zest strips. Bring the mixture to a simmer over medium heat, stirring to dissolve the sugar.

2. One variety at a time, gently poach the dried fruits in the syrup, covering the saucepan, until the fruit is plump and tender but not mushy. As each fruit is done, transfer it with a slotted spoon to a bowl. The timing will depend on the size and dryness of the fruit, but nectarines and figs may take 20–30 minutes, while raisins will take only 5 minutes. Quarter the larger poached fruits such as figs, pears, and nectarines; halve the smaller fruits such as apricots.

3. When all the fruits are poached, remove the syrup from the heat and let cool completely. Stir in the brandy. Strain over the fruits. Cover and refrigerate to chill thoroughly.

4. At serving time, in a small bowl, whisk the mascarpone, adding enough of the poaching syrup—2–3 tablespoons—to give it the consistency of softly whipped cream.

5. Divide the fruits and remaining syrup among balloon wineglasses. Top each serving with a dollop of mascarpone.

SERVES 6

NUTRITIONAL ANALYSIS PER SERVING
Calories 432 (Kilojoules 1,814); Protein 3 g; Carbohydrates 90 g; Total Fat 9 g;
Saturated Fat 6 g; Cholesterol 16 mg; Sodium 19 mg; Dietary Fiber 5 g

Classic Pecan Tart

PASTRY DOUGH

1¼ cups (5 oz/155 g) soft winter-wheat flour, such as White Lily brand, or cake (soft-wheat) flour

½ teaspoon salt

¼ cup (2 oz/60 g) solid vegetable shortening, chilled

¼ cup (2 oz/60 g) chilled unsalted butter, cut into small cubes

3–6 tablespoons (1½–3 fl oz/45–90 ml) ice water

¾ cup (6 oz/185 g) sugar

¾ cup (7½ oz/235 g) light corn syrup

⅓ cup (3 oz/90 g) unsalted butter, melted

3 eggs, lightly beaten

2 tablespoons bourbon (optional)

1 tablespoon grated orange zest

1 teaspoon vanilla extract (essence)

¼ teaspoon salt

1 cup (4 oz/125 g) pecan halves, plus ⅓ cup (1½ oz/45 g) coarsely chopped

The pecan tree grows wild in many areas of the temperate South. On chilly autumn mornings you'll find kids and grown-ups alike scurrying in their yards, bucket in hand, trying to beat the squirrels to this prized nut. Bourbon and orange zest add subtle flavor to this cherished Southern dessert.

1. To make the pastry, in a bowl, stir together the flour and salt. Add the shortening and cut in with a pastry blender, 2 knives, or your fingers until the mixture resembles cornmeal. Add the butter and cut in until it forms tiny balls about the size of peas. Add the ice water, a little at a time, stirring and tossing with the pastry blender or a fork until the mixture holds together. Gather the dough into a ball and flatten into a disk. Wrap in plastic wrap and refrigerate for 30–60 minutes.

2. On a lightly floured work surface, roll out the dough into a round about 11 inches (28 cm) in diameter and ⅛ inch (3 mm) thick. Fold the round into quarters and place in a 10-inch (25-cm) tart pan with a removable bottom. Unfold, then press gently into the bottom and sides of the pan. Trim the overhang even with the pan rim. Refrigerate until ready to fill.

3. Position a rack in the lower third of the oven and preheat to 325°F (165°C).

4. In a bowl, stir together the sugar, corn syrup, melted butter, eggs, bourbon (if using), orange zest, vanilla, salt, pecan halves, and chopped pecans. Pour into the chilled pastry and place on a baking sheet.

5. Bake until the center is slightly soft to the touch, the edges are set, and the crust is golden brown, 45–55 minutes. Transfer to a wire rack to cool for 30 minutes, then remove the pan sides and slide the tart off the pan bottom onto a serving plate. Serve warm or at room temperature.

SERVES 8

NUTRITIONAL ANALYSIS PER SERVING
Calories 543 (Kilojoules 2,281); Protein 5 g; Carbohydrates 60 g; Total Fat 33 g; Saturated Fat 12 g; Cholesterol 118 mg; Sodium 275 mg; Dietary Fiber 1 g

Mixed Berry Crisp

TOPPING

½ cup (2 oz/60 g) walnut pieces

¾ cup (4 oz/125 g) unbleached all-purpose (plain) flour

3 tablespoons firmly packed brown sugar

2 tablespoons granulated sugar

¼ teaspoon ground cinnamon

pinch of salt

6 tablespoons (3 oz/90 g) unsalted butter, cut into small pieces

⅓ cup (1 oz/30 g) old-fashioned rolled oats

FILLING

6 cups (1½ lb/750 g) mixed berries such as raspberries, blackberries, loganberries, and olallieberries, in any combination

¾ cup (6 oz/185 g) granulated sugar, or to taste

¼ cup (1 oz/30 g) quick-cooking tapioca

A California summer announces itself in a flood of berries. Bring home a berry medley and make a mixed-fruit crisp to serve with vanilla ice cream.

1. To make the topping, preheat the oven to 325°F (165°C). Spread the walnuts on a baking sheet and toast until fragrant and lightly colored, about 25 minutes. Let cool and then chop coarsely. Raise the oven temperature to 375°F (190°C).

2. In a stand mixer fitted with the paddle attachment, combine the flour, brown and granulated sugars, cinnamon, and salt. Mix on low speed until blended. Add the butter and mix until the flour-coated pieces of butter are the size of peas. Add the walnuts and oats and mix on medium-low speed until the mixture begins to clump; it may take 2–3 minutes. Cover and refrigerate until needed.

3. To make the filling, in a large bowl, combine the berries, ¾ cup (6 oz/185 g) granulated sugar, and tapioca. Stir gently with a large rubber spatula, then let stand for 15 minutes. Taste and add more sugar, if desired.

4. Pour the filling into a 10-inch (25-cm) pie plate or an oval baking dish about 13 inches (33 cm) long by 8 inches (20 cm) wide. Top evenly with the walnut mixture.

5. Bake until the filling is bubbling and the topping is lightly browned, 55–60 minutes. Let cool for 30 minutes before serving.

SERVES 6

NUTRITIONAL ANALYSIS PER SERVING
Calories 476 (Kilojoules 1,999); Protein 5 g; Carbohydrates 77 g; Total Fat 18 g; Saturated Fat 8 g; Cholesterol 31 mg; Sodium 52 mg; Dietary Fiber 7 g

Sopaipillas with Canela-Vanilla Ice Cream

ICE CREAM

2 cups (16 fl oz/500 ml) heavy
(double) cream

2 cups (16 fl oz/500 ml) milk

1 vanilla bean, split lengthwise

2 canela or cinnamon sticks

pinch of kosher salt

¾ cup (6 oz/185 g) sugar

8 egg yolks

SOPAIPILLAS

¾ cup (4 oz/125 g) unbleached all-
purpose (plain) flour

¼ cup (1½ oz/45 g) *panocha* flour
or whole-wheat (wholemeal) flour

½ teaspoon kosher salt

½ teaspoon baking powder

1 tablespoon sugar

1 tablespoon lard or solid vegetable
shortening, at room temperature

¼–⅓ cup (2–3 fl oz/60–80 ml)
buttermilk

canola oil for deep-frying

1. To make the ice cream, pour the cream and milk into a saucepan. Scrape the seeds from the vanilla bean into the pan, then add the pod halves. Add the canela or cinnamon and salt and bring just to a boil. Remove from the heat, cover, and set aside for 30 minutes.

2. Remove the vanilla bean pods and canela or cinnamon and discard. Add ½ cup (4 oz/125 g) of the sugar and bring to a simmer over medium heat, stirring to dissolve the sugar. In a bowl, whisk together the remaining ¼ cup (2 oz/60 g) sugar with the egg yolks. Slowly whisk 1 cup (8 fl oz/250 ml) of the hot cream mixture into the egg mixture. Then slowly return it to the saucepan, whisking constantly. Cook over low heat, stirring constantly, until thick enough to coat a spoon, 8–10 minutes. Pour through a fine-mesh sieve, let cool, cover, and refrigerate to chill well.

3. Transfer the custard to an ice-cream maker and freeze according to the manufacturer's instructions. Freeze until serving.

4. To make the sopaipillas, in a food processor, pulse together the flours, salt, baking powder, and sugar. Add the lard or shortening and pulse to combine. Add the buttermilk and pulse until a moist dough forms. Transfer to a lightly floured work surface, and knead several times until it binds into a cohesive mass. Cover with plastic wrap and let rest for 30 minutes.

5. Pour oil to a depth of 4 inches (10 cm) into a heavy saucepan and heat to 375°F (190°C). Meanwhile, divide the dough in half. On a lightly floured work surface, roll out half of the dough ⅛–¼ inch (3–6 mm) thick. Cut into 6 squares or triangles. Drop 2 cutouts, one at a time, into the hot oil and fry, rolling them over, until golden, 40–50 seconds. Drain on paper towels. Repeat with the remaining dough.

6. Serve at once on warmed individual plates with scoops of the ice cream.

SERVES 6

NUTRITIONAL ANALYSIS PER SERVING
Calories 723 (Kilojoules 3,037); Protein 11 g; Carbohydrates 58 g; Total Fat 50 g;
Saturated Fat 24 g; Cholesterol 408 mg; Sodium 325 mg; Dietary Fiber 1 g

Pear Gingerbread

1 tablespoon unsalted butter, plus ½ cup (4 oz/ 125 g), at room temperature

1 large, firm but ripe pear *(see note)*, peeled, cored, and cut into ½-inch (12-mm) dice

1½ cups (7½ oz/235 g) all-purpose (plain) flour

¾ cup (4 oz/125 g) whole-wheat (wholemeal) flour

1½ teaspoons baking soda (bicarbonate of soda)

1 teaspoon ground ginger

1 teaspoon ground cinnamon

½ teaspoon salt

¼ teaspoon ground nutmeg

1¼ cups (9 oz/280 g) firmly packed brown sugar

¾ cup (9 oz/280 g) unsulfured molasses

2 eggs

2 teaspoons peeled and grated fresh ginger

1 cup (8 fl oz/250 ml) buttermilk

2 cups (16 oz/500 g) plain yogurt

Pears are an important crop in the Rogue and Hood River valleys of Oregon, and because many of the varieties store well, the fruits are available throughout the year. Anjou or Bosc, both of which have slightly less moisture than many other varieties, will work well in this spicy gingerbread.

1. Preheat the oven to 350°F (180°C). Grease a 7-by-11-inch (18-by-28-cm) baking pan with butter. Dust the pan with flour, tapping out the excess.

2. In a large frying pan over medium-high heat, melt the 1 tablespoon butter. Add the pear and cook, stirring often, until softened, 3–4 minutes. Transfer to a small bowl and let cool.

3. In another bowl, sift together the all-purpose and whole-wheat flours, baking soda, ground ginger, cinnamon, salt, and nutmeg. Set aside.

4. In a separate bowl, using an electric mixer set on medium speed, beat together the ½ cup (4 oz/125 g) butter and ¾ cup (6 oz/180 g) of the brown sugar, until light and fluffy, 2–3 minutes. Gradually beat in the molasses. Add the eggs one at a time, beating well after each addition. Beat in the fresh ginger.

5. With the mixer on low speed, beat the flour mixture into the egg mixture in three batches alternately with the buttermilk, beginning and ending with the flour. Beat just until mixed. Stir in the pear. Pour into the prepared pan.

6. Bake until a cake tester inserted into the center comes out clean, 45–50 minutes. Transfer the pan to a rack and let cool for 15 minutes.

7. While the cake is cooling, in a small bowl, stir together the yogurt and the remaining ½ cup (3 oz/100 g) brown sugar. Cut the cake into squares and serve warm with dollops of the yogurt.

SERVES 8

NUTRITIONAL ANALYSIS PER SERVING
Calories 555 (Kilojoules 2,331); Protein 10 g; Carbohydrates 93 g; Total Fat 17 g; Saturated Fat 10 g; Cholesterol 98 mg; Sodium 482 mg; Dietary Fiber 3 g

Apple-Raisin Bread Pudding

2 tablespoons unsalted butter

2 large tart apples such as Jonathan, Northern Spy, or Granny Smith, about 1 lb (500 g) total weight, peeled, halved, cored, and roughly chopped

2 tablespoons granulated sugar

4 whole eggs, plus 2 egg yolks

½ cup (3½ oz/105 g) firmly packed light brown sugar

1½ cups (12 fl oz/375 ml) milk

1½ cups (12 fl oz/375 ml) heavy (double) cream

2 tablespoons maple syrup

1 tablespoon bourbon

1 teaspoon vanilla extract (essence)

⅛ teaspoon salt

8 slices day-old white bread, ½ inch (12 mm) thick, crusts removed and bread torn into 1-inch (2.5-cm) pieces (about 7 cups/14 oz/440 g)

¾ cup (4 oz/125 g) raisins, soaked in hot water to cover for 30 minutes and drained

New England's repertoire of pudding recipes is long and varied: hasty pudding, bird's nest pudding, Indian pudding, popcorn pudding, summer pudding, and so forth. This cozy creation can be served plain or dressed up with a custard sauce or heavy cream.

1. Preheat the oven to 375°F (190°C). Butter a 2½-qt (2.5-l) soufflé or baking dish.

2. In a large frying pan over medium heat, melt the butter. Add the apples and granulated sugar and sauté, stirring often, until the apples are nicely glazed and most of the liquid has evaporated, 5–8 minutes. Remove from the heat and set aside.

3. In a large bowl, whisk together the whole eggs, egg yolks, and brown sugar until well mixed. Whisk in the milk, cream, maple syrup, bourbon, vanilla, and salt. Add the bread pieces and let them soak for 10–15 minutes. Stir in the apples and the drained raisins. Pour the mixture into the prepared baking dish.

4. Set the baking dish in a larger roasting pan and place the pan on the center rack of the oven. Add hot water to the roasting pan to reach about halfway up the sides of the dish.

5. Bake the pudding until set and a knife inserted into the center comes out almost clean, 1–1½ hours. The timing will depend on the depth of the baking dish. Transfer the pudding to a wire rack to cool.

6. Serve the pudding warm or at room temperature.

SERVES 8

NUTRITIONAL ANALYSIS PER SERVING
Calories 539 (Kilojoules 2,264); Protein 11 g; Carbohydrates 65 g; Total Fat 27 g; Saturated Fat 15 g; Cholesterol 236 mg; Sodium 384 mg; Dietary Fiber 3 g

Blue Ribbon Cinnamon Buns

DOUGH

2½ teaspoons (1 package) active dry yeast

¼ cup (2 fl oz/60 ml) warm water (105°–115°F/41°–46°C)

2½ cups (12½ oz/390 g) all-purpose (plain) flour, or as needed

¼ cup (2 oz/60 g) granulated sugar

1 teaspoon salt

2 eggs, lightly beaten

¼ cup (2 fl oz/60 ml) milk

1 teaspoon vanilla extract (essence)

¼ cup (2 oz/60 g) unsalted butter, at room temperature

FILLING

½ cup (3½ oz/105 g) firmly packed dark brown sugar

2 teaspoons ground cinnamon

1 teaspoon freshly grated nutmeg

ICING

¼ lb (125 g) cream cheese, at room temperature

¼ cup (2 oz/60 g) unsalted butter, at room temperature

1 teaspoon vanilla extract (essence)

1–1¼ cups (4–5 oz/125–155 g) confectioners' (icing) sugar, sifted

pinch of salt

1. To make the dough, in a large bowl, sprinkle the yeast over the warm water and let stand until foamy, about 5 minutes. Using a wooden spoon, mix in ½ cup (2½ oz/75 g) of the flour, the granulated sugar, salt, eggs, milk, and vanilla until blended. Gradually stir in the remaining 2 cups (10 oz/315 g) flour until the dough comes together. Turn out the dough onto a lightly floured surface and knead until smooth and elastic, adding more flour if necessary to prevent sticking, 7–10 minutes. Knead in the butter until incorporated. Shape into a ball, place in a large buttered bowl, and turn to coat the dough with butter. Cover loosely with plastic wrap and let rise in a warm place until doubled in size, about 1½ hours.

2. Punch down the dough, turn out onto a lightly floured surface, and knead briefly. Return the dough to the bowl, again cover loosely with plastic wrap, and again let rise until doubled in size, about 1 hour.

3. Butter a 9-by-13-inch (23-by-33-cm) baking pan. Punch down the dough and, on a floured surface, roll out into a 16-by-12-inch (40-by-30-cm) rectangle. To make the filling, mix together the brown sugar, cinnamon, and nutmeg. Sprinkle evenly over the rectangle. Starting from a long side, roll up as you would a jelly roll. Cut into 8 equal slices and arrange, cut side down, in the prepared pan. Cover loosely with plastic wrap and let rise until doubled, about 1 hour. Preheat the oven to 350°F (180°C).

4. Bake the rolls until golden, about 30 minutes. Meanwhile, prepare the icing: In a bowl, using an electric mixer, whip together the cream cheese and butter until light and fluffy. Beat in the vanilla, then gradually beat in the confectioners' sugar and salt until light and smooth.

5. Let the rolls cool in the pan on a rack for 5 minutes, then transfer to a platter and spread with the icing. Serve hot, warm, or at room temperature.

MAKES 8 BUNS

NUTRITIONAL ANALYSIS PER BUN
Calories 475 (Kilojoules 1,995); Protein 8 g; Carbohydrates 68 g; Total Fat 19 g;
Saturated Fat 12 g; Cholesterol 103 mg; Sodium 379 mg; Dietary Fiber 1 g

Blue Ribbons

In the Heartland, flaky pie crusts and delicate cakes have always been yardsticks of a cook's skills. But venture through the home arts pavilion at any Midwest state fair, and you'll find that the competition is not just about sweets. Since the 1800s, fair judges have been awarding blue ribbons in dozens of categories of homemade food, from baked goods to tart pickles, all made by entrants who have cooked their way through a series of qualifying rounds at the county, district, and regional levels.

Some national cooking contests are sponsored by major food corporations, including the Midwest's Pillsbury, General Mills, and Land O'Lakes, and the contest winners receive handsome prize money for their efforts. The first national baking competition was hosted by Pillsbury in Minneapolis in 1949, and soon became known simply as the Pillsbury Bake Off, the most renowned of all such contests. Over the years, the winning recipes have been published in a series of cookbooks that have helped shape the way we bake today.

A Tunnel of Fudge Cake, the 1966 winner, popularized the then little-known Bundt pan. Some winning recipes have had grocers scrambling to order special ingredients, such as the Starlight Mint Surprise cookies that cleaned out the supply of Mint Wafers in a single day.

The stakes are high at state fairs, too. Food producers often purchase winning recipes for jams, jellies, pickles, and preserves, then award the creator a residual on every jar sold.

Hotly contested baking and cooking competitions at Midwestern state fairs earn the winners more than just blue ribbons and a little recognition.

Shortcakes with Berries & Crème Fraîche

2½ cups (12½ oz/390 g) soft winter-wheat self-rising flour such as White Lily brand

½ cup (2½ oz/75 g) yellow cornmeal

1 teaspoon baking soda (bicarbonate of soda)

1 teaspoon ground cinnamon

½ teaspoon salt

¼ cup (2 oz/60 g) firmly packed light brown sugar

½ cup (4 oz/125 g) plus 2 tablespoons chilled unsalted butter, cut into ½-inch (12-mm) cubes

1 cup (8 fl oz/250 ml) buttermilk

1 cup (8 oz/250 g) sour cream

½ teaspoon vanilla extract (essence)

3 tablespoons milk

3 tablespoons granulated sugar mixed with ½ teaspoon ground cinnamon

1 cup (4 oz/125 g) sliced strawberries

3 cups (12 oz/375 g) mixed blackberries, raspberries, and blueberries

½ cup (4 oz/125 g) granulated sugar

2 cups (16 fl oz/500 ml) crème fraîche, sour cream, or whipped heavy (double) cream

fresh mint sprigs

Shortcake has long been a summertime favorite. This updated version is still right at home served with barbecue and lemonade on the Fourth of July.

1. Preheat the oven to 450°F (230°C). Lightly butter a large baking sheet.

2. In a bowl, sift together the flour, cornmeal, baking soda, cinnamon, and salt. Then, push the brown sugar through the sieve into the bowl with your fingers or a spoon. Using a pastry blender or 2 knives, cut in the butter until the mixture resembles a coarse meal. In a small bowl, whisk together the buttermilk, the 1 cup (8 oz/250 g) sour cream, and the vanilla. Make a well in the center of the flour mixture and pour in the buttermilk mixture. Stir with a fork to moisten evenly; a wet dough will form.

3. Drop the dough by heaping spoonfuls (about ½ cup/4 oz/125 g each) into 8 equal mounds on the prepared baking sheet, spacing them about 2 inches (5 cm) apart. With floured hands, lightly shape each mound into a 3-inch (7.5-cm) round about ½ inch (12 mm) thick. Brush the tops with the milk and sprinkle with the sugar-cinnamon mixture.

4. Bake until golden brown, 15–18 minutes. Transfer to a wire rack to cool completely.

5. In a large bowl, stir together the strawberries, blackberries, raspberries, blueberries, and granulated sugar until the sugar dissolves.

6. With a serrated knife, cut the cooled shortcakes in half horizontally and place the bottoms, cut sides up, on 8 dessert plates. Place a dollop of the crème fraîche, sour cream, or whipped cream on each bottom. Top with some of the berries and crown with an additional dollop of cream. Position the top of each shortcake slightly offset from the bottom. Garnish the plates with the remaining berries and the mint. Serve at once.

SERVES 8

NUTRITIONAL ANALYSIS PER SERVING
Calories 746 (Kilojoules 3,133); Protein 10 g; Carbohydrates 77 g; Total Fat 44 g; Saturated Fat 27 g; Cholesterol 105 mg; Sodium 962 mg; Dietary Fiber 4 g

Tres Leches Flan

1 can (12 fl oz/375 ml) evaporated milk

1 can (14 fl oz/440 ml) sweetened condensed milk

1 cup (8 fl oz/250 ml) heavy (double) cream

pinch of kosher salt

½ teaspoon freshly ground canela or ¼ teaspoon ground cinnamon

1 tablespoon Grand Marnier, Cointreau, or other orange-flavored liqueur

1 tablespoon vanilla extract (essence)

⅔ cup (5 oz/155 g) sugar

2 whole eggs plus 6 egg yolks

Typically, the *tres leches*—"three milks"—combination is used to make celebratory cakes in Mexico, particularly in the northwestern coastal state of Sinaloa, across the border from the American Southwest. That proximity explains the use of the same trio to make this thick, creamy custard.

1. In a saucepan, combine the evaporated milk, sweetened condensed milk, cream, salt, canela or cinnamon, liqueur, and vanilla and bring just to a boil. Remove from the heat and set aside to cool.

2. In a small, heavy frying pan over medium-high heat, melt the sugar, without stirring, until it becomes a clear amber syrup, 6–8 minutes. Pour it quickly into a 9½-inch (24-cm) ring mold (5-cup/40–fl oz/1.25-l capacity). Holding the mold with potholders, carefully and quickly rotate it to spread the caramelized sugar over the bottom and up the sides, coating evenly. Set aside to cool and set.

3. Position a rack in the lower third of the oven and preheat the oven to 325°F (165°C).

4. In a small bowl, whisk together the whole eggs and yolks, and then whisk them into the steeped milk mixture. Pour into the caramel-lined ring mold. Place the mold in a baking pan. Pour hot water into the baking pan to reach three-fourths of the way up the sides of the mold.

5. Bake until the custard is set but still jiggles in the center, about 40 minutes. Transfer the mold to a rack and let cool completely.

6. To unmold, run a thin knife blade around the inside edge of the mold and invert onto a serving plate. The caramel will run down over the edges. Cut into 8–10 portions, transfer to individual plates, and spoon a little of the caramel over each serving.

SERVES 8–10

NUTRITIONAL ANALYSIS PER SERVING
Calories 413 (Kilojoules 1,735); Protein 10 g; Carbohydrates 46 g; Total Fat 21 g; Saturated Fat 12 g; Cholesterol 252 mg; Sodium 139 mg; Dietary Fiber 0 g

Old-Fashioned Sundae with Fresh Cherries

ICE CREAM
3½ cups (28 fl oz/875 ml) heavy (double) cream

1 cup (8 fl oz/250 ml) milk

1 cup (8 oz/250 g) sugar

½ vanilla bean, or 2 teaspoons vanilla extract (essence)

CHOCOLATE SAUCE
6 oz (185 g) semisweet (plain) chocolate, chopped, or chocolate chips

½ cup (4 fl oz/125 ml) strong brewed coffee

½ teaspoon vanilla extract (essence)

CHERRIES
1 cup (4 oz/125 g) cherries, pitted

2 tablespoons sugar, or to taste

Two Rivers, Wisconsin, was home to the original sundae, created in 1881 by Ed Berners in his tiny ice-cream parlor when a customer requested chocolate sauce on his dish of vanilla ice cream. The recipe for this ice cream, made with cream but not eggs, is easy because the base doesn't need to be cooked.

1. To make the ice cream, in a large bowl, combine the cream, milk, and sugar. If using the ½ vanilla bean, split it lengthwise and, using the tip of a knife, scrape the seeds into the cream mixture. If using vanilla extract, add it to the cream mixture. Stir to dissolve the sugar and mix the ingredients thoroughly. Cover and refrigerate for at least 2 hours or for up to overnight.

2. Pour the cream mixture into an ice-cream maker and freeze according to the manufacturer's instructions.

3. To make the sauce, combine the chocolate and coffee in the top pan of a double boiler placed over simmering water in the lower pan. Heat, stirring often, until melted and smooth. Remove from over the water and stir in the vanilla.

4. To prepare the cherries, in a small saucepan over low heat, stir together the cherries and sugar. Warm just until the sugar melts. Do not allow the cherries to cook.

5. To serve, scoop the ice cream into large tumblers or bowls. Crown each serving with a few cherries and spoon the warm sauce over the top.

SERVES 6–8

NUTRITIONAL ANALYSIS PER SERVING
Calories 703 (Kilojoules 2,953); Protein 5 g; Carbohydrates 59 g; Total Fat 53 g; Saturated Fat 32 g; Cholesterol 168 mg; Sodium 66 mg; Dietary Fiber 2 g

Blackberry Slump

4 cups (1 lb/500 g) blackberries

¾ cup (6 oz/185 g) sugar

¼ cup (2 fl oz/60 ml) fresh lemon juice

2 teaspoons grated lemon zest

BISCUITS

1 cup (5 oz/155 g) all-purpose (plain) flour

2 tablespoons sugar

1 teaspoon baking powder

¼ teaspoon baking soda (bicarbonate of soda)

pinch of salt

3 tablespoons unsalted butter, melted

½ cup (4 fl oz/125 ml) buttermilk

Slumps, grunts, buckles, and cobblers are all colonial desserts of fruit with a biscuit topping. What sets slumps apart, however, is that they are simmered on the stove top, rather than baked in the oven. Serve with heavy (double) cream, softly whipped cream, or vanilla ice cream.

1. To prepare the fruit, in a Dutch oven or a wide, heavy saucepan with a tight-fitting lid, combine the berries, sugar, lemon juice, and lemon zest. (Heavy-duty aluminum foil will also work as a lid.) Set aside.

2. To make the biscuits, in a bowl, stir together the flour, sugar, baking powder, baking soda, and salt. Stir in the melted butter and buttermilk briefly to form a soft, lumpy dough.

3. Set the pan holding the berries over high heat, cover, and bring to a boil, stirring to ensure that the sugar dissolves. Reduce the heat to medium-low and drop spoonfuls of the biscuit dough onto the simmering fruit, spacing them evenly. Replace the cover and simmer gently until the biscuits are firm and dry to the touch, about 20 minutes. Avoid lifting the lid too frequently and allowing steam to escape.

4. Spoon the slump into warmed dessert bowls. A slump is unthickened, so a spoon is the best utensil for eating it.

SERVES 6

NUTRITIONAL ANALYSIS PER SERVING
Calories 314 (Kilojoules 1,319); Protein 4 g; Carbohydrates 62 g; Total Fat 6 g; Saturated Fat 4 g; Cholesterol 16 mg; Sodium 179 mg; Dietary Fiber 4 g

Classic Southern Pralines

3 cups (1½ lb/750 g) sugar

3½ cups (14 oz/440 g) pecan halves

1⅓ cups (11 fl oz/345 ml) buttermilk

6 tablespoons (3 oz/90 g) unsalted butter

¼ teaspoon salt

1 teaspoon vanilla extract (essence)

½ teaspoon almond extract (essence)

1½ teaspoons baking soda (bicarbonate of soda)

Although the idea of mixing nuts (traditionally almonds) with caramelized sugar is French in origin, these pralines are Louisiana ingenuity pure and simple. The earliest recipes called for locally grown pecans and raw sugar brought into the port of New Orleans from Cuban cane fields. Avoid making pralines on a humid day; they will not set up properly.

1. Line 2 baking sheets with waxed paper.

2. In a large, heavy saucepan over low heat, combine the sugar, pecan halves, buttermilk, butter, and salt. Cook, stirring occasionally, until the sugar dissolves completely, about 10 minutes. Do not allow the mixture to boil before the sugar dissolves or it may crystallize and become grainy. Raise the heat to medium-high and bring to a boil, stirring occasionally but being careful not to scrape any hardened candy mixture from the sides of the saucepan. Cook to the soft-ball stage, 236°–239°F (113°–115°C) on a candy thermometer, about 15 minutes.

3. Remove from the heat and stir in the vanilla and almond extracts and the baking soda. As soon as you add the baking soda, the mixture will become lighter in color and foamy in texture. Beat rapidly with a wooden spoon until the mixture begins to cool, thicken, and lose some of its shine, 5–7 minutes.

4. Working quickly, drop the candy by heaping tablespoonfuls, using one spoon to scoop and another to push the mixture onto the prepared baking sheets. Let stand at room temperature until firm, about 1 hour. Eat immediately, or store between layers of waxed paper in an airtight container for up to 10 days.

MAKES ABOUT 3 DOZEN PRALINES

NUTRITIONAL ANALYSIS PER PRALINE
Calories 168 (Kilojoules 706); Protein 1 g; Carbohydrates 21 g; Total Fat 9 g; Saturated Fat 2 g; Cholesterol 6 mg; Sodium 78 mg; Dietary Fiber 1 g

Deep-Dish Apple-Blueberry Pie

Pie Pastry *(page 161)*

3 cups (12 oz/375 g) blueberries

2 apples, peeled, halved, cored, and cut into ½-inch (12-mm) pieces

½ cup (4 oz/125 g) sugar, or to taste

Make this pie early in the fall when the new apples are tart and the late-season blueberries are slightly overripe and very sweet. Wild or low-bush blueberries are smaller and snappier than cultivated high-bush berries. They grow along the rocky shores of northern lakes and throughout the boggy woods.

1. Prepare the pastry dough and chill as directed.

2. Preheat the oven to 350°F (180°C).

3. On a floured pastry cloth or waxed paper, roll out half of the dough into a 13-inch (33-cm) round about ⅛ inch (3 mm) thick. Drape around the rolling pin and carefully transfer to a 9-inch (23-cm) deep-dish pie dish, pressing it gently into the bottom and sides of the dish. Trim the edge, leaving a ½-inch (12-mm) overhang.

4. In a large bowl, gently toss together the blueberries, apples, and sugar. Pour into the pastry-lined pie pan.

5. On a lightly floured pastry cloth or waxed paper, roll out the remaining dough and transfer to the top of the pie in the same way. Press firmly around the edges to seal the crusts together, trimming away any excess overhang, then fold the overhang under itself all around and flute the edge attractively. Make three slashes 2 inches (5 cm) long in the pastry.

6. Bake the pie until the crust is golden brown and firm and the juices have bubbled through the slashes, 50–60 minutes. Transfer to a wire rack to cool for 15–20 minutes. Serve warm or at room temperature.

SERVES 8–10

NUTRITIONAL ANALYSIS PER SERVING
Calories 368 (Kilojoules 1,546); Protein 6 g; Carbohydrates 60 g; Total Fat 12 g; Saturated Fat 7 g; Cholesterol 75 mg; Sodium 265 mg; Dietary Fiber 3 g

Maple Rum Custard

2 cups (16 fl oz/500 ml) light (single) or heavy (double) cream

3 whole eggs, plus 2 egg yolks

2 tablespoons sugar

½ cup (5½ fl oz/170 ml) maple syrup

2 tablespoons dark rum

whipped cream (optional)

In the seventeenth century, much of the New England economy depended on importing raw molasses and distilling it into what was known as New England rum. Although little rum is produced in the Northeast today, more rum is consumed per capita here than elsewhere in the country.

1. Preheat the oven to 300°F (150°C).

2. Rinse a heavy saucepan with water and leave the inside slightly damp (this helps prevent the cream from scorching). Pour the cream into the saucepan, place over medium heat, and heat until small bubbles appear along the edges of the pan. Remove from the heat.

3. In a bowl, whisk together the whole eggs, egg yolks, sugar, and maple syrup until just blended. Gradually whisk the hot cream into the egg mixture without making it too frothy. Stir the rum into the custard. Pour into a large measuring pitcher or bowl with a pouring lip. Divide the custard evenly among six ⅔–¾-cup (5–6–fl oz/160–180-ml) custard cups or ramekins. Set the cups in a roasting pan or baking dish and place it on the middle rack of the oven. Add hot water to the pan or dish to reach halfway up the sides of the cups.

4. Bake the custards until set but the center still jiggles slightly when a cup is shaken, about 50 minutes. Let the custards cool for about 20 minutes in the water bath. Remove the custards from the water bath and set on a wire rack.

5. Serve the custards while still slightly warm. Or let cool completely, cover with plastic wrap, refrigerate for up to 2 days, and serve chilled, with dollops of whipped cream, if desired.

SERVES 6

NUTRITIONAL ANALYSIS PER SERVING
Calories 298 (Kilojoules 1,252); Protein 6 g; Carbohydrates 25 g; Total Fat 20 g; Saturated Fat 11 g; Cholesterol 230 mg; Sodium 68 mg; Dietary Fiber 0 g

The Sugar Maple

The majestic and stalwart sugar maple dominates the character and landscape of much of New England. These cherished trees can live for up to four hundred years and account for almost 25 percent of all the native trees in the region. Every autumn, a steady stream of "leaf peeping" tourists comes to view the flashy display of fiery red, orange, and yellow. Beyond their great beauty, sugar maples, also known as rock maples, are the source of pure maple syrup and maple sugar, two fundamental ingredients in the local cuisine and economy.

Toward the end of the long northern winter, the sturdy sugar maple offers the earliest glimpse of spring when the sap, spurred by the first warm days of the season, rises from the frozen earth to fill collecting buckets and tanks. Then, for days and nights, wood smoke mingled with sweet steam pours forth from sugar shacks, as sugar makers—often farmers welcoming a chance for income during the off-season—boil down the sap to produce exquisitely flavored maple syrup. It takes an average of 40 gallons (160 l) of sap to produce one precious gallon (4 l) of syrup.

Friends and neighbors gather together to help with sugaring—the local term for making maple syrup—and to celebrate the season with a traditional sugar-on-snow party. Bowls are filled with fresh snow or shaved ice, and then some of the boiling maple syrup is poured on top, making a chewy caramel confection.

At the annual celebration, sour dill pickles, old-fashioned dougnuts, and hot coffee are traditionally served alongside the sugar-on-snow.

Sour Cream–Brown Sugar Cookies

1 cup (7 oz/220 g) firmly packed brown sugar

½ cup (4 oz/125 g) unsalted butter, at room temperature

1 egg

1 teaspoon vanilla extract (essence)

2½ cups (12½ oz/390 g) all-purpose (plain) flour

1 teaspoon baking powder

¼ teaspoon baking soda (bicarbonate of soda)

½ teaspoon salt

½ cup (4 oz/125 g) sour cream

¼ cup (2 oz/60 g) granulated sugar

These old-fashioned cookies are as essential on the farm as a tractor. Grab a handful, a big glass of cold lemonade, and a book and go sit for a while under the shade of a tree. Sour cream makes these cookies soft, moist, and tangy. Bake an extra batch to freeze for another day.

1. Preheat the oven to 375°F (190°C). Lightly butter baking sheets or line with parchment (baking) paper.

2. In a large bowl, using an electric mixer set on medium-high speed, beat together the brown sugar and butter, stopping often to scrape down the sides of the bowl, until creamy, 1–2 minutes. Beat in the egg and vanilla.

3. In another bowl, sift together the flour, baking powder, baking soda, and salt. Add the flour mixture in 3 batches to the butter mixture alternately with the sour cream, beginning and ending with the flour mixture and mixing well after each addition.

4. Have ready a small shallow bowl filled with water and a second bowl holding the granulated sugar. Drop the dough by rounded teaspoonfuls 3 inches (7.5 cm) apart onto the prepared baking sheets. Dip the bottom of a flat juice glass first into the water, and then into the sugar, and lightly press on each mound of dough to form a round about 2 inches (5 cm) in diameter.

5. Bake the cookies, 2 sheets at a time, rotating and switching the sheets at midpoint, until the cookies are golden brown and set, 10–12 minutes. Transfer the cookies to racks to cool. Store in airtight containers for up to 1 week or freeze for up to 1 month.

MAKES 4–5 DOZEN COOKIES

NUTRITIONAL ANALYSIS PER COOKIE
Calories 64 (Kilojoules 269); Protein 1 g; Carbohydrates 10 g; Total Fat 2 g; Saturated Fat 1 g; Cholesterol 10 mg; Sodium 40 mg; Dietary Fiber 0 g

Glossary & Basic Recipes

ALLSPICE The berry of a tropical evergreen tree, allspice possesses a complex flavor that hints at cinnamon, nutmeg, and cloves. It appears in both sweet and savory cooking.

ANCHOVY FILLETS A tiny relative of the sardine that once thrived off California's coast, the anchovy is most often enjoyed in the form of salt-preserved, oil-packed fillets that lend briny flavor to everything from Caesar salads to pasta sauces to pizzas.

APPLE CIDER, FRESH Sometimes called sweet cider or apple juice, fresh apple cider refers to unpasteurized, unfiltered apple juice and is used as an ingredient in recipes and as a beverage. It is not to be confused with hard, or alcoholic, cider, which is slightly fermented, resulting in a low alcohol content ranging from 3 to 7 percent. Ciders often contain the juice of several apple varieties, particularly Red Delicious and McIntosh.

ARUGULA Also known as rocket, these small, notch-edged leaves have a mildly bitter taste and tender texture that can be appreciated raw in salads or briefly cooked.

BACON Made from the belly cut of the pig, which lies just below the spareribs, bacon is cured with salt and typically smoked. Most early smokehouses used smoldering hickory logs to provide the flavor for the meats hung from their eaves, and many cooks—and eaters—still consider fragrant hickory smoke ideal for bacon. Although presliced, plastic-wrapped bacon is widely available, look for slab bacon, which can be sliced as desired, for the best quality. Canadian bacon, or back bacon as it is known in Canada, comes from the loin along the back of the hog. Leaner, drier, and fully cooked, it has a mild flavor and meaty texture that is more similar to ham than to bacon. It is sold both presliced and in large pieces for slicing at home.

BALSAMIC VINEGAR Based on condensed grape juice, aged and reduced for years in a succession of ever-smaller barrels made from different aromatic woods, balsamic vinegar develops a heady sweet-sour flavor and an almost syrupy consistency. It is a specialty of the area around Modena, Italy.

BASIL In addition to common fresh sweet basil, a favorite year-round Mediterranean seasoning, look for the highly aromatic Asian or Thai basil, distinguished by dark green leaves on purple-tinged stems.

BAY LEAVES Pungent and spicy, the dried whole leaves of the bay laurel tree are used to flavor sauces, marinades, and pickles.

BELL PEPPERS Roasting softens and sweetens the flesh of bell peppers (capsicums) while also loosening their skin to facilitate peeling. To roast, peel, and seed bell peppers, follow the instructions given for chiles (page 311).

BIRD'S EYE CHILES Varying from hot to sweet, these peppers resemble cherries, under which name they are often sold.

BUTTERMILK The thick, tangy, butter-flecked liquid left as a by-product of churning butter, buttermilk has been an American standby since the arrival of the Puritans. Today, most buttermilk for sale is cultured, that is, factory-made by fermentation. But commercial products yield fine results in the many savory and sweet dishes that buttermilk enriches.

CABBAGE Napa cabbage, also known as Chinese or celery cabbage, has long, pale yellow-green crinkly leaves, with wide, white veins. Its delicate texture and relatively loosely layered leaves make it ideal for using fresh as a wrapper around savory fillings. Red cabbage, with its deep color, thicker leaves, and slightly peppery flavor, is excellent for cooking and for adding raw to salads.

CAPERS These small gray-green buds of a Mediterranean evergreen bush are commonly preserved in salt and sold packaged in either salt or vinegar for use as a zesty garnish for appetizers or salads or as a flavoring in sauces.

CARAWAY SEEDS These small, curving, brown seeds give rye bread its characteristic nutty, anisey flavor. Caraway is used to flavor meats, cabbage, sausages, cheese, and breads.

CARDAMOM Related to ginger, the highly aromatic pods of the cardamom plant hold tiny black seeds that have a warm, sweet flavor. Native to India, it is also widely used in fruit dishes and baked desserts.

CAYENNE PEPPER A source of heat in many regional dishes, including Creole and Cajun favorites, this fine brownish red powder is ground from the dried small, hot red chile of the same name.

CHERVIL This fresh herb has leaves resembling a pale, lacy form of flat-leaf (Italian) parsley. Chervil adds a subtle flavor resembling anise and parsley to eggs and sauces.

Cheeses

BLUE, OREGON In the Oregon town of Central Point in the 1950s, cheese maker Tom Vella began making Roquefort-style blue cheeses with a culture he carried back from a trip to the famed French region. Today, Oregon blues are prized for their savory but not overly salty character and their smooth, soft texture.

CHEDDAR Made from cow's milk, cheddar, the most popular cheese produced in the United States, comes in a range of tastes, from mild to sharp (aged) and tangy.

GOAT, FRESH Smooth, white, creamy, and tangy fresh cheeses made from goat's milk are readily available throughout the United States.

MASCARPONE A thick, almost fluid, slightly soured cream cheese, mascarpone is most often used in desserts or to enrich sweet or savory sauces.

MONTEREY JACK Named for a late-19th-century businessman in Monterey, California, who began producing this smooth, mild, semisoft cow's milk cheese, Monterey jack has become a common substitute for similar traditional cheeses produced in Mexico.

PARMESAN The best of this type of firm, nutlike, salty-tasting Italian cheese is generally acknowledged to be Parmigiano–Reggiano, produced from cow's milk mid-April to mid-November in a region that embraces Parma, Modena, Mantua, and Bologna, and aged for at least 14 months. Buy Parmesan in block form, selecting pieces with a good, deep yellow color and even, grainy texture; grate it fresh, just before use.

PECORINO ROMANO This popular Italian cheese resembles Parmesan but has a sharper, tangier flavor, a result of the sheep's milk from which it is made.

QUESO AÑEJO Literally "aged cheese," this mature version of fresh Mexican-style cow's milk cheese (see *queso fresco,* below) is often used crumbled as a garnish. Grated pecorino cheese may be substituted.

QUESO FRESCO Made from cow's milk, this "fresh cheese" of Mexico, also produced north of the border, is appreciated for its soft, somewhat crumbly consistency and salty, fresh yet tangy flavor. It may be sliced or crumbled as an ingredient that cooks in a dish or added at the end as a garnish. Mild feta cheese may be substituted.

CHILES, ROASTING Roasting develops the flavor of fresh chiles and makes removing their slightly bitter skins easier. To roast chiles, use metal tongs to hold them over the flame of a gas-stove burner until their skins blacken and blister on all sides, about 5 minutes. Alternatively, roast them on the grill rack of a hot gas or charcoal grill, or place them under a preheated broiler (grill). In both cases, turn them occasionally until evenly blackened and blistered, about 10 minutes. Using the tongs, slip the roasted chiles into a paper or heavy-duty plastic bag, or place in a heatproof bowl and cover with a heavy kitchen towel. Leave to cool for about 5 minutes, during which time the steam will help loosen the skins further. With your fingertips, peel away the skins. If the chiles are to be left whole, slit carefully along the length, leaving the stems intact, and, with your fingertips, a small spoon, and/or the tip of a small, sharp knife, remove the seeds and white ribs or veins. If the chiles are to be cut up, cut or pull away the stems, slit them lengthwise, lay the chiles flat, remove the seeds and ribs, and then cut as directed.

Caution: Chiles contain essential oils that can cause a painful burning sensation on contact with eyes, cuts, or other sensitive areas. Handle chiles carefully, wearing rubber kitchen gloves if you have particularly sensitive skin. After handling, wash hands, gloves, and utensils thoroughly with warm, soapy water.

CHIVES A relative of the onion, this grasslike herb has a mild, sweet taste reminiscent of the pungent bulb. Fresh chives go well with eggs, cream cheeses, vegetables, soups, and salads.

CHORIZO Flavored with ground red chile, garlic, oregano, and cumin, this fresh, coarse-textured Mexican-style pork sausage adds rich, spicy flavor to many savory dishes. If unavailable, substitute top-of-the line spicy Polish kielbasa or Cajun andouille.

CILANTRO Also known as Chinese parsley or fresh coriander, these bright green leaves of the coriander plant deliver a pungent—and pleasing—flavor.

CINNAMON Sweet spice derived from the aromatic bark of a type of evergreen, sold as whole dried strips—cinnamon sticks—or in ground form.

COCONUT MILK, UNSWEETENED Sold canned or frozen and used as an enrichment in many Southeast Asian recipes, this rich-tasting liquid is made by grating fresh coconut meat and combining it with hot water, then straining out the particles from which all the milky essence has been extracted. If left undisturbed, a thick layer of coconut cream will have risen to the surface of the milk. Shake well before opening to blend the cream into the milk, or lift off the cream for a lower-fat milk. Avoid sweetened "coconut cream," commonly used as an ingredient in tropical cocktails, unless called for by name.

CORIANDER SEEDS Small, citrusy, sharp-tasting seeds of the coriander plant. Used whole or ground as a seasoning.

CRAWFISH and CRAB BOIL This traditional commercial blend of seasonings is added to a pot of boiling water in which crustaceans are about to be cooked, seasoning them as they simmer. The mixture usually includes bay leaf, dried chile, and clove, among other seasonings.

CREMA The Mexican term for a cultured, slightly soured heavy (double) cream found in Mexican markets and well-stocked food stores. It is used as a sauce enrichment and as a garnish. The most similar and widely available substitute is the French-style cultured cream known as crème fraîche. In a pinch, substitute lightly whisked sour cream only if the cream will not be cooked, or it will curdle.

CRÈME FRAICHE Literally "fresh cream," this typical French product, now widely available throughout the United States, is in fact a lightly soured cream used in both sweet and savory dishes. Crème fraîche may be stirred into sauces or other preparations as an enrichment and does not curdle like sour cream. At its simplest, a chilled dollop may be spooned atop fresh fruits such as berries.

CREOLE Term applied to a New Orleans–style blend of seasonings that, depending on the brand, might typically include such ingredients as paprika, cayenne pepper, allspice, cumin, black pepper, lemon zest, and thyme.

CUMIN SEEDS Strong, aromatic, dusky-tasting Middle Eastern spice, sold either as whole, small, crescent-shaped seeds or ground.

CURRY POWDER, MADRAS Each region of India seasons its signature dishes with unique blends of spices, known and sold generically as curry powders outside of India. Those in the style of Madras, on the southeastern coast, often heavily favor coriander, along with cumin, black peppercorns, turmeric, black mustard seeds, chili powder, and ginger. Try to buy in small quanity and use quickly.

DILL This feathery-leaved herb has a sweet, aromatic flavor well suited to pickling brines, vegetables, seafood, chicken, veal, and pork. It is used fresh and dried.

FILÉ POWDER Made from the bark of the sassafras tree, filé powder is a thickening agent and is most commonly used to thicken gumbo. It can also be sprinkled, sparingly, on a dish to lend a very particular earthy flavor.

FISH SAUCE Made from salted and fermented fish, this thin, amber liquid plays a role in Southeast Asian kitchens similar to that of soy sauce in China and Japan. Depending on their country of origin or manufacturer, fish sauces vary in taste and intensity but are generally interchangeable. Thai fish sauce is known as *nam pla,* Vietnamese fish sauce as *nuoc mam.*

GINGER The rhizome of a tropical plant, ginger is prized around the world for its warm, citruslike flavor. Fresh ginger is grated or sliced and added to sauces, soups, and marinades to add a singular, refreshing note. Dried, finely ground ginger is an essential ingredient in spiced cakes and cookies. Cooked in syrup and then coated with sugar, crystallized ginger adds a sweet-spicy accent to breads, fruit compotes, and desserts.

HOJA SANTA Large and heart shaped, this green "sacred leaf," a common seasoning in Mexico, has a taste resembling those of sassafras and licorice. Also known as *hierba santa,* it is used primarily to season sauces and as a wrapper for steamed foods and is believed to aid digestion.

HORSERADISH Central European immigrants established horseradish farms in the rich Mississippi River basin of eastern Illinois. Long summers allowed excellent growth, and cold winters encouraged the dormancy required to develop the pungency of the gnarled, dark-skinned root. Once the creamy-white flesh is grated or ground, horseradish releases its characteristic mustardlike odor and flavor. Prepared horseradish is available widely, but it is worth finding the fresh root for its clean, sharp flavor.

HOT-PEPPER SAUCES Made by blending, distilling, and preserving various types of hot chiles, hot-pepper sauces range from mild to ferociously hot and from sharp to full bodied. Read label descriptions and sample several varieties to find those that suit your taste.

JICAMA Native to Mexico and to parts of Central and South America, this large, bulbous tuber is enjoyed for its crisp, refreshingly juicy, snowy white flesh, which has a mild, slightly sweet taste. Once the thick, fibrous brown skin is peeled away, jicama is cut into sticks or wedges for eating as a snack with a squeeze of lime and a sprinkling of salt or chile; or it is chopped, diced, or shredded for inclusion in salads.

LARD Rendered pork fat, commonly known as lard, is a popular medium for frying in the Southwest, imparting rich, full flavor to refried beans, traditional deep-fried breads, and other foods. Look for good-quality lard rendered by a butcher; it will have a flavor superior to that of packaged processed lard sold in food stores.

LEMONGRASS A common seasoning in Southeast Asia now also grown in California and other parts of the United States, this stiff, reedlike grass has a sharp, citrus-like flavor. The best flavor comes from the heart of lemongrass, reached by peeling away the tough outer leaves down to the stalk's inner pale purple ring. Lemongrass is usually chopped or bruised to release its fragrant oils.

MADEIRA This rich-tasting fortified wine is available in five styles corresponding to sweetness: dry Sercial, medium-dry Verdelho and Rainwater, medium-sweet Bual, and sweet Malmsey. Named for the Portuguese island where it is produced, Madeira is used today in both savory and sweet dishes. Dry, medium-dry, or sweet sherries, traditional Spanish fortified wines, may be substituted in most cases.

MARJORAM A milder relative of oregano, marjoram is used fresh to bring out the flavors of tomatoes, legumes, lamb, poultry, or eggs.

MINT The refreshing flavor of mint brightens lamb and poultry dishes, vegetables, salads, and desserts. Although many varieties are cultivated, spearmint is the most readily available.

MOLASSES American colonial traders brought home this dark, thick, sticky by-product of sugar processing from the West Indies, and molasses' rich flavor and consistency, not to mention its economical price, won favor in the young nation's kitchens. Molasses still sweetens many traditional dishes, from baked beans to cookies. Light molasses results from the first boiling of the syrup, and dark molasses from the second. Blackstrap molasses, the darkest of all, has a distinctive hint of bitterness to complement its sweetness.

OKRA Native to Africa, okra was brought to the South by slaves. The slender, tapered, gray-green pods grow up to 9 inches (23 cm) long, but they are best eaten small, young, and tender. They have crisp exterior flesh, slightly gummy interiors, and an earthy, slightly acidic flavor. Okra is outstanding when pickled or deep-fried, and it also adds body to such stews as the burgoo of Kentucky and Louisiana's gumbos, which take their name from the original African word for okra, *ngombo* or *kingombo*. Although fresh okra is at its peak in summer, the vegetable also freezes well and can be found frozen in most markets.

OREGANO, MEXICAN Mexican varieties of this popular herb tend to have a more pronounced flavor than other varieties. Look for dried whole leaf oregano in Mexican markets and, as with any dried herb, crush it in your palm with your thumb to help release its essential oils just before adding it to a dish.

PANOCHA FLOUR This finely milled flour, sometimes labeled *harina para panocha,* is ground from sprouted wheat and is used in the Southwest to make a traditional Native American pudding known as *panocha.* Whole-wheat flour may be substituted.

PAPRIKA A bright red powder ground from the pepper (capsicum) of the same name. A popular ingredient in Hungarian cooking, paprika is used to flavor sauces, braises, or stews or as a colorful garnish on finished dishes. Two basic types, sweet and hot, are the most widely available.

PARSLEY, FLAT-LEAF (ITALIAN) This widely popular, fresh-tasting herb of southern European origin has a deeper, more complex flavor than the more familiar curly parsley, which is generally employed as a garnish.

PEA SHOOTS The sweet, tender baby leaves and tendrils of the snow pea, these are enjoyed raw, steamed, stir-fried, or simmered in soups.

PECANS The seeds of a hickory tree native to Mississippi and Alabama, pecans were long ago enjoyed by the region's Chickasaw, Choctaw, and Natchez tribes. In fact, in some parts of the South, they were known as Natchez nuts, as well as by such variations on their common spelling as peccans and pecawns. Harvested in the fall, the sweet, crunchy nutmeats, which resemble elongated walnuts, store well in their shells for up to nine months in the freezer or up to two months at cool room temperature. Although sometimes ground to use as a thickener for stews, most often they are showcased in candies and desserts, from pralines and brittles to pecan pies.

PEPPERCORNS The most common of all savory spices is best purchased as whole peppercorns, to be crushed or ground as needed. Pungent black peppercorns are slightly underripe pepper berries whose hulls have oxidized during drying. Hotter white peppercorns come from fully ripened, husked berries. Green peppercorns are the same fruits but harvested at an earlier stage. They are available dehydrated or packed in water or brine.

RHUBARB Although it is a vegetable, rhubarb is generally treated as a fruit, and its asser-tively tart flavor mellows when cooked with sugar. It is a classic pie filling, especially when paired with strawberries, and its ruby hue ensures attractive jams and jellies. The plant's heart-shaped leaves are mildly toxic and should always be discarded. In grocery stores, the scarlet stalks are trimmed and sold in bunches like celery. Select the thinnest, reddest stalks for the best flavor and color.

RICE VINEGAR Clear, clean-tasting rice vinegar, made from rice wine, is used to add bright flavor to sauces, salad dressings, and

pickles. Unseasoned varieties allow home cooks more latitude in seasoning dishes to taste, while seasoned versions contain salt and sugar. Japanese rice vinegars tend to be milder in flavor than those from China.

ROSEMARY This Mediterranean herb, used fresh and dried, has a strong, pleasantly resinous flavor well suited to lamb, veal, poultry, seafood, and vegetables.

RUM, DARK Some of the molasses brought home from the West Indies by New England traders was distilled to make rum, which remains a popular regional flavoring. Dark rums, also known as Demerara rums, carry some of the caramel color and robust taste associated with molasses.

SAGE Popular throughout Europe, North Africa, and the Middle East, this pungent, mildly camphorous herb goes particularly well with fresh or cured pork, lamb, veal, or poultry. It is used fresh and dried.

SARDINES Maine is America's leading source of these slender, silvery members of the herring family. In springtime, they may be enjoyed freshly caught, simply cooked with tomatoes, fried, or grilled. At other times of year, sardines are available in their ubiquitous canned form.

SCOTCH BONNET CHILES A close cousin to the habañero chile, this highly aromatic variety is thought to be a thousand times more fiery than the jalapeño. It is popular throughout Latin America.

SHALLOTS Relatives of the onion, these small brown-skinned bulbs with purple-white flesh

are popular as a seasoning. Some people describe their flavor as a combination of onion and garlic.

SORREL A sharp, lemony flavor distinguishes these elongated green leaves. When very young and mild in taste, they may be included in salads. Otherwise, sorrel leaves are best cooked in soups, sauces, or stuffings, during which they break down into a puréelike consistency.

SOY SAUCE A flavorful, salty liquid fermented from soybeans and some form of grain, usually wheat, soy sauce is one of the most common seasonings in China and Japan. Chinese cooks use two types of soy sauce: dark, which is aged longer and includes a touch of molasses, is usually added to more robust dishes such as these featuring red meat; while light soy is most commonly used in dipping sauces and soups and with seafood and vegetables. Japanese soy sauce contains a higher percentage of wheat and is actually closer in color and flavor to Chinese light soy sauce.

SPICES, TOASTING AND GRINDING To bring out the full flavor of spices, such as coriander and cumin seeds, purchase them whole and toast and grind them at home, preparing only what you need at the time. To toast them, put the seeds in a dry, heavy frying pan over medium heat and warm them until they are fragrant and just begin to change color, shaking the pan as necessary to prevent scorching. This should take only a few minutes. Pour onto a plate, let cool, then grind in a spice grinder or with a mortar and pestle.

SWEET POTATO Southerners favor the deep orange–fleshed variety of this tuber over its pale-fleshed cousin more common in the North. Both types fall under the botanical classification *Ipomoea batatas,* a relative of the morning glory. Despite the fact that Southerners refer to their sweet potatoes as "yams," these sweet potatoes are unrelated to the much larger and blander true yams of the Caribbean.

TAMARI A type of Japanese soy sauce made without the wheat that traditionally accompanies soybeans in the fermentation process. It has a thicker consistency and stronger flavor than ordinary soy sauces.

TAMARIND CONCENTRATE The dark reddish brown pulp inside the pods of the tropical tamarind tree has a tangy sweet-sour flavor that complements both savory and sweet dishes. Ethnic markets sell the pods loose or the pulp in blocks or concentrate form. The last, sold in small jars, is the easiest to use.

TARRAGON With its delicate perfume reminiscent of anise, this classic French herb flatters eggs, seafood, green beans, asparagus, and poultry. It is frequently infused in vinegar for use in sauces or salad dressings.

TEQUILA, GOLD Fermented and distilled from the juice of the blue agave cactus, this signature spirit of Mexico is available under many brands. All tequila must contain at least 51 percent spirit from blue agave, which is combined with other forms of alcohol. Mexican government regulations do not specify aging for gold tequilas, but the better ones are aged at least a couple of months in oak and are smoother than unaged white (silver) tequilas. Gold tequilas get their color from the addition of caramel. They are not, however, as rich or complex as aged (*añejo*) tequilas, which are kept in oak for at least a year.

THYME This small-leaved herb of Mediterranean origin has a clean, aromatic character that adds flavor to many poultry, light meat, seafood, and vegetable dishes. It is used fresh and dried.

WALNUTS Close to 100 percent of the walnuts sold in the United States are grown in California. Although walnuts are an autumn harvest, they keep extremely well. In their shells, the nuts stay fresh for up to three months under cool, dry conditions. Shelled, the nutmeats will keep in an airtight container for up to six months in the refrigerator or a year in the freezer.

FRESH TOMATO SALSA

3/4 cup (4 1/2 oz/140 g) *each* yellow, red, and
   orange cherry tomatoes, stemmed and
   halved lengthwise
1 small red onion, finely diced
1 tablespoon snipped fresh chives
1 tablespoon chopped fresh cilantro (fresh
   coriander)
2 teaspoons chopped fresh mint
2 serrano chiles, minced
2 tablespoons white wine vinegar
1–2 tablespoons lime-flavored oil
pinch of sugar
kosher salt to taste

In a bowl, combine all the cherry tomatoes, the onion, chives, cilantro, mint, and chiles. Stir gently to combine. Add the vinegar, lime-flavored oil, sugar, and salt and toss to mix. Let the mixture stand for 10 minutes. Taste and adjust the seasoning. Serve immediately.

CORNMEAL COATING

1 1/2 cups (7 1/2 oz/235 g) stone-ground
   yellow cornmeal
1/4 cup (1 1/2 oz/45 g) masa harina
6 tablespoons (1 oz/30 g) ground Chimayó
   chile
1 1/2 teaspoons freshly ground coriander
1 teaspoon freshly ground cumin
1 tablespoon kosher salt
1 teaspoon freshly ground pepper

In a bowl, combine the cornmeal, masa harina, ground chile, coriander, cumin, salt, and pepper. Whisk to combine.

SEASONED WHITE RICE

2 tablespoons olive oil or vegetable oil
1 cup (7 oz/220 g) long-grain white or
   basmati rice
1 small yellow onion, chopped
2 bay leaves
1 teaspoon salt
1 1/2 cups (12 fl oz/375 ml) water

In a 2-qt (2-l) saucepan over medium heat, warm the oil. Add the rice and stir until the grains turn opaque, 3–4 minutes. Add the onion, bay leaves, and salt and continue to stir until the rice is light tan, 2–3 minutes longer. Add the water, stir well, and bring to a boil. Cover the pot, reduce the heat to low, and cook until all the liquid has been absorbed and the rice is tender, 25–30 minutes. Uncover, stir the rice, re-cover, remove from the heat, and let "steam" for 5 minutes longer.

Fluff the rice with a fork, discard the bay leaves, and transfer to a serving dish. Serve immediately.

Index

First published in the USA by Time-Life Custom Publishing.
Originally published as Williams-Sonoma New American Cooking:
The South, California, New England, The Pacific Northwest,
The Southwest, and *The Heartland*
Copyright © 2000-2001 Weldon Owen Inc.
and Williams-Sonoma, Inc.

Oxmoor House®

Oxmoor House books are distributed by Sunset Books
80 Willow Road, Menlo Park, CA 94025
Telephone: 650-321-3600 Fax: 650-324-1532

Oxmoor House and Sunset Books are divisions of
Southern Progress Corporation

SUNSET BOOKS

Vice President, General Manager: Rich Smeby
Vice President, Editorial Director: Bob Doyle
National Account Manager: Brad Moses

WILLIAMS-SONOMA, INC.

Founder and Vice-Chairman: Chuck Williams

WELDON OWEN INC.

Chief Executive Officer: John Owen
President and Chief Operating Officer: Terry Newell
Creative Director: Gaye Allen
Publisher: Hannah Rahill
Editor: Val Cipollone
Editorial Assistant: Juli Vendzules
Design and Production: Todd Rechner
Production Director: Chris Hemesath
Color Manager: Teri Bell

NEW AMERICAN COOKING

Conceived and produced by
WELDON OWEN INC.
814 Montgomery Street, San Francisco, CA 94133
Telephone: 415-291-0100 Fax: 415-291-8841

In Collaboration with Williams-Sonoma, Inc.
3250 Van Ness Avenue, San Francisco, CA 94109

A WELDON OWEN PRODUCTION

Copyright © 2005 Weldon Owen Inc.
and Williams-Sonoma, Inc.

All rights reserved, including the right of
reproduction in whole or in part in any form.

First printed in 2005
10 9 8 7 6 5 4 3 2 1
ISBN 0-8487-3059-3
Printed by Midas Printing Limited
Printed in China

RECIPE & TEXT CREDITS

Beth Dooley: 32, 42, 43, 70, 92, 122, 136, 137, 150, 156, 158, 176, 200, 202, 218, 228, 229, 292, 293, 298, 304, 308; **Janet Fletcher:** 20, 21, 26, 36, 37, 48, 54, 62, 63, 74, 96, 97, 112, 113, 114, 142, 146, 152, 154, 174, 182, 188, 189, 220, 234, 238, 240, 258, 272, 273, 276, 280, 284; **Jean Galton:** 12, 18, 34, 44, 56, 57, 64, 72, 88, 94, 106, 110, 144, 145, 162, 166, 172, 190, 194, 224, 225, 230, 248, 249, 250, 256, 268, 278, 288; **Kathi Long:** 14, 22, 28, 30, 31, 40, 46, 60, 82, 84, 90, 104, 120, 138, 164, 170, 186, 192, 204, 206, 207, 232, 244, 245, 260, 274, 286, 296; **Ray Overton:** 24, 78, 80, 81, 100, 102, 103, 118, 130, 134, 140, 178, 184, 214, 222, 226, 236, 237, 246, 262, 266, 282, 294, 302; **Molly Stevens:** 16, 38, 50, 52, 53, 58, 68, 76, 77, 86, 98, 108, 124, 126, 128, 132, 148, 160, 161, 180, 196, 198, 208, 212, 216, 217, 242, 254, 264, 270, 290, 300, 306, 307.

ACKNOWLEDGMENTS

Weldon Owen would like to thank Desne Ahlers, Adrienne Aquino, Carrie Bradley, Ken DellaPenta,
Arin Hailey, Tanya Henry, Renée Myers, and Victoria Spencer for their assistance in producing this book.